Brian Friel
in Conversation

EDITED BY PAUL DELANEY

Ann Arbor

THE UNIVERSITY OF MICHIGAN PRESS

Copyright © by the University of Michigan 2000
All rights reserved
Published in the United States of America by
The University of Michigan Press
Manufactured in the United States of America
⊗ Printed on acid-free paper

2003   2002   2001   2000   4   3   2   1

A CIP catalog record for this book is available from the British Library.

Library of Congress Cataloging-in-Publication

Friel, Brian.
    Brian Friel in conversation / edited by Paul Delaney.
      p.   cm. — (Theater—theory/text/performance)
    Includes bibliographical references and index.
    ISBN 0–472-09710-5 (alk. paper) — ISBN 0-472-06710-9
(pbk. : alk. paper)
      1. Friel, Brian—Interviews.   2. Dramatists, Irish—20th
century—Interviews.   3. Ireland—In literature.
4. Drama—Technique. 5. Playwriting.   I. Delaney, Paul, 1948–   .
II. Title.   III. Series.
PR6056.R5 Z469 2000
822'.914—dc21   99-006947

For Patrick, William and Hugh,
my three degrees of separation
from pre-famine Ireland

and for Arthur,
who may in the fifth generation
become an Irish-American playwright

Contents

Preface

My great-grandfather left Ireland at the time of the famine and settled in Kentucky where he orphaned two boys, one of whom became a farmer, whose youngest son became a preacher, whose eldest son became a professor in California. When I returned to Ireland with my son, who wants to become a playwright, we found the land of our heritage welcoming to two members of the Irish diaspora. During the cease-fire of 1995 we were able to travel freely throughout the North as well as the Republic, and it was strangely soothing to listen to The Cast singing about one who had left Kilkelly, Ireland—and the ones left behind. It was dusk when we found ourselves in Kilkelly geographically as well as emotionally. But we still had miles to go—after a day that included visits to libraries and newspaper offices in Derry and Belfast—and could not linger. Nevertheless, what my son found "luminous," in Seamus Heaney's phrase, was The Cast's poignant chronicle of separation and loss, and when I let him choose how we would spend our last full day in Ireland we drove back to see what we could find "down at Kilkelly churchyard." That night, staying in a pre-famine cottage that may have been like my great-grandfather's boyhood home, we watched our host herd his cows across the road past the cottage in which he had grown up. But when we struck up a conversation, the talk turned to Patrick Kavanagh and Seamus Heaney. I had known men who herded cattle and men who discussed poetry appreciatively, but they hadn't been the same men. Brian Friel says he finds it hard to explain what he gained from his first trip to America, although he describes his "parole from inbred claustrophobic Ireland" as "a kind of explosion in the head." I find it hard to explain what my son and I gained from our trip to Ireland; but a poignant sense of separation and loss was assuaged by a sense of coming full circle, of connections lost and reestablished.

I am grateful to Tony Lennon, the brother of Peter Lennon who conducted the first substantive interview with Brian Friel, for warmly welcoming us to the clippings library of *The Irish Times*. His successors were equally cordial in 1997. I am also happy to express gratitude for access to the clippings libraries of the Independent Newspapers, Dublin (the *Irish Independent, Sunday Independent,* and *Evening Herald*), the *Belfast Telegraph,* the *Irish News* (Belfast), and the *Derry Journal.* I received gracious assistance from staff members at the *Sunday Tribune,* Radio Telefís Éireann, the Gate Theatre, the National Library in Dublin, the Linen Hall Library in Belfast, and the libraries of Trinity College, Dublin, Queen's University in Belfast and Magee College in Derry. In England, the BBC Written Archives Centre provided access to transcripts; the National Sound Library provided access to recordings; and the National Theatre Press Office, the British Library, the British Library Newspaper Library, and Cambridge University Library provided access to a wide variety of published material.

Melissa Michaels offered support and encouragement throughout the project—as, indeed, throughout her tenure as student and secretary. She decoded indecipherable microfilm (giving me new appreciation for the term *translations*), typed interviews, and served as a reliable communication cord when I was at distant research sites. Elizabeth Delaney typed interviews and corrected typescripts; helped with correspondence, faxes, and telephone messages; and deserves primary credit for indexing the volume. Arthur Delaney was patient and appreciative throughout our time in Ireland and, back in California, volunteered to type interviews. I am happy to express my gratitude to Stan Gaede, provost of Westmont College, for support in the form of a sabbatical and for additional assistance during the final preparation of the volume. Finally, I want to thank my wife, Dianne, once again for reading and discussing and raising queries and offering suggestions. Without her assistance the pieces would not have become a quilt. Again.

Acknowledgments

Grateful acknowledgment is made to the following authors, publishers, and journals for permission to reprint previously published materials.

Belfast Telegraph Newspapers for "After *Philadelphia*," by John Fairleigh, *Belfast Telegraph,* 9 August 1966, p. 6, copyright © Belfast Telegraph 1966; for "Why Friel and Rea are Having a 'Field' Day," by Lynne Riddel, *Belfast Telegraph,* 15 September 1980, p. 8, copyright © Belfast Telegraph 1980. Reprinted by permission of Belfast Telegraph.

Eavan Boland for "Brian Friel: Derry's Playwright," *Hibernia,* 16 February 1973, p. 18. Copyright © 1973 Eavan Boland. Reprinted by permission.

The Christian Science Monitor for "Frank Talk from Friel," by Alan N. Bunce, *Christian Science Monitor,* 27 November 1968, p. 13. Copyright © 1968 The Christian Science Publishing Society. All rights reserved. Reprinted with permission from The Christian Science Monitor.

The Dramatic Publishing Company for "Interview with Brian Friel," by Lewis Funke, *Playwrights Talk about Writing: 12 Interviews with Lewis Funke* (Chicago: Dramatic Publishing Co., 1975), pp. 111–33. Copyright © 1975 by The Dramatic Publishing Company. Printed in the United States of America. All Rights Reserved. This interview is protected by copyright and all rights are reserved. No part of this interview may be reproduced or transmitted in any form or by any means, electronic or mechanical, including photocopy, recording, or any information storage and retrieval system without permission from The Dramatic Publishing Company. All inquiries should be addressed to Dramatic Publishing Company, 311 Washington St., Woodstock, IL 60098. Phone: (815) 338–7170. Fax: (815) 338–8981. Reprinted by permission.

Brian Friel and the British Broadcasting Corporation for "The Green Years: A Talk by Brian Friel," broadcast on the BBC Radio Northern Ireland Home Service, 30 April 1964; for "An Observer in Minneapolis," broadcast on the BBC Radio Northern Ireland Home Service, 16 August 1965; for "Philadelphia, Here the Author Comes!" broadcast on the BBC Radio Northern Ireland Home Service, 21 July 1966; for "Soundings," with John Boyd, broadcast on the BBC Radio Northern Ireland Home Service, 2 August 1970; for "Self-Portrait: Brian Friel Talks about His Life and Work," broadcast on the BBC Radio Northern Ireland Home Service, 19 December 1971. Material held in the BBC Written Archives

Centre, Caversham Park, Reading. Copyright © 1964, 1965, 1966, 1970, 1971 Brian Friel and the British Broadcasting Corporation. Reprinted by permission.

Brian Friel and Radio Telefís Éireann Archive for "Brian Friel and Field Day," transmitted on RTÉ, 14 February 1983. Copyright © 1983 Brian Friel and Radio Telefís Éireann. Reprinted by permission.

The Guardian for "Playwright of the Western World," by Peter Lennon, *The Guardian,* 8 October 1964, p. 9, copyright © The Guardian 1964; for "Mapping Cultural Imperialism," by Stephen Dixon, *The Guardian,* 27 September 1980, p. 11, copyright © The Guardian 1980. Reprinted by permission.

Bobbie Hanvey for "Brian Friel Never Gives Interviews and Writes with a 2B Pencil," by Bobbie Hanvey, *Belfast News Letter,* 12 June 1999, p. 15. Copyright © 1999 Bobbie Hanvey. Reprinted by permission.

Independent Newspapers, Dublin, for "Broadway? Who Cares?" by Ronan Farren, *Evening Herald,* 28 August 1980, p. 8, copyright © 1980 Independent Newspapers plc; for "Finding Voice in a Language Not Our Own," by Ciaran Carty, *Sunday Independent,* 5 October 1980, p. 16, copyright © 1980 Independent Newspapers plc. Reprinted by permission.

Irish Press Plc for "Brian Friel's Other Island: Aodhan Madden Talks to Ireland's Top Dramatist about His New Play," by Aodhan Madden, *Sunday Press,* 28 November 1971, p. 31, copyright © 1971 Irish Press Newspapers; for "Can the Critics Kill a Play?" by Fachtna O'Kelly, *Irish Press,* 28 March 1975, p. 9, copyright © 1975 Irish Press Newspapers; for "New Play to Set Fire to the Foyle?" by Liam Robinson, *Evening Press,* 19 September 1980, p. 6, copyright © 1980 Irish Press Newspapers; for "Friel and a Tale of Three Sisters," by Donal O'Donnell, *Sunday Press,* 30 August 1981, p. 19, copyright © 1981 Irish Press Newspapers; for "Friel's Sense of Conflict," by Michael Sheridan, *Irish Press,* 1 October 1986, p. 9, copyright © 1981 Irish Press Newspapers. Reprinted by permission of Irish Press Plc.

The Irish Times for "Press Diary: Unsinkable Brian Friel," *Irish Times,* 11 April 1969, p. 17, copyright © 1969 The Irish Times; for "Is the Play Still the Thing?" by Elgy Gillespie, *Irish Times,* 28 July 1978, p. 8, copyright © 1978 The Irish Times; for "The Saturday Interview: Brian Friel," by Elgy Gillespie, *Irish Times,* 5 September 1981, p. 14 ("Weekend" sec., p. 6), copyright © 1981 The Irish Times; for "An Irishman's Diary," by Niall Kiely, *Irish Times,* 17 September 1981, p. 9, copyright © 1981 The Irish Times; for "Rehearsing Friel's New Farce," by Ray Comiskey, *Irish Times,* 14 September 1982, p. 8, copyright © 1982 The Irish Times; for "Field Day's New Double Bill" by Patrick Quilligan, *Irish Times,* 18 September 1984, p. 10, copyright © 1984 The Irish Times; for "Drama of Love: From One Great Master to Another," by Eileen Battersby, *Irish Times,* 1 August 1992, "Weekend" sec., p. 2, copyright © 1992 The Irish Times; for "Playwright Brian Friel Quits Field Day," by Gerry Moriarty, *Irish Times,* 3 February 1994, p. 7, copyright © 1994 The Irish Times. Reprinted by permission of The Irish Times.

Julie Kavanagh for "Friel at Last," by Julie Kavanagh, *Vanity Fair,* October 1991, pp. 128, 130, 134, 138. Copyright © 1991 Julie Kavanagh. Reprinted by permission.

John Lahr and Georges Borchardt, Inc., for "In *Dancing at Lughnasa,* Due on Broadway this Month, Brian Friel Celebrates Life's Pagan Joys," by John Lahr, *Vogue* (American), October 1991, pp. 174, 176, 178–79. Copyright © 1991 John Lahr. Reprinted by permission of Georges Borchardt, Inc., for the author.

Vincent Brown (editor) and *Magill* magazine (Dublin, Ireland) for " 'Talking to Ourselves': Brian Friel Talks to Paddy Agnew," by Paddy Agnew, *Magill,* 4, no. 3 (December 1980), pp. 59–61, copyright © 1980 Magill. Reprinted by permission.

The New York Times for "From Ballybeg to Broadway," by Mel Gussow, *New York Times Magazine,* 29 September 1991, pp. 30, 55–61. Copyright © 1991 by the New York Times. Reprinted by permission.

Fintan O'Toole for "The Man from God Knows Where: An Interview with Brian Friel," by Fintan O'Toole, *In Dublin,* no. 165 (28 October 1982), pp. 20–23, copyright © 1982 Fintan O'Toole. Reprinted by permission.

The Sunday Tribune for "Friel Takes Derry by Storm," by Ulick O'Connor, *Sunday Tribune,* 6 September 1981, p. 2, copyright © 1981 Tribune Publications. Reprinted by permission.

Telegraph Group Limited, London, for "How *Dancing with Lughnasa* Writer Put Glenties Squarely on the Map" by James Delingpole, *Daily Telegraph,* 2 June 1992. Copyright © Telegraph Group Limited, London, 1992. Reprinted by permission.

The University of Ulster, Magee College Library, for "An Ulster Writer: Brian Friel," by Graham Morison, *Acorn,* no. 8 (Spring 1965), pp. 4–15. Copyright © 1965 Magee University College. Reprinted with permission of the University of Ulster, Magee College Library.

Matt Wolf, London theatre critic of *Variety* and a regular contributor to *The New York Times* and *The Times* of London, for "Brian Friel's Ireland: Both Private and Political," *New York Times,* 30 April 1989, sec. 2, pp. 7, 8. Copyright © 1989 Matt Wolf. Reprinted by permission.

The Word and Divine Word Missionaries (Donamon, Co. Roscommon, Ireland) for "Kathleen Mavourneen, Here Comes Brian Friel," by Desmond Rushe, *The Word: An International Catholic Pictorial Magazine,* February 1970, pp. 12–15. Copyright © 1970 The Word. Reprinted with permission from *The Word.*

Every effort has been made to trace the ownership of all copyrighted material in this book and to obtain permission for its use.

Chronology

1929	Born outside Omagh, Co. Tyrone, on 9 January or 10 January (according to two conflicting birth certificates).
1939	Family moves to Derry.
1941–45	Attends St. Columb's College, Derry.
1945–48	Attends St. Patrick's College, Maynooth, a Catholic seminary outside Dublin; receives B.A. degree, 1948.
1949–50	Takes teacher training course at St. Mary's Training College (now St. Joseph's College of Education), Belfast.
1950–60	Schoolteacher in primary and intermediate schools in Derry.
1951–52	Begins writing for publication; first essay appears in the *Irish Monthly;* first short story in *The Bell.*
ca. 1952	Writes his first play, *The Francophile.*
1954	Marries Anne Morrison, with whom he will have four daughters and one son.
1958	*A Sort of Freedom* and *To This Hard House* on BBC Radio (Northern Ireland). *The Francophile* accepted by the Group Theatre, Belfast, with the suggestion that it be renamed *The Doubtful Paradise.*
1959	Short stories begin appearing in *The New Yorker.*
1960	*The Francophile* staged at the Group Theatre, Belfast, as *A Doubtful Paradise.*
1961	*King's Son of Reddened Valour* accepted by the Abbey Theatre, Dublin, and renamed *The Enemy Within.*
1962	*A Doubtful Paradise* on BBC Radio (Northern Ireland). *The Enemy Within* staged at the Abbey Theatre, Dublin. Publishes *The Saucer of Larks,* a collection of short stories. Begins writing a weekly column for the *Irish Press* (Dublin).
1963	*The Blind Mice* staged at the Eblana Theatre, Dublin (February). *The Blind Mice* and *The Enemy Within* on BBC Radio

	(Northern Ireland). Friel goes to Minneapolis, at the invitation of Tyrone Guthrie, to observe rehearsals for the first season of the Tyrone Guthrie Theater.

1964   *Philadelphia, Here I Come!* staged at the Gaiety Theatre, Dublin (September), and becomes the hit of the Dublin Theatre Festival. *Three Fathers, Three Sons* televised on Radio Telefís Éireann (RTÉ); *The Founder Members* on BBC Radio.

1965   *The Enemy Within* televised on the BBC. *Philadelphia, Here I Come!* on the BBC Third Programme.

1966   First Broadway production of *Philadelphia, Here I Come!* runs for nine months. *The Loves of Cass McGuire* on the BBC Third Programme and staged at the Helen Hayes Theatre, New York (October), where it closed after 20 performances. Publishes *The Gold in the Sea,* a collection of short stories.

1967   Moves six miles from Derry in Northern Ireland to the village of Muff, Co. Donegal, in the Republic of Ireland. First Dublin production of *The Loves of Cass McGuire* at the Abbey Theatre is well received. *Lovers* staged at the Gate Theatre, Dublin (July).

1968   First New York production of *Lovers,* initially starring Art Carney at Lincoln Center (July) and then at the Music Box, runs for four months. Friel participates in civil rights demonstrations in Derry; on 5 October the police beat five organizers of a civil rights rally. *Crystal and Fox* staged at the Gaiety Theatre, Dublin (November).

1969   *Crystal and Fox* on the BBC Third Programme. *The Mundy Scheme,* rejected by the Abbey Theatre (May), is staged at the Olympia Theatre, Dublin (June) and then closes in New York after just two performances at the Royale Theatre (December).

1970–71   Visiting Writer at Magee University College, Derry.

1971   *The Gentle Island* staged at the Olympia Theatre, Dublin (November).

1972   British troops kill thirteen civilians in the Bogside area of Derry on Bloody Sunday (30 January).

1973   *The Freedom of the City* staged at the Abbey Theatre, Dublin (February) and in a separate production at the Royal Court Theatre, London, one week later. First New York production of *Crystal and Fox* (March). *The Gentle Island* on BBC Radio Four (October).

1974   First New York production of *The Freedom of the City* closes after nine performances (February).

1975   *Volunteers* staged at the Abbey Theatre, Dublin (March), prompts *Times Literary Supplement* article by Seamus Heaney, "Digging Deeper," in response to negative review.

1976   Writes an unproduced play called *Bannermen*, originally intended to be staged during the Queen's Festival, Belfast. "Farewell to Ardstraw" and "The Next Parish" televised on BBC Northern Ireland television.

1977   *Living Quarters* staged at the Abbey Theatre, Dublin (March).

1979   *Aristocrats* staged at the Abbey Theatre, Dublin (March). *Faith Healer* staged at the Colonial Theatre, Boston (February), prior to opening on Broadway at the Longacre Theatre (April), where it closes after a week despite some favorable reviews.

1980   Friel and Stephen Rea found the Field Day Theatre Company (June). First Dublin production of *Faith Healer* at the Abbey (August). *Translations*, the first Field Day production, staged at the Guildhall, Derry, and receives ecstatic response (September); becomes the hit of the Dublin Theatre Festival (October). The playlet *American Welcome* staged by the Actors Theatre of Louisville (February).

1981   First London production of *Faith Healer* at the Royal Court Theatre (March). First New York production of *Translations* at the Manhattan Theatre Club (April). First London production of *Translations* at the Hampstead Theatre (May), declared "a national classic," transfers to the National Theatre (August). Friel and Rea add four additional directors to Field Day. Friel's version of Chekhov's *Three Sisters* begins its Field Day tour at the Guildhall, Derry (September).

1982   *The Communication Cord* begins its Field Day tour at the Guildhall, Derry (September), and plays at the Olympia Theatre in Dublin (November). Moves from Muff to Greencastle, twenty miles further into Co. Donegal.

1983   Radio Telefís Éireann (RTÉ) documentary on "Brian Friel and Field Day" (February).

1985   First Belfast production of Friel's 1977 *Living Quarters*.

1986   Announces plans to publish a Field Day anthology of Irish literature.

1987   Friel and other Field Day directors on fund-raising tour of

United States (March). Friel is appointed to the Irish Senate (May) and serves until 1989. *Fathers and Sons,* Friel's dramatization of the novel by Turgenev, staged at the National Theatre, London (July).

1988   First London production of Friel's 1979 *Aristocrats* at the Hampstead Theatre (June) receives *Evening Standard* best play award. *Making History* staged in a Field Day production at the Guildhall, Derry (September). Field Day production of *Making History* transfers to the National Theatre, London (December). Dublin revival of *The Gentle Island* directed by Frank McGuinness (December).

1989   BBC Radio launches a "Brian Friel Season" of six plays by Friel, the first living playwright to be thus honored (April). First New York production of Friel's 1979 *Aristocrats* at the Manhattan Theatre Club (April) wins New York Drama Critics Circle award for best new foreign play.

1990   *Dancing at Lughnasa* staged at the Abbey Theatre, Dublin (April); transfers to the National Theatre in London (October). *The London Vertigo,* a version of a play by Charles Macklin, published.

1991   Abbey Theatre production of *Dancing at Lughnasa* named play of the year at the Olivier awards in London (April); plays one night in Glenties, Co. Donegal (August); then receives rave reviews on Broadway (October). Three-volume *Field Day Anthology of Irish Writing* published (December).

1992   *The London Vertigo* staged in a Gate Theatre production at the Andrews Lane Theatre, Dublin (January). *Dancing at Lughnasa* receives eight Tony nominations and wins three Tony awards, including best play; *Lughnasa* is named best play by the New York Drama Critics Circle. *A Month in the Country,* a version of the play by Turgenev, staged at the Gate Theatre, Dublin (August).

1993   *Wonderful Tennessee* staged at the Abbey Theatre, Dublin (June). First Broadway production of *Wonderful Tennessee* closes after nine performances (October).

1994   Friel resigns from Field Day (February). *Molly Sweeney* staged at the Gate Theatre, Dublin, directed by Friel (August); transfers to the Almeida Theatre, London (November).

1995   Broadway revival of Friel's 1980 *Translations* (March) closes after twenty-five regular performances and fifteen previews.

1996   First New York production of *Molly Sweeney* directed by Friel at the Roundabout Theatre (January) is named best foreign play by the New York Drama Critics Circle.

1997   *Give Me Your Answer, Do!* staged at the Abbey Theatre, Dublin, directed by Friel (March).

1998   First London production of *Give Me Your Answer, Do!* at the Hampstead Theatre (March). Film version of *Dancing at Lughnasa* starring Meryl Streep and Michael Gambon opens in Ireland (September) and in the United States (November). Friel's version of Chekhov's *Uncle Vanya* staged at the Gate Theatre as part of the Dublin Theatre Festival (October). First British production—by the Royal Shakespeare Company (RSC)—of Friel's version of *A Month in the Country* (December).

1999   *Ballymore*, an opera by Richard Wargo based on *Lovers* by Friel, staged at the Skylight Opera Theatre, Milwaukee (January). A Friel Festival (in the year of the playwright's seventieth birthday) includes productions of eight plays at six theaters in Dublin and one in Belfast (April–August). Two Friel Festival events—the Abbey's production of *The Freedom of the City* and the Gate's production of *Aristocrats*—along with the Gate's 1998 production of *Uncle Vanya* appear as part of the Lincoln Center Festival in New York (July). First New York production of *Give Me Your Answer, Do!* by the Roundabout Theatre (September). *Dancing at Lughnasa,* directed by Peter Brook's daughter Irina Brook, performed in English as part of the Tokyo International Festival of Performing Arts (October).

Introduction

In 1963, when he had just published his first book (a collection of short stories), a "33-year-old ex-schoolmaster" from Derry told the *Belfast Telegraph* that his ambition was to write the "great Irish play." Brian Friel, the author at the time of three unpublished plays, only one of which had been performed on stage, said the great Irish play would be "one where the author can talk so truthfully and accurately about people in his own neighbourhood and make it so that these folk could be living in Omagh, Omaha or Omansk."[1] With *Dancing at Lughnasa* (1990), Friel may have realized his early ambition. Although Friel was born in Omagh, his mother hailed from Glenties. And *Dancing at Lughnasa*, deeply rooted in the small Donegal town of Glenties, speaks to audiences from Glendale to Glinka. *Dancing at Lughnasa* creates on stage—through a play written in English—an experience "as if language had surrendered to movement" and invokes a realm in which "words were no longer necessary . . ."[2] But by the time *Dancing at Lughnasa* was communicating worldwide—albeit in part wordlessly—Friel had decided that in at least one other way words were no longer necessary.

Preparations for the Abbey Theatre opening of Friel's next play, *Wonderful Tennessee* (1993), were "conducted in a shroud of secrecy. No interviews. Not even with director Patrick Mason or any of the actors."[3] "We are all taking our cue from Brian Friel," said one Abbey Theatre insider who declined to be named. "He rarely talks to anyone and he keeps telling us not to talk to the press or anyone about the play until it opens."[4] But, come opening night, "the shy man of Irish drama" was still not to be heard from and almost not to be seen. Three months later, when *Wonderful Tennessee* would follow *Dancing at Lughnasa* to Broadway,

---

1. "Brian Friel's First Book," *Belfast Telegraph*, 25 February 1963, p. 3.
2. Brian Friel, *Dancing at Lughnasa* (London and Boston: Faber, 1990), p. 71.
3. Harry McGee, "In Search of the Real Brian Friel," *Sunday Press*, 27 June 1993, sec. 2 "Leisure," p. 1.
4. Mary Carr, "Is There Life after Lughnasa?" *Evening Herald*, 24 June 1993.

Friel was still not talking. For a Radio Telefís Éireann (RTÉ) documentary Noel Pearson was preparing on the making of *Wonderful Tennessee,* Friel agreed to appear on camera but declined to speak into a microphone.[5] Friel declined all requests for interviews regarding *Molly Sweeney* (1994) even though he directed the play himself in Dublin, in London and on Broadway. Nor would he give any answers regarding his next play, the pointedly named *Give Me Your Answer, Do!* (1997).

Friel's aversion to interviews has become legendary among journalists who swap stories not just about refusals but about interviews agreed to and then cancelled at the last moment, or about requirements that all questions be submitted—and answered—in writing. A title like *Brian Friel in Conversation* must strike some would-be interviewers as something of an oxymoron. Noting the imminent appearance of the film version of *Dancing at Lughnasa,* the London production of *Give Me Your Answer, Do!* and a Dublin festival of Friel plays, one London journalist could opine: "As usual, your man will not be coming down from the mountain to tell us about any of the above."[6]

And yet journalists who do meet Friel are struck by the affability of "a Puckish, dapper man of immense good humour [with] the looks and manner of a particularly amiable and philosophical publican."[7] The playwright who sends apologetic notes to press officers asking pardon for his inability to engage in self-promotion[8] has repeatedly been described as affable, mild-mannered,[9] "infinitely courteous"[10] and "genial."[11] Noel Pearson, the producer who has been mounting Friel's plays for ten years, acknowledges that Friel's refusal in recent years to give interviews has inadvertently shrouded him with a certain mystique. "I don't think he does that intentionally, but it does have that effect," Pearson says. "He's not that calculating at all. He's a very shy man. But he's not like Beckett or anything. He loves a sing song, puffs away on his cigar. He's great company."[12]

---

5. Alex Witchel, "Life May Be a Madness, but It's Also a Poem," *New York Times,* 17 October 1993, sec. 2, p. 5.

6. Jasper Rees, "A Bright Light in Search of the Shadows," *The Independent,* 26 March 1998, "Features" section, p. 6.

7. Stephen Dixon, "Mapping Cultural Imperialism," *The Guardian,* 27 September 1980, p. 11.

8. Douglas Kennedy, "Success Went to His Feet," *Sunday Telegraph,* 14 October 1990, "Review" section, p. 8.

9. Ray Comiskey, "Rehearsing Friel's New Farce," *Irish Times,* 14 September 1982, p. 8.

10. Charles Spencer, "Friels on Wheels . . . ," *The Standard* (London), 15 May 1981, p. 24.

11. Julie Kavanagh, "Friel at Last," *Vanity Fair,* October 1991, p. 130.

12. Rees, "A Bright Light in Search of the Shadows," p. 6.

His avoidance of interviews, however, is not just attributable to shyness. When Friel offered a "Self-Portrait" on BBC Radio in 1971, he began with a mock interview of himself. That mock interview, in a talk contained in this volume, displays Friel's self-deprecating wit but also needles interviewers for frequently repeated "chestnuts" and displays something of his distaste for the interview format itself:

> *When did you know, Mr. Friel, that you were going to be a writer?*
> The answer is, I have no idea.
> *What other writers influenced you most strongly?*
> I have no idea.
> *Which of your plays, Mr. Friel, is your favorite?*
> None of them.
> *Which of your stories?*
> Most of them embarrass me.
> *Do you think, Mr. Friel, that the atmosphere in Ireland is hostile or friendly to the artist?*
> Uh, I'm thinking of my lunch.
> *Do you see any relationship between dwindling theatrical audiences all over the world and the fragmentation of what we might call the theatrical thrust into disparate movements like theatre of cruelty, tactile theatre, nude theatre, theatre of despair, etc., etc., or would you say, Mr. Friel, that the influence of Heidegger is only beginning to be felt in the drama and that Beckett and Pinter are John the Baptists of the great new movement?*
> Well, in answer to that, I'd say that—I'd say that I'm a middle-aged man and that I tire easily and that I'd like to go out for a walk now; so please go away and leave me alone.[13]

Friel's antipathy to interviews has deep roots. As early as 1964, when *Philadelphia, Here I Come!* had just opened in Dublin, the play's "shy, modest and thoughtful" thirty-five-year-old author would confess that meeting the press was "rather frightening."[14] Even this early in his career he was letting it be known that he "prefers to let his plays speak for them-

---

13. Brian Friel, "Self-Portrait," BBC Radio Four Northern Ireland, 19 December 1971 (recorded 21 October 1971).

14. Gus Smith, "'I've Yet to Make Money from My Plays' Says Festival Dramatist Brian Friel," *Sunday Independent* (Dublin), ca. 4 October 1964. (Undated clipping from the *Sunday Independent* clippings library does not appear in the edition on microfilm. *Philadelphia, Here I Come!* opened on 28 September 1964 as part of the Dublin Festival that closed on 4 October 1964. Internal evidence suggests the interview occurred during the Festival.)

selves."[15] In 1969 Friel did complain to the press about the Abbey Theatre's rejection of *The Mundy Scheme*. But a week later, when the play went into rehearsals at the Olympia Theatre, journalists who broached the subject found that Friel, "who is reticent by nature, declined to talk about the affair."[16]

Despite his legendary reticence, Friel has from time to time been surprisingly forthright in talking about thematic implications of his plays. During the late 1960s and very early 1970s, Friel gamely agreed to a series of extensive interviews. Refusing to term *Philadelphia, Here I Come!* an emigrant play, Friel says he did not so much focus on emigration as on three other concerns: "a boy belatedly becoming a man; a relationship between a father and son not coming to fruition; and a love affair that never flowered simply because of incoherence or shyness or whatever."[17] Although *The Enemy Within* (1965) is about the exile of St. Columba, Friel describes the play not so much as historical or ecclesiastical in its focus but as a "kind of venture . . . into an analysis of family relations."[18] The saint, "a thick, big, 'get' of a fella,"[19] left Ireland, Friel says, because "it was politically too hot for him" and because "his family were driving him up the walls, literally."[20]

Throughout, Friel emphasizes the ordinariness of his characters, contrasting his dramatic approach with that of Tennessee Williams. Whereas Williams "starts off with unbelievable characters and then sets out to make them credible," Friel says he relies on the stock characters of Irish drama and "then ha[s] to make something of them."[21] Friel says he hopes to encourage "sympathy and intelligence and understanding"[22] for the people he writes about while avoiding any suggestion of crusading for them.

While writing about people who are ordinary, Friel has from the first engaged in extraordinary experiments in dramatic form. Indeed, the

---

15. "Tatler's Parade: Brian Friel's Latest Play Opens Next Week," *Irish Independent,* 7 November 1968, p. 12.

16. Gus Smith, "Why Friel Doesn't Write about Civil Rights," *Sunday Independent,* 1 June 1969, p. 20.

17. Lewis Funke, "Interview with Brian Friel," in *Playwrights Talk about Writing: 12 Interviews with Lewis Funke* (Chicago: Dramatic Publishing Co., 1975), p. 122.

18. John Boyd, "Soundings," BBC Radio Four Northern Ireland, 2 August 1970 (recorded 17 June 1970).

19. Peter Lennon, "Playwright of the Western World," *The Guardian,* 8 October 1964, p. 9.

20. Boyd, "Soundings."

21. John Fairleigh, "After *Philadelphia,*" *Belfast Telegraph,* 9 August 1966, p. 6.

22. Graham Morison, "An Ulster Writer: Brian Friel," *Acorn* (English Department, Magee University College, Derry, now a campus of the University of Ulster), no. 8 (Spring 1965), p. 5.

very form of *Philadelphia, Here I Come!* in which the protagonist is divided into Public Gar, a shy, quiet man who cannot communicate with those around him, and Private Gar, a confident and verbal Greek chorus, may reflect something of Friel's own inner division. That inner division, in turn, may be reflected in Friel's alternating willingness and reluctance to communicate regarding his work. During his early career Friel gave a number of radio talks and discussed the thematic implications of his early plays on the BBC Northern Ireland Home Service.

But after his 1971 "Self-Portrait" containing his parodic self-interview, Friel's contacts with the press became increasingly limited. He did speak briefly about *The Gentle Island* (1971) and *The Freedom of the City* (1973). But by the end of the decade he was forswearing all interviews. When *Living Quarters* (1977) and *Aristocrats* (1979) opened in Dublin, and even when *Faith Healer* (1979) opened in New York, Friel refused to meet with any journalists. Producer Noel Pearson first met Friel in New York in 1979, where the critics had not been kind to his ballet of *The Playboy of the Western World* or to Friel's *Faith Healer.* "I was staying at the Royalton then, back in the days when the roaches did jigs at the end of the room, and Brian Friel was staying across the street at the Algonquin," says Pearson. "He was drinking sizable gins and feeling sore and we started to talk."[23] Friel may have been willing to commiserate with a fellow sufferer. But a journalist—like Elgy Gillespie who wanted to know "Is the Play Still the Thing?"[24]—could attempt to pluck out the heart of Friel's mystery only by submitting questions in writing to which he would respond, if at all, in writing. Apart from such written communication, the rest was silence.

Then Friel founded Field Day. The venture that Friel and actor Stephen Rea embarked on in 1980 would, over the next fourteen years, have constantly evolving goals. Field Day was going to escape the theatrical orthodoxies of both London and Dublin, bring theater of professional caliber to Irish people, free Irish voices to speak to Irish ears without pitching their words to sound acceptable to London or Broadway or even Dublin ears. Based in the North but embracing the entire island, Field Day would generate creative energy for the closing decades of the twentieth century as Yeats and the Abbey Theatre had provided earlier in the century, provide an artistic basis for some kind of reconciliation of the majority and minority cultures in the North, and even serve as a fifth column that might ultimately lead to "a more generous and noble

---

23. Witchel, "Life May Be a Madness, but It's Also a Poem," p. 5.
24. Elgy Gillespie, "Is the Play Still the Thing?" *Irish Times,* 28 July 1978, p. 8.

notion of Irishness"[25] for the whole island. If the evolving visions for what Field Day might accomplish were immense, so were the challenges. Immediately to hand were the tasks of casting a play, hiring a director, securing multiple venues for a touring production, organizing the logistics of transportation and lodging for a theater troupe. Friel and Rea secured grants from both the Northern Ireland Arts Council and the Arts Council in Dublin, but the money was never enough to provide financial security. Donations were needed and corporate sponsorships and audiences for the plays. The generation of donations and audiences provided a compelling need for publicity and lots of it. What Friel had become unwilling to do in order to promote his own plays was now incumbent upon him if the shared vision of Field Day was to prosper. Brian Friel started talking.

In the early 1980s Friel spoke with more journalists in Northern Ireland, in the Republic, and even in Britain than he had in the rest of his career combined. He agreed to multiple radio and television interviews with the BBC and RTÉ and was interviewed several times for an RTÉ documentary on "Brian Friel and Field Day." Friel's newfound expansiveness coincided with the Field Day production of *Translations* (1980), by any reckoning one of Friel's masterpieces. Besides discussing the genesis of the play, Friel was willing to explore the thematic implications of *Translations* and the way those themes coalesced with his vision for Field Day. Friel's willingness to meet with the press also coincided with the first Dublin and London productions, in 1980 and 1981, of another of his masterpieces, *Faith Healer*. Referring to *Faith Healer* as "some kind of metaphor for the art, the craft of writing,"[26] Friel acknowledged to one interviewer that the "austere form" of that play—with its monologues that contradict each other—involves the audience in wrestling with questions about the nature of truth.[27] In each of several interviews, Friel offered generous commentary on his translation of Chekhov's *Three Sisters* (1981) and his farce *The Communication Cord* (1982), which were Field Day's second and third productions.

But when he realized that people were referring to the entire enterprise of Field Day as "Friels on Wheels," he decided his own work should have a lower profile in the venture. Even in interviews when *The Commu-*

---

25. Patrick Quilligan, "Field Day's New Double Bill," *Irish Times,* 18 September 1984, p. 10.

26. Fintan O'Toole, "The Man from God Knows Where: An Interview with Brian Friel," *In Dublin,* no. 165 (28 October 1982), p. 22.

27. Ronan Farren, "Broadway? Who Cares?" *Evening Herald* (Dublin), 28 August 1980, p. 8.

nication Cord was in rehearsal, Friel was saying the need "to protect myself and protect my work" was in competition with his desire "to keep this enterprise of Field Day vibrant."[28] "I don't know whether I'll be able to do these two things; maybe one will have to go," said Friel, "because there certainly is a conflict between appearing in public as I'm doing at this moment and suppressing the personality, which is necessary for the work."[29]

Friel continued, albeit at a reduced level, to speak out on occasion for Field Day, but he drastically reduced other contact with the press. In 1984 he made one brief statement to the *Irish Times* about his hopes for Field Day;[30] in 1986 he offered brief remarks when Field Day's plan to publish an anthology of Irish writing was announced;[31] and in 1987 he and other Field Day directors promoting the anthology participated in a fund-raising trip to the United States. But when *Living Quarters* (1977) had its first Belfast production in 1985, Friel gave no interviews. When *Philadelphia, Here I Come!* was revived in Dublin in 1986, Friel stayed at home while his wife attended the opening.[32] And by 1986 Friel was again requiring journalists to submit their questions to him in writing. Even written questions were not answered regarding *Fathers and Sons* (1987) when it opened in London, and Friel took the further precaution of leaving his telephone off the hook.[33] He even stopped granting interviews regarding Field Day productions of his plays when *Making History* (1988) opened in Derry, leaving that task to Stephen Rea and other actors.

Therefore, Friel's willingness to grant three substantial interviews for *Dancing at Lughnasa*, even if the journalists were required to come to Co. Donegal, was all the more extraordinary. Talking to Mel Gussow, John Lahr, and Julie Kavanagh[34] about his extraordinary masterpiece, Friel may have resisted questioning even as he advised his questioners to "Persist! Persist!"[35] Taken together the three interviews—which appeared in *The New York Times Magazine, Vogue* and *Vanity Fair* and are all reprinted in this volume—offer a compelling account of the genesis of

---

28. Quoted in "Brian Friel and Field Day," RTÉ, 14 February 1983.
29. Quoted in "Brian Friel and Field Day," RTÉ, 14 February 1983.
30. Quilligan, "Field Day's New Double Bill," p. 10.
31. Martin Cowley, "Field Day Has Made a Permanent Mark," *Irish Times,* 5 May 1986, p. 12.
32. "The Night Brian Sent His Missus to Philadelphia," *Irish Independent,* 17 April 1986.
33. Michael Davie, "A Novel Way to Write a Play," *The Observer,* 12 July 1987, p. 16.
34. Mel Gussow, "From Ballybeg to Broadway," *New York Times Magazine,* 29 September 1991, pp. 30, 55–61; Kavanagh, "Friel at Last," pp. 128, 130, 134, 138; John Lahr, "In *Dancing at Lughnasa,* Due on Broadway this Month, Brian Friel Celebrates Life's Pagan Joys," *Vogue* (American), October 1991, pp. 174, 176, 178–79.
35. Gussow, "From Ballybeg to Broadway," p. 56.

Dancing at Lughnasa, of Friel's concern for language, and of his desire to incarnate the spiritual in his play in a way that transcends language. While saying that *Lughnasa* is "about the necessity for paganism," he indicated his next play would be about "the necessity for mystery. It's mystery, not religion, but mystery finds its expression in this society mostly in religious practice."[36] Although Friel was calling his next play *The Imagined Place,* his remark to Gussow may stand as his only published description of *Wonderful Tennessee,* the title his next play had when it opened in 1993. But by then the veil had descended. Friel has, to date, given no further interviews.

Although Friel's aversion to interviews may to some extent be explained by a simple desire to be left alone, the reason he has most often given is that he does not want to upstage his own plays: "I don't think that the worker should distract from the work."[37] But beyond his innate shyness and even beyond his desire not to distract from the work is Friel's desire to honor the complexity of experience. Victoria Radin came away from her interview with the impression that "Brian Friel qualifies his every statement." In conversation with Radin, Friel said that writing overtly political plays like *The Freedom of the City* was a kind of emotional inflammation. But he questioned the value of what he had done even as he also turned the tables on his interviewer:

> Was it, he wondered, an abdication of real, more humane things, under the pressure and hysteria of the moment? What did I think?
>
> He is apt to ask you questions like that—and not just rhetorically. He is a medium-sized man with a slight Northern lilt and a very direct blue gaze. Sometimes it feels inquisitorial—he never, says one of his writer-friends, the poet and professor of English, Seamus Deane, stops gathering information. It seems to be partly genuine interest and partly writer's antennae. At times during our interview I wondered who would finally get written up.[38]

Other interviewers seem equally certain about Friel's lack of certitude. Charles Spencer describes Friel as an "infinitely courteous man

---

36. Gussow, "From Ballybeg to Broadway," p. 61.

37. Justine McCarthy, "Friel Day: Justine McCarthy Tries to Pin Down the Elusive Genius of Secretive Playwright Brian Friel." *Irish Independent,* 19 January 1991, "Weekender" section, p. 13.

38. Victoria Radin, "Voice from Ireland: Victoria Radin talks to Brian Friel," *The Observer,* 1 March 1981, p. 34.

who hedges his judgements with qualification and speaks clear sense in the diffident tones of one who suspects he might have got it all wrong."[39] Elgy Gillespie, who describes Friel as having "an exceedingly gentle manner, and a beautiful voice with very musical modulations," found it easy to understand why he would loathe interviews. "He is so mild and equivocal in manner," says Gillespie, "that it is easy, even inevitable, for journalists to put their own bias or construction upon his words, by quite unconsciously giving them certain inflections."[40] Concurring with Radin and Spencer about Friel's questioning, self-qualifying mode of discourse, Gillespie puts her finger on why even a verbatim transcript of Friel's words may be misleading:

> His passionate involvement in Field Day, we can safely hazard, is not about nationalism in a narrow way. It's about questioning everything, just the way he questions everything as he talks. The journalists would easily put them down as statements, if they were taping them and relaying word for word. This, he explains, is why he's no good at them. "Things seem so much more definite in the way I'm quoted in interviews."[41]

Friel's perception that his views "seem so much more definite" in the interviews suggests that readers should approach statements in his interviews with caution. Any interviewer might be tempted to make things sound just a bit more definite than does Friel when he says—on a given issue—"Maybe not. . . . But I feel perhaps yes."[42] Any journalist might not depict the precise degree of qualification conveyed when Friel, as part of his response to a question, "makes a little movement of his head, approximating to a shrug, the better to downplay commitment."[43]

To be sure, Friel himself may on occasion have succumbed to the impulse to make things seem a bit more definite than he felt them to be. "The interview situation changes you," as British playwright Tom Stoppard has said. "You're trying to oblige somebody by making more sense of things than you normally feel. So you end up as somebody who has much clearer positions, much more definitive positions on all kinds of

---

39. Spencer, "Friels on Wheels . . . ," p. 24.
40. Elgy Gillespie, "The Saturday Interview: Brian Friel," *Irish Times*, 5 September 1981, p. 14 ("Weekend" section, p. 6).
41. Gillespie, "The Saturday Interview."
42. Radin, "Voice from Ireland," p. 34.
43. Gillespie, "The Saturday Interview."

topics because you somehow didn't realize you could sit there and say, 'Actually, I have no idea.'"[44] Actually, on one occasion Friel had tried sitting there and saying "I have no idea"—in his parodic self-interview in "Self-Portrait." But at other times, the attempt to translate Friel's shrugs and hesitancies and self-questioning is, as one of his friends puts it, like "shifting smoke with a pitchfork."[45]

Indeed, for a playwright "whose reclusiveness in recent years has bordered on fetish,"[46] according to a *New York Times* reporter, even the statement that Friel avoids interviews may seem too definite. At a reception, the playwright was visibly ruffled by a journalist's stark question "Why do you not give interviews, Mr. Friel?"

> "Oh, don't put it like that," he pleaded, looking aghast, the puppy dog eyes in his caricatural face pleading for understanding. "I just never know what to say."[47]

And yet. Over the course of four decades, Friel has had quite a lot to say. Although his reticence has vied with periods of expansiveness, his willingness to grant interviews has fortuitously coincided with the productions of his pivotal works. As a result, some of his most reflective interviews have turned out to be about his best plays. *Brian Friel in Conversation* includes much material that until now has been virtually inaccessible to many readers, including surprisingly extensive comments on his work by a playwright known for his legendary reluctance to talk to the press.

Indeed, one of the reasons Friel's conversations have seemed so rare has been the relative inaccessibility of many of his interviews. Consulting Friel's early BBC broadcasts requires access to the BBC Written Archives Centre in Reading or the National Sound Archive in London. During rehearsals of *The Communication Cord* Friel participated in several interviews for a Radio Telefís Éireann documentary on "Brian Friel and Field Day,"[48] videotape of which is held at RTÉ headquarters in Dublin.

Conversations disseminated on the airwaves may be expected to be ephemeral, but some of Friel's conversations in print pose their own

---

44. Sean Mitchell, "Just Who, Really, Is Tom Stoppard?" *Los Angeles Herald Examiner,* 18 December 1986; reprinted in *Performing Arts* microfiche, vol. 13 (November 1986–February 1987), card 110:A5–A6.

45. Gussow, "From Ballybeg to Broadway," p. 55.

46. Witchel, "Life May Be a Madness, but It's Also a Poem," p. 5.

47. McCarthy, "Friel Day," p. 13.

48. "Brian Friel and Field Day," RTÉ, 14 February 1983.

challenges in terms of accessibility. Three of the most substantive interviews of Friel's career appeared in the pages of *Acorn, The Word,* and *In Dublin.* In 1965 Friel talked at length about his aims and writing methods to the associate editor of *Acorn,* the literary magazine of the English Department of Magee University College in Derry. But the particular issue of *Acorn* that contains Friel's interview[49] is not to be found in the British Library, the Cambridge University Library, the National Library in Dublin, nor the libraries of Trinity College, Dublin, or Queen's University, Belfast. A pilgrimmage to Derry is rewarded by helpful librarians who have that particular *Acorn* safely squirreled away in the Magee College Special Collections. But not everyone interested in *Philadelphia, Here I Come!* can come to Derry to read about Friel's aims in writing.

Friel's most extended consideration of religious questions—including his views on God, the afterlife, and the Catholic Church—are contained in *The Word,*[50] a Catholic pictorial magazine once published by the Divine Word Missionary Brothers at St. Richard's College of Hadzor, near Droitwich, Worcestershire. But God knows where to find "The Man from God Knows Where: An Interview with Brian Friel,"[51] a poignant discussion with Fintan O'Toole of Friel's sense of exile. O'Toole's interview, contained in this volume, originally appeared in *In Dublin,* an arts and culture listing once put out by Tribune Publications. But *In Dublin* is now under separate management, which no longer has the issue containing "The Man from God Knows Where."

Most of Friel's interviews have, of course, been with Irish interviewers, and Friel's career spans a time period for which, unfortunately, no indexes exist for Irish newspapers. *Brian Friel in Conversation* is based on research in the offices of *The Irish Times,* the Independent Newspapers, Dublin *(Irish Independent, Sunday Independent, Evening Herald),* the *Sunday Tribune,* the *Belfast Telegraph* and the *Irish News,* all of which granted access to their files of clippings. Drawing on that wealth of material, *Brian Friel in Conversation* includes some interviews never listed in any Friel bibliography. The volume concludes with the most extensive bibliography and discography of Friel interviews ever compiled.

The chronologically arranged conversations begin at the beginning with Friel talking about growing up as a "thieving little street urchin" on

49. Morison, "An Ulster Writer: Brian Friel," pp. 4–15.

50. Desmond Rushe, "Kathleen Mavourneen, Here Comes Brian Friel," *The Word: An International Catholic Pictorial Magazine* (Divine Word Missionaries, formerly of St. Richard's College, Hadzor, Droitwich, Worcestershire, England; now published at Donamon, Co. Roscommon, Ireland), February 1970, pp. 12–15.

51. O'Toole, "The Man from God Knows Where," pp. 20–23.

the streets of Derry.[52] Friel mingles his affection for the city by "the winding Foyle" with vivid memories of knowing as a twelve-year-old boy that
taking shoes to be repaired meant entering an area where "if the Protestant boys caught you . . . they'd kill you."[53] But the young Catholic who
faced possible death at the hands of Protestant boys also found it "a very
disturbing thing"[54] at age sixteen to enter Maynooth, the Catholic seminary outside Dublin. He alludes to his seminary education as a
"tragedy,"[55] calling it "an awful experience" that "nearly drove me
cracked."[56] By contrast, his 1963 trip to America—where he observed
Tyrone Guthrie rehearsing for his opening season in Minneapolis—was,
Friel says, "my first parole from inbred, claustrophobic Ireland."[57] Friel
describes that "sense of liberation"[58] as a "kind of explosion in the
head,"[59] resulting in the writing of *Philadelphia, Here I Come!*—the play
that would take the young Irish writer not just to Philadelphia but to
Broadway.

Friel's vivid descriptions of what it was like to grow up as a member
of the minority in the North provide a telling biographical backdrop.
But interviews with Friel are not, finally, primarily valuable for what they
reveal of Friel the man but for what they may reveal of Friel's plays. Friel's
later reticence in interviews may, in part, be attributed to his recognition
of just how self-revealing the plays are. Although he has resisted attempts
to find a pattern in the carpet of the many plays he has woven, he has
acknowledged "a projection of some kind of dual personality in a lot of
the plays."[60] "I discover this now in looking back over the bulk of the
work," Friel explained, "that there are very often two characters: one
who is a very extrovert, quick-talking, glib character and another who's a
kind of morose and taciturn and . . . less immodest, let's say. And in some
way I think perhaps those reflect some aspect of myself and perhaps
some aspect of a member of the minority living in the North."[61]

Those who have followed Friel's career will not expect an easy resolution to the contrast between an affable, genial Friel who is willing to

---

52. Brian Friel, "The Green Years: A Talk by Brian Friel," BBC Radio, Northern Ireland
Home Service, 30 April 1964 (recorded 30 April 1964).
53. Rushe, "Kathleen Mavourneen, Here Comes Brian Friel," p. 13.
54. Rushe, "Kathleen Mavourneen, Here Comes Brian Friel," p. 13.
55. Rushe, "Kathleen Mavourneen, Here Comes Brian Friel," p. 13.
56. Lennon, "Playwright of the Western World," p. 9.
57. Friel, "Self-Portrait."
58. Friel, "Self-Portrait."
59. Lahr, "In *Dancing at Lughnasa*, Due on Broadway this Month, Brian Friel Celebrates
Life's Pagan Joys," p. 179.
60. "Brian Friel and Field Day," RTÉ, 14 February 1983.
61. "Brian Friel and Field Day," RTÉ, 14 February 1983.

talk and a reticent Friel who is kind of morose and taciturn. Friel insists that the primary concern of *Translations* is not so much with the historical transformation of Irish place names as with the continuing, contemporary need to "look at ourselves, recognize and identify ourselves."[62] But the process of identifying ourselves is fraught with complexities. Indeed, throughout his career Friel has been inclined to subvert oversimplifications of his work or of his perception of truth. He says that after *Translations* he wrote the farcical *Communication Cord* "because I was being categorised in some sort of a way that I didn't feel easy about, and it seemed to me that a farce would disrupt that kind of categorising."[63] Despite—or perhaps because of—the staggering Broadway success of *Dancing at Lughnasa,* Friel upended his audience's expectations by following that play's raucous celebration of paganism with the quietly evocative religious mystery of *Wonderful Tennessee.* The playwright who has written whole plays to subvert his audience's expectations may rightly be wary of being pinned down too definitively in the context of an interview. Readers should be wary of taking any single statement as definitive rather than viewing it in the full complex round of Friel's work and words about his work. Yet the insights Friel offers into his background and his intentions for his plays should be of interest to anyone who has been puzzled, intrigued, or fascinated by a Friel play and has harbored a desire to engage Brian Friel in conversation.

---

62. Paddy Agnew, "'Talking to Ourselves': Brian Friel Talks to Paddy Agnew," *Magill* (Dublin), 4, no. 3 (December 1980), p. 61.

63. O'Toole, "The Man from God Knows Where," p. 21.

The Green Years:
A Talk by Brian Friel

Brian Friel / 1964

Despite his wariness of self-revelation, in his early thirties Friel agreed to write a humor column for the *Irish Press* in Dublin based on everyday events in his life. Although Friel had published stories in *The New Yorker*—and BBC Northern Ireland had broadcast one of his plays—the column offered no indication that Friel was an author of such works. In his first column, under a banner headline—"The Lighter Side of Life: Meet Brian Friel who has undertaken to entertain you here every Saturday"—Friel confessed to worries about his mortgage and got some comic mileage out of having two birth certificates ("one which says my birthday falls on January 9th, another which favours January 10th"). But the tone turned more serious when he talked about starting his schooling at age seven with his father as his teacher: "He always thought I should have been his brightest pupil, and I think he suspected that I was dull on purpose, just to annoy him." A few months after the column began to appear, Friel went to the studios of the BBC Northern Ireland Home Service to record the first of several autobiographical radio talks. That first talk, "Some People and Places," focussed on his difficulty in transforming his warehouse of "dull, embarrassing, uneasy memories" into accounts that were "attractive" or "hilarious" or "respectable"—"the stuff of conventional autobiography." Still, Friel continued writing for the *Irish Press* about incidents from his life even after he left for

Transmitted on the BBC Northern Ireland Home Service, 30 April 1964 (recorded 30 April 1964).

America in March 1963, when the column appeared for three
months as "Brian Friel's American Diary." Back in Northern
Ireland after his American sojourn, Friel resumed his association with the BBC, reviewing books and on occasion serving as
host for "The Arts in Ulster." He also continued to offer autobiographical talks. Of these, "The Green Years" returns to his
uneasy relationship with his father but also offers the most
poignant account of his first response to Derry and his abiding
affection for his adopted home.

I spent the first ten years of my life in a place called Culmore, outside the
town of Omagh, and if the Jesuits are right in saying, "Give us the first
seven years and you can keep the rest," then Culmore had my formative
years and three more for good value. It wasn't until I was ten that we
moved to Derry, in 1939, when the world that our fathers knew began to
break up. But for a young boy of ten it wasn't such a bad year at all—
apart from sweet rationing. To begin with, there was snow on the ground
that winter, and the great city of Derry with its dizzy hills was obviously
designed for sleighing. There was, besides, the wonderful position of our
new house, the last in a terrace and directly opposite the army barracks.
From our drawing-room window I'd an upper circle view of the whole
drama of military life—of marching soldiers, and tanks, and artillery,
and bayonet practice—a splendid and continuous tattoo, and all put on
just for my entertainment. And on our right hand side, and separated
from us only by the width of a street, was a Presbyterian church; and of
that I have particularly happy memories because I was then preparing
for an entrance examination to a grammar school, and my father, who
was a teacher, was coaching me. Now I don't remember the details of
those private lessons, but I *do* know that they always ended with my father
in a towering rage and me in tears, and I *have* a vivid recollection of
crawling up to bed night after night, weighed down by the very *terrible*
and apparently imminent prospect of turning into a "Yahoo". But what
exactly a Yahoo was I wasn't at all sure, but it was certainly the inevitable
fate of people who couldn't learn algebra, and the fact that it was an
amorphous, faceless thing made it all the more terrifying. Anyhow, as I
lay in bed contemplating this damnation, the Presbyterian congregation
next door consoled me with their hymns. They were fine lusty singers,
and I had a good ear, and within a month I knew all their pieces and was
able to join in with them. The only snag was that I had to stop and listen
every so often to make sure that we were all keeping together. But they
brought me great solace and great comfort, and although it may not

have been the height of mystical experience I can heartily recommend hymn-singing to all those who labour and are burdened.

My first disappointment with Derry was really a misunderstanding. Long before I came, I heard the term, "the Strand"—people walked along the Strand, and shopped there, and went to films there, and had afternoon tea there. Heaven alone knows what sort of a concept I had of this place—it was a beach and a lido and a promenade and a fun-palace and a civic centre all rolled into one. But the dominant feature, the one constant in my ever-changing image was the beach. A strand to me meant a beach and a sea. There was a sea-shore bang in the centre of Derry City! Obviously my geography was as weak as my algebra. However, on my first excursion down town my one ambition was to get to the Strand. We got there. It was just another street. I kept asking, "But where's the strand? Where's the strand?", and my mother kept saying, "We're in it! We're on it! *This* is the Strand." And with the growing realisation that the Strand was not, after all, a strand, an image withered, and sunny days of bathing and sand-castles went suddenly black, and the town for me lost its best amenity. Even now I still think it's a bit sharp calling the Strand the Strand when it's not a strand.

What did we do? What was our fun? What was the atmosphere of city life for a child in those days? Well, of course, there was school, primary school and then grammar school; and for an apprentice Yahoo, school was merely a marking time until you got out at 3.00 o'clock in the afternoon. Then you stopped being a vegetable and you came to life. I'd like to imagine that my friend, John, and I went for long walks around the high periphery of the town, and looked down on the winding Foyle and the smoking factories and the lazy docks, and thereby laid the foundation of sweet memories that would quicken and renew us in later years. Or I'd like to be able to claim that we grew flowers in grimy windowboxes or traced the footsteps of Saint Columba when he lived here, or did regular tours of the city's fine, solid walls. But—we did none of these idyllic things. Indeed, we were as insensitive to the beauty and the history of the town as we were to the terrible holocaust that was going on in Europe just then. To certain things, though, we responded actively, even violently. One of these was a dumpy little WREN who was in digs in our street. Her name was Jill—Jill Hunt; and we both loved her; and we were both resolved to marry her. The detail that she could have been our mother and that we were both in short pants was trivial. How many times we came to blows over her I've *no* idea. In retrospect I see us forever wrestling and punching and clawing at each other—but perhaps the vividness of this memory is merely significant of the depth of my passion at the time. We really *can't* have fought over her all that much because I have another memory of us, equally vivid, tearing down Abercorn Road on roller skates; and now that I think of it, we must have fought very little over dumpy Jill because I seem to remember us *living* on those skates. Abercorn Road was wonderful for skating. The gradient was steep, enough without being terrifying. And when you got to the bottom—and by then you were doing a reckless three or four miles per hour—you had to zig-zag between huge cement blocks that were flung up in the middle of the road to smash invading German tanks. Sometimes your navigation was off; sometimes the police were hot on your tail; and sometimes you were so intoxicated by speed that your judgment was impaired. But for one reason or another you frequently met the fate that was intended for the Germans. Then you would pick yourself up and crawl to the footpath—always smiling, of course, the desperate smile never left your face—and in the secrecy of some doorway with tender fingers you examined the bleeding knees and the raw hands and the bruised shins; and if the wounds were near-mortal you slipped off those treacherous skates and pretended that you were wanted for your tea. But it wasn't the injuries that were important, I remember. It was the secrecy, the compulsion to conceal the suffering, the obligation to walk *back up* Abercorn Road without a trace of a limp. And that, I suppose, marked the end of childhood and the beginnings of manhood.

I think we were vandals. I know we had no civic sense whatever, and to this day I have an odd twinge of conscience when I recall the amount of damage we did. Those were the days of air-raid shelters, and on the corners of those shelters there were reflectors, circles of red glass set in chrome rings, just like the reflectors on the back of a bicycle. And when we should have been employed in healthy pursuits like bird-nesting or stamp collecting, we collected those reflectors and stored them in the shelter in our own street. We had in all 164 at one time—I remember the number vividly because I myself wrenched number 164 from a shelter at the foot of Bishop Street. Now assuming that there were four reflectors on each shelter, this meant that we stripped forty-one shelters; and if that figure is correct, we must have gone looting all over the town. The things were valueless, you couldn't play with them, they were too hot to swop. I can only conclude, then, that we were disturbed by some sort of paranoia that led us to believe that by squatting in a dark, smelly shelter and gloating over a hoard of worthless glass we believed ourselves to be Ben Gunn or Long John Silver. But no! That's ridiculous—that's the mistake all adults make when they try to interpret the behaviour of children by the doubtful criteria of grown-ups. We suffered from no paranoia. We were just thieving little street urchins, and the only therapy we needed was a kick in the pants.

When an affection for Derry grew in me I don't know, and I think that's as it should be. As a child your home-place is something you take for granted, like meals on the table and clean shirts in your drawer. It's only when you grow older that you *consciously* categorize, that you look for neat beginnings and endings, and that you apply a system of selection and rejection. I *think* I can recall when I first knew that I loved Derry; but again, as I say, this is the unreliable casting-back of an adult. We were coming home from holidays on the old G.N.R. line which follows the river north from Strabane; it was a rich August evening; we had just turned the last bend that concealed the town; and there, suddenly, it was: the docks and the bridge and the black plane of the river and the trees and the sleeping ships. And I can recall the flood of happy recognition and joy and love and peace that suffused me. And this is a memory that I don't suspect, because that view of Derry, no matter how often I see it, sparks off the same reaction. Now, of course, it's heightened by a vague wistfulness and by a recollection of that early epiphany. But that first awareness was precious and illuminative and permanent; and from then on every going away was a wrench and every return a fulfilment.

And talking of going away reminds me of a faculty that seems to be more acute and more developed in Derry people than it is in other Irish people—that is their attachment to their city. Put a Derryman in Belfast and he is uneasy. Put him in Birmingham and he is miserable. Put him in Boston and he breaks his heart. The reason, I suspect, is that, much as we boast of our city-status, we're not really a city at all. We haven't the drive nor the vitality nor the impermanence nor the anonymity of a city. And if it goes to that, the texture of city life doesn't appeal to us. We are all villagers at heart, or at best inhabitants of a market town. We have our industries, but they haven't made us industrial. We have a port that sees ships from every nation, but we scarcely know what the word cosmopolitan means. We are concerned about the individual, and if we don't know him personally at least we know his brother or his wife's aunt or a cousin of his father's uncle. Stewart? . . . Stewart, aye, he'd be one of the Stewarts from the Brandywell, or else he'd be married on one of Jock Stewart's daughters—you know Jock that used to be the great doggy man. The inquisitiveness of villagers; the complacency of a market town. In one sense it's an easy atmosphere to live in, and in another sense it imposes its own rigid rules of conduct because respectability here is equated with virtue, and the trouble is that respectability is not an absolute standard, but dependent on what people respect here and now. Aye, that's the rub.

I am tempted at times to pull up my stakes and go and live in a real city, for there I will have theatre and good talk and the intellectual excitement that these places promise. And occasionally I go, not pulling up my stakes and not with my family, but on a sort of try-out pioneering expedition by myself. And for a few nights or for a week I enjoy the theatre and the good talk and the intellectual excitement. But then nostalgia begins to gnaw at me, and I have to get back, urgently, desperately, if only to walk round the high periphery of the town, and look down on the winding Foyle and the smoking factories and the lazy docks—if only to do all those things that a born Derryman did in his youth and then forgot about them, and that I, who came here almost too late, have never fully assimilated yet. Maybe in time I will acquire detachment. Maybe a day will come when Derry means little to me. But if that day comes, I believe I will really have become a Yahoo then.

Playwright of the Western World

Peter Lennon / 1964

Friel's play *Philadelphia, Here I Come!* was first performed on 28 September 1964 as part of the Dublin Theatre Festival, which closed on 4 October. Despite garnering accolades from critics, the play did not run long enough to garner much in the way of box office receipts. Friel may have written a "hit," but in early October 1964 the author still had no income to show from his career as a playwright. After the play opened to critical acclaim in Dublin, Friel's immediate concern—expressed to Gus Smith of Dublin's *Sunday Independent*—was that the festival did not run long enough to "give the playwright a really good chance of making money." A few days later Friel could be more philosophical in talking to Peter Lennon. Although the interview appeared in *The Guardian,* a British newspaper, Peter Lennon is an Irishman who would immediately recognize Maynooth as a seminary and would not need a gloss for Friel's reference to "a thick, big, 'get' of a fella." Speaking to Lennon, Friel could talk freely about what Hilton Edwards as an Englishman had trouble grasping about the play he had just directed in Dublin. Despite Friel's sense of some cultural gap between his Irish play and its English director, Friel came to Edwards's defense when the eminent Irish short story writer Frank O'Connor attacked him as a "wicked . . . old magician" who turned Friel's "beautiful, gentle play" into "a rip-roaring revue." In a letter to the editor to the *Sunday Independent* on 11 October 1964, Friel said he was "grateful to Mr. Edwards for the magic he worked with my play" and defended the magic as "always discreet and in tone."

From *The Guardian*, 8 October 1964, p. 9.

Before writing *Philadelphia, Here I Come!* which was the undisputed hit of the Dublin Theatre Festival, Brian Friel had already acquired a modest international reputation with his *New Yorker* stories and two plays. His first play *The Blind Mice* has been on BBC television; his second, *The Enemy Within,* had brief life at the Abbey, Dublin. A collection of short stories, *A Saucer of Larks,* published this year won critical acclaim both in England and the United States.

Friel is a former schoolteacher from Omagh, an old garrison town in the predominately Catholic county of Tyrone. Married with three children he gave up his teaching job in Derry to concentrate on writing when he landed a contract with the *New Yorker.* He is 35.

"Are you a practising Catholic?"

"I am. I was in Maynooth even, for two years when I was 16. An awful experience, it nearly drove me cracked. It is one thing I want to forget. I never talk about it—the priesthood. You know the kind of catholicism we have in this country, it's unique. Then I got a job teaching with the Christian Brothers which was nearly as bad as Maynooth. I was with them for ten years. Then I gave it up altogether. Last year I got an Arts Council award of £1,000 to go to Tyrone Guthrie's theatre in Minneapolis. I was there for six months. I had no real function, but the Americans handed me that nice label 'an observer.'

"I live in Derry now," he said with that familiar northern drone, in his case soft and full of nervous and alert overtones. "I'm a Nationalist too, you know. I feel very emotionally about this country. I wouldn't attempt to rationalise about my feelings, but I get myself involved in stupid controversies about the border. . . I don't know why.

"That first play *Blind Mice* was very poor. No I'm not being modest. It's a play I'm sorry about, you know the way it is, you think you have something but somehow it does not work. It was a good theme. An Irish missionary comes home to the North after signing a "confession" in a Communist concentration camp. It describes how people react when they find out. It was too solemn, too intense—I wanted to hit at too many things. I know now that people who go all flowery aren't going to get anywhere.

"Some people think that if they write a play and get it put on at the Gaiety they'll change the world. But while you may move a lot of people for the moment there will be only a very few who will think about it afterwards. Maybe lie awake in bed for half an hour thinking over what you said. That's all I want. You are never going to move people intellectually in the theatre. If there is one thing I learned from Tyrone Guthrie, it's that people at the theatre are moved by their hearts and their stomachs.

As Brendan Behan said to me once, 'make them laugh and then stick them.'

"*The Enemy Within* was about St. Columba. It was a realistic play with no thee's and thou's in it. St. Columba was a thick, big, 'get' of a fella. I think he was anyway, and he was responsible for a hell of a lot of wars and butchery. I wanted to discover how he acquired sanctity. Sanctity in the sense of a man having tremendous integrity and the courage to back it up. In that sense Joyce was probably a saint."

"And how did he acquire integrity?"

"By turning his back on Ireland and on his family."

"Isn't that the theme of *Philadelphia, Here I Come!*?"

"Yes. Gareth was leaving home not only in a local sense but in a spiritual sense too. Even if his inarticulate father had responded to him at the crucial moment it would only have postponed the departure. He would have had to get away. I took that quotation from the Bible. *The Enemy Within* as meaning literally Saint Columba's family. You have to get away from a corrupting influence. I think in Ireland we feed on each other a lot, we batten on each other. But the corruption I'm talking about a man finds anywhere around him—in Dublin or in Winesburg, Ohio."

"*Philadelphia, Here I Come!* is a rather subtle and gentle play. Did you have any problems with the interpretation?"

"It's really an angry play. It was very raw at the beginning but I toned it down. Then Hilton Edwards the producer is an Englishman. He did a very fine job but there were some things he found it hard to grasp. For example the man travelling around with the Irish couple from America.

"What relationship had this man with the woman, he wanted to know—or even with the husband? But there was no definite relationship. I think you find that a lot in Irish marriages, there is another man floating like a satellite around the couple. A person in whom the wife confides, probably. There is nothing sinister in this and certainly nothing sexual, but English people would find that very hard to grasp. And people want to know whether Gareth's old girlfriend who comes to say good-bye is still in love with him even though she is now married and a mother.

"But in Ireland many people would never admit such a possibility. They pull down the blinds. The Irish mind has many windows and the blinds are often down. In England they might have made love and it would have been tragic—or worse they might have made love and it would have made no difference. But not in Ireland."

"Do you think Ireland is a good place to work?"

"Dublin isn't. In Dublin your friends are legion—apparently. And it's too self-consciously literary. There is too much cheap chat. But you notice the amount of work that comes out of Dublin is negligible. I can work better in Derry."

"But in a small town would people not interfere more?"

"Ach no. They are more concerned about how you dress or whether you shave in the morning."

An Ulster Writer: Brian Friel

Graham Morison / 1965

When the editors of *Acorn*, the literary magazine of Magee University College, interviewed the most promising local author, what loomed largest in the interviewer's mind was the career of a playwright who had just had one play on national BBC radio, another on BBC television, and a forthcoming production on Broadway. But Brian Friel was still thinking of himself as a short story writer, despite having been acclaimed in Dublin as "in the front line of our contemporary writers for the theatre" for writing "the finest new Irish play . . . of this year" and acclaimed in Belfast as one of "The 'Big Five' of Ulster Drama." Whether Friel—in pursuing his literary craft on a partitioned island— was perceived as writing an "Irish play" or "Ulster drama" depended in large part on the political orientation of the observer. But both unionists and nationalists of Friel's adopted town—called Derry by nationalists and Londonderry by unionists—had been united in Spring 1965 in their hopes that Northern Ireland's second university would be sited in the province's Second City. Those hopes centered on the prospect that Magee, a two-year institution that sent its graduates to the University of Dublin, would be granted university status and then rapidly expand. *Acorn* had been founded in 1961 by the English Department of Magee out of the conviction that craftsmanship in writing could strike a blow against "the sloppiness, the pretentiousness and the vulgarity that confront us everywhere in print today." In his interview, *Acorn* assistant editor

From *Acorn* (English Department, Magee University College, Derry, now a campus of the University of Ulster), no. 8 (Spring 1965), pp. 4–15.

Graham Morison clearly wanted to focus on what Friel had to say about the craft of writing plays and short stories. Responding to questions about his work schedule and how he gets and develops ideas for stories, Friel may or may not offer guidance for aspiring undergraduate writers, but he certainly goes into the greatest detail of his career in describing his methods of composition.

MORISON: I gather that you have just returned from a visit to New York in connection with a production later this year of *Philadelphia, Here I Come!* When did you write your earlier play *The Enemy Within?*

FRIEL: I'm very bad on dates—I would think about three years ago.

MORISON: Have you been writing many short stories since that play or have you been concentrating on the theatre?

FRIEL: I don't concentrate on the theatre at all. I live on short stories. This is where my living comes from. As for playwriting it began as a sort of self-indulgence and then eventually I got caught up more and more in it. But the short story is the basis of all the work I do.

MORISON: Doesn't a play tend to involve the writer too much?

FRIEL: The short story is more self-contained. You write a short story and you're totally responsible for it. You can delude yourself that the people who read it think exactly as you think and are highly appreciative. It never occurs to you that it's being read by people in dentists' waiting rooms or waiting for a train.

MORISON: While writing, do you have an ideal reader in mind?

FRIEL: I don't think you have anybody specifically in mind. You try to be as lucid as you possibly can and you try to be as attractive as you can. I wouldn't put it any more rigidly than that.

MORISON: But you must entertain?

FRIEL: Yes. And you must keep the reader with you. You can't risk that he throws the damn thing aside after two and a half paragraphs and says, "I couldn't read any more of that." But you must also persuade him to your point of view, to the particular vision of these people that you're writing about.

MORISON: Do you see the writer's job as one of breaking down barriers?

FRIEL: No.

MORISON: I don't mean political or religious ones. But of getting one section of the community to take a closer look at another.

FRIEL: I would agree with that. But never in the role of a crusader. I hope to encourage sympathy for the people I'm writing about. Sympathy and intelligence and understanding for these people. But never crusading for them, nor suggesting for a minute that these people I write about are more important than anybody else.

MORISON: Do you think that would be presumptuous?

FRIEL: I do.

MORISON: What do you think of those plays that put across a social message?

FRIEL: I don't agree with it at all. I think people like Wesker did a tremendous lot of good, though, and Osborne, too; not for a class, but for the drama itself. Osborne rescued theatre and changed the direction of theatre. This doesn't mean that I think he's a major playwright by any means. He was an instrument in the course of the drama. He turned the direction of it. And was and is a good dramatist. But not a major dramatist, because I think that he lost something of himself through the cause he was fighting for—getting theatre away from Shaftesbury Avenue, or trying to do this.

MORISON: The new playwrights were often criticised for being more destructive than constructive. They never offered anything to replace the ruins.

FRIEL: Well, of course—and I'm not defending Osborne in saying this—I don't think this is the writer's job. All any writer does, whether he's a dramatist or a short-story writer, is to spotlight a situation. In other words, he presents a set of people and a situation with a certain clarity and understanding and sympathy and as a result of this one should look at them more closely; and if one is moved then that one should react accordingly. This is the responsibility of a reader or an audience, but I don't think it's the writer's.

MORISON: How do you want people to react? Do you want them to be angry?

FRIEL: This is a technique, a theatrical technique. Anger is a theatrical technique. The theatre is altogether so different from a short story anyhow. You get a group of people sitting in an audience and they aren't individual thinking people any longer once they're in an audience. They are a corporate group who act in the same way as a mob reacts—react emotionally and spontaneously. Now you can move these people by making them angry. You can make them sympathetic. You can make them laugh. You can make them cry. You can do all these things. And this emotional reaction doesn't live very long, doesn't last very long; I mean, they will not storm out of a theatre and pull down a Government. Or they will not storm out of a theatre and build homes for people that haven't got houses. But there is always the chance that a few people will retain a certain amount of the spontaneous reaction that they experienced with the theatre building and that they will think about this when they come outside. And perhaps they may do something. But this is not the end purpose. The end purpose is to move them, and you will move them, in a theatre anyhow, not through their head but through their heart. Brendan Behan used to say that you keep the people laughing in a theatre for five minutes and then in the sixth minute, when they're helpless laughing, you plug your message, if you want to plug a message.

MORISON: In a short story is it the characters or the plot that most interests you?

FRIEL: It's both. It's the characters in a particular situation. It's these particular people, caught in these particular circumstances at this particular time. This is the basis for your short story. Now if you can capture this with sufficient vividness and sufficient understanding, you will have seen them at a characteristic point in their lives and as a result of that you'll be able to gauge to an extent what they were like before this situation happened and you'll be able to forecast, generally, how they'll behave in the future. Obviously you haven't got the time for character development in a short story so that how they're going to behave is naturally surmised. But I think it should be apparent from their actions and thought at the time you have captured them what their future is going to be like.

MORISON: What about place? There is a terrific emphasis on place in your work. For example, in the first story of *The Saucer of Larks,* the place is very important. Does that place exist?

FRIEL: Well, almost. I couldn't point it out to you in a map, but I could point out four places that go to make up this one place. The general region, of course, is accurate. But the particular place within this general region is made up of three or four places within a broader area in the west of Donegal.

MORISON: Do you think a writer could go through all the elements of his story and identify their counterparts in his own past life?

FRIEL: Yes.

MORISON: Do you have a strong memory, yourself?

FRIEL: Not for everyday matters. After you've gone I won't be able to remember the questions you've asked me.

MORISON: Do you have a strong memory of place?

FRIEL: Yes. A memory of atmosphere, perhaps. The atmosphere of a place or the atmosphere of a person. They say, you know, that nothing important ever happens to you after you're ten or so. That could be very true. I'm a very strong believer in this theory, though I have never analysed it in any psychological sense. But I believe that it's very true. And I've also a strong belief in racial memory. This is a theory that Sean O'Faolain holds very dearly, and I think it's very true.

MORISON: It is said that a producer will often uncover strata of meaning in a play of which the author was unaware. Has this happened with you?

FRIEL: No, but this is a theory that is widely held and generally accepted.

MORISON: Do you accept it?

FRIEL: It could be true. But a certain arrogance keeps me from accepting it. This is about all I can say. I would like to think that I was fully conscious of every nuance of meaning that goes into everything I write; and I think: "How dare anyone suggest that there's something in this that I don't understand fully!" But it's very likely true. For example, if ten people go into a room and look at a painting it'll mean perhaps ten different things. Maybe it's nothing more significant than that.

MORISON: What was your first play?

FRIEL: The first play I did was a play called *This Doubtful Paradise,* and it was done in the Group Theatre in Belfast about six years ago. This was the old Group Theatre—before it collapsed. It was a dreadful play. I don't think the Group Company collapsed because of it, but it didn't do them any good! It was a very bad play and I like to forget about it. Then I did *The Blind Mice,* which was also a bad play and which I have now withdrawn. The next one was *The Enemy Within,* which was a solid play.

MORISON: Are you happier about it?

FRIEL: No, I'm not. It's not good, but it was a commendable sort of a play. I wouldn't put it any stronger than that. There's nothing very wrong with it and there's certainly nothing very good about it. It's a solid play.

MORISON: Did you ever find your plays getting out of hand? Characters running away?

FRIEL: No, I don't believe this theory at all. Somebody was talking to me recently about this and maintained that the characters in her novels become dictators and she has no control over them. But I don't believe this. What can happen, however—and it's happened in a play I'm working on at the moment—is that you lose it half-way through. This doesn't mean that the characters have got out of hand. I've lost a certain excitement about it. I think maybe that in this particular case I worked too hard on it before I began writing it.

MORISON: Is this preparatory work mental?

FRIEL: No, it's writing out notes—analyses of the different characters: what they did before the play opened and all sorts of details about them to get a very detailed knowledge of them. But I think that I overdid it this time. The result was I lost a certain interest in them: perhaps I got to know too much about them. The play is now half done and I haven't looked at it for the past six weeks. I've the feeling I've lost it. And three or four months' work.

MORISON: Do you often have to throw material overboard?

FRIEL: No. But it has happened once with a play I did that was a complete write-off. I had to scrap it altogether. It doesn't happen often in the case of the short story. I've written a lot of short stories that are bad. Very bad. Stories that appeared in the collection *The Saucer of Larks* should never have gone into it. Many of them are not good at all. I regret that now.

MORISON: Are you more cautious now about letting your work see the light of day?

FRIEL: Yes. There was a time when I could write ten stories a year without any great effort. Now I write four or five a year at the most. And even that is a great effort.

MORISON: Couldn't this be because you're not getting the same impetus to write as you used to?

FRIEL: I'm not very inventive anyhow, at the best of times. Perhaps now I'm more critical. A lot of the stories that appeared in *The Saucer of Larks* and which I thought when I had done them were marvellous and were for all time, are utter rubbish, I can now see. When I am writing now I can detect this so much more easily and so much more quickly.

MORISON: When did you start writing?

FRIEL: I imagine when I was about 21. I'm 36 now.

MORISON: You weren't writing at school?

FRIEL: Only the obligatory essays at week-ends!

MORISON: You left school and went into teaching?

FRIEL: Yes, well, first I was at Maynooth for two and a half years, left that and went to St. Mary's for their one-year graduate course.

MORISON: Were you writing then?

FRIEL: I did a bit of journalism.

MORISON: This wasn't fiction, was it?

FRIEL: Yes, I must have been doing stories. It's very hard to remember, you know. I think I did some stories then too. That was when I was about twenty, I imagine. It's a long time ago.

MORISON: You taught in Derry for about ten years?

FRIEL: Yes, I stopped in 1960.

MORISON: When did you get your first story published?

FRIEL: The first story I ever published was in *The Bell* magazine—it was an Irish "little" magazine and had a very strong literary tradition. Its editors had included Sean O'Faolain and Peadar O'Donnell. It's dead now for ten years.

MORISON: Did you ever have any doubts about going into teaching?

FRIEL: Well, no, though going to an ecclesiastical college was a very disturbing experience, I found I liked teaching very well. I suppose it was an obvious thing to do. I had a pass B.A. degree, which was useless for making a career. My father had been a teacher; two sisters were teachers. It was the obvious and easy thing to slip into. And I liked it very well. Loved it. I was very lucky.

MORISON: Then you were running two careers?

FRIEL: I was writing more and more while I was teaching. And it got to the stage when I had to decide which I would do.

MORISON: What swung the balance?

FRIEL: £250. This is what I had in capital and I decided I could live on that for, say, six months or so.

MORISON: This was a bit of a risk to take, surely?

FRIEL: Well, people say it was a very courageous thing to do. I don't see anything courageous about it.

MORISON: You must have had a great confidence in yourself at the time.

FRIEL: No, I don't think so. I don't agree with this at all.

MORISON: Did you consider when you gave up teaching that you might be coming back to it sometime?

FRIEL: Oh, yes. I was quite prepared for this in fact. I was sure I couldn't make a living as a writer. In fact this doubt has only been removed within the past year and a half. And it still could happen. If I were ill for six months, I'd be in serious financial bother again.

MORISON: There's no real security at all for the creative artist.

FRIEL: This is the anxiety. And it's a constant anxiety. Even when I've made some money on a story this worry is always there. The £250 comes back to me now. While I was teaching, any money I made in writing was always spent on silly things like buying a fridge or something like that. And then eventually I said, well this is stupid living like this; we'll save up whatever money I made. And when I had this amount of money, I said, "Right!" Of course what happened then was I was able to do a lot more work. You were fresh when you began working in the morning. It was what the Americans call "moonlighting"—having a second job. Of course it isn't off the cards that I might still have to go back to teaching. But it doesn't disturb me. On the other hand I'm lucky to the extent that most of my work sells in America, which means I get paid by American standards. Living here in Ireland costs about a third of what it does in America. I couldn't live in America on what I earn in American money.

MORISON: Apart from financial considerations, would you like to live in America?

FRIEL: I'd be very lonely, I think, in the way a child is lonely. I get very nostalgic and very homesick.

MORISON: What is the longest time you have spent in America?

FRIEL: I was out there for four months.

MORISON: Without the family?

FRIEL: I was part of the time on my own and then Anne and the children came out. I was at the Guthrie Theatre in Minneapolis.

MORISON: Is Tyrone Guthrie there permanently?

FRIEL: The theatre is called the Tyrone Guthrie Theatre and he is artistic director. They do four plays each season and this year he is doing one. He's doing one next year too.

MORISON: He's a man that seems to be everywhere at the one time.

FRIEL: He is. He's a marvellous, marvellous man. He's the "greatest." A great man in every way. Not only a great man of the theatre. But a great man—without qualification.

MORISON: When you're at home here working, do you have a working schedule?

FRIEL: In theory I have a schedule, which I never once hit. Roughly the schedule is that I work from, say, half-nine in the morning until lunchtime—that's about twelve o'clock. And then maybe from half-one till three o'clock. In theory. But I never, ever hit this schedule. I usually get upstairs maybe about ten o'clock and answer letters. This takes me about an hour or so. And I try to get some work done then. Or else somebody calls. Or something else turns up. I may get an average three hours done in the day.

MORISON: How does your inspiration come?

FRIEL: Oh, I haven't got any. Don't believe in it at all.

MORISON: Does this mean that when you're going to write a short story you simply sit down and say, "Right, I'll write a short story"?

FRIEL: No. This isn't how I work. This is an individual thing, of course. It varies from writer to writer. There's no set pattern for me. What I do is, I get an idea for a story. It could begin anywhere or with anything. It begins with the smallest possible idea which I write down in a notebook which I carry with me. And then I read this maybe three times a week. And then maybe after two months or three months I'll read it again and then I may fill in a few other details on the other side of the page. And then I'll leave this again. And maybe after three or four months I will then set to and start working on it. People say to me, "How long does it take you to write a short story?" Well, you see, I can't answer that question. I don't know how long it takes. Generally I will spend three weeks in the actual writing of the story. Doing that and absolutely nothing else. Working at it, day after day.

MORISON: Do you actually write? In longhand?

FRIEL: Yes, with a pencil. And then type it out myself afterwards.

MORISON: When it's typed out is that it finished? Or can you still change it about?

FRIEL: No, I'm usually finished when it's typed out.

MORISON: I've heard it said that a writer will often be able to view his work more objectively when it's typed out. Do you consciously become objective to your own writing after you have finished the composition of it?

FRIEL: No. Not for maybe a year afterwards.

MORISON: Until after it's finished?

FRIEL: Oh, long after it's printed. After it's printed I can read it and think that that's certainly not good, or something like this. But this is a long, long time afterwards. I find that you're so close to it and you're with this story for so long—it probably extends over a period of six months I imagine—that you're not objective and cannot see the thing at all.

MORISON: You might be thinking of two or three stories running?

FRIEL: Oh, yes. There are always two or three going at the same time. I've as many as twenty in my notebook at the moment. And if I get two out of them, this will be the height of it.

MORISON: So you often get bogus ideas down the left-hand page?

FRIEL: Oh, of course.

MORISON: And you look at them in a couple of days and they mean nothing to you?

FRIEL: Well, I always know what it meant at the time, but whether I can make anything of it or whether it can be developed and extended is another problem. There are very few editors that you can respect. My editor at *The New Yorker* is a writer himself, Roger Angell, a stepson of E. B. White. He has a book of short stories called *The Stone Arbour*—most of the *New Yorker* editors are short story writers. And when he gets a story of mine, he may very often say that they just don't like it. But if he says that they like it, he may then suggest certain things about it. And in that case I will change the story. He always maintains that I understate stories, that I am always underwriting. I agree thoroughly with this because I think there's nothing as annoying as an overstated story. And it's a fault I have of underwriting. The result is that he often likes me to expand—frequently a last paragraph, which is the conclusion, the summing up, the whole point of the thing. And if he likes a story he will very often write back and say something like "Right! this is fine. I am confused with the motivation of your last paragraph. Could you expand it slightly? You have the old man walking up the slipway from the harbour, looking back over his shoulder. But it isn't obvious why he is looking back. Perhaps you could just give us a line in there." Very often, I think, Angell's right.

I'm talking now about the ordinary changes made in a story. The sort of thing that people will level at you as a sinister criticism is to say, "Do you change your stories for *The New Yorker*?" In other words, "Do you produce a *New Yorker* type story?" Well, no, I don't produce a *New Yorker* type story, but I do change things for *The New Yorker*. I can't answer the question with a flat yes or no. But I will do this sort of thing: if I've used a word or a phrase that isn't intelligible to American readers, I would change it. It is my function to be intelligible to these people.

The editor will never suggest a major revision of a story. He'll just say, "I'm sorry. This story isn't successful." There are no other editors—no other magazines—that I would do this sort of thing for.

MORISON: Isn't the short story market a very limited one?

FRIEL: It is on this side of the Atlantic. It's a different thing over there.

MORISON: After *The New Yorker* I think of *The Saturday Evening Post*.

FRIEL: Yes, I've had stories in *The Saturday Evening Post*. Mediocre stories. Well, first of all they are always stories which *The New Yorker* rejects. I'm under contract to them.

MORISON: This means they have first refusal?

FRIEL: Yes.

MORISON: It isn't a contract to produce and present to them a certain number of stories a year?

FRIEL: No, no. There's no obligation at all. What they do is they pay you a retainer if you sign the contract and then they have to see everything that you write and they pay you twice as much as they would do if you weren't under contract.

MORISON: Well, it's no trouble for you to let them see your work first. I suppose it's quite an honour too that they think so highly of your work.

FRIEL: Oh, of course, it's marvellous. If it weren't for *The New Yorker* I couldn't live. Couldn't live at all. And they're so—I hate to use the word—they're so respectful. It sounds a pompous thing to say, but you know what I mean in the context. They have such respect for work and for their contributors.

I think I'm a sort of a peasant at heart. I'm certainly not "citified" and I never will be. There are certain atmospheres which I find totally alien to me and I'm much more at ease in a rural setting.

MORISON: You would never think of going to live in New York?

FRIEL: Oh, lord, no. I love it though. It's a very exciting place. I like American people. The pace of life is exciting—for a time. There's a great sense of unreality about it which I find very interesting. Somebody once said that when you're walking along underneath these vast skyscrapers, you feel that they're great Hollywood sets and that if you walk round to the back of them you'll see they're being held up by props and that they're only a front. And it's this unreality about the place which I find very exciting. They're a very interested people, too. People who are associated with writing or theatre are much more engaged than we are and not so ashamed of talking about it as we are. They have great dedication to their work.

MORISON: You mean they talk night and day about it?

FRIEL: No, this is what they don't do. This is what you find very often in Dublin where they talk and talk and talk about their work. And, dammit, not a lot of work is produced in Dublin. Whereas in America there's not so much talk but there's a lot of work done. American actors, for example, all go in for calisthenics. Now if you gathered a company together in Dublin to put on a play and suggested to them that for three quarters of an hour before the rehearsal they do physical education— well, there'd be a mass walk-out. Yet this is a very important thing, because they've got to be physically very agile and on top of their form, especially for strenuous roles. This is a form of embarrassment which we have here, but which the Americans wouldn't have.

An Observer in Minneapolis

Brian Friel / 1965

In March 1963 Brian Friel went to America to spend four
months observing Tyrone Guthrie at work as he prepared for
the initial season of the theatre in Minneapolis that bears his
name. Although he continued writing his weekly column for
the *Irish Press,* Friel was not employed by the Guthrie Theater as
a playwright-in-residence, and he had virtually no income.
Years later Friel would acknowledge that his parents and his
wife's people both thought he was crazy to cross the ocean just
to sit and watch rehearsals. But Friel would look back on the
time he spent in Minneapolis as "some kind of explosion in the
head." After returning home, Friel published a glowing tribute
in the pages of *Holiday* to Sir Tyrone Guthrie as "The Giant of
Monaghan." A year later Friel offered "An Observer in Minneapolis" as an autobiographical talk on the BBC Northern Ireland Home Service. For the BBC talk, Friel drew on his *Holiday*
description of Guthrie's appearance and rehearsal process. But
Friel confided to his BBC listeners a more personal account not
only of how he secured Guthrie's permission to come and "just
hang around" but also of the self-consciousness and uncertain-
ties he experienced while Guthrie's vision of theatre sparked
the explosion in his head.

On a glorious spring morning just over two years ago my plane from New
York touched down at the municipal airport of St. Paul. Now I would like
to be able to tell you—just for the sake of filling in the background—how
the state capital of Minnesota looked that beautiful day, and what my first

Transmitted on the BBC Northern Ireland Home Service, 16 August 1965 (recorded 21
May 1965).

impressions and reactions were. But the only thing I remember is the feeling of utter relief and gratitude at being delivered safely from that wretched plane; because no sooner had we taken off from New York than the captain made an announcement: "Ladies and gentlemen"—it was the yawning casualness of his attitude that terrorized me even more than the message itself—"Ladies and gentlemen, I would ask you to—ah—ah—keep your safety belts fastened throughout the entire trip because we're—ah—ah—going to have to fight our way right through—ah—lots and lots of thunderstorms. Ah—ah—welcome aboard and have a nice journey." Suffice it to say that we battled our way through.

St. Paul and Minneapolis are twin cities wedded together and at the same time divorced by the Mississippi River. They complement one another because Minneapolis is the active, pushing, go-ahead commercial centre, and St. Paul is easy-going, mellow, a city with a sense of its history and beauty and dignity. And yet, as might be expected, it was Minneapolis that coaxed Tyrone Guthrie to build his theatre there; and it was to Minneapolis that I was going, to watch that theatre being built, to see a new repertory company being formed and shaped, and to soak in as best I could as much as I could of the performing side of the art of theatre.

The story of the creation of the Tyrone Guthrie Theatre in the mid-West is a tale in itself. Very briefly what happened was this. Two young Americans, Peter Zeisler and Oliver Rea, who had worked and sweated on Broadway, decided that commercial interests were too strong there for the proper presentation of classical theatre. They wanted to get together a first-class repertory company to do first-class plays with first-class producers. Fair enough. Many young men have had similar dreams. They wrote to Tyrone Guthrie, explained their modest proposals, and asked him would he work with them—just about as brash a suggestion as if I were thinking of opening a sweetie-shop in the front room and were to write to Sir Isaac Wolfsen to come and manage it. By return post came Guthrie's reply: Delighted. And from then on, miraculously, the project never looked back. At least four American cities offered sites, money, support, red carpet, white wine; and after cautious selection Minneapolis was decided on for all sorts of good reasons. Plans for a theatre seating 1400 people were drawn up; money was raised; actors from all over the States were auditioned in New York; and by the time I reeled into the building late that spring afternoon after riding out the thunderstorms, *Hamlet* was in rehearsal, and a blond young man called George Grizzard was proclaiming my very own thoughts—"I could a tale unfold, whose lightest word would harrow up thy soul; freeze thy young blood; make thy two eyes, like stars, start from their spheres".

Like Zeisler and Rea, I, too, had written to Sir Tyrone Guthrie some months previously. I said that I knew of his new theatre and asked him would he mind if I were to go out there and . . . well, just hang around. I got the same reply that the other two got—and I was off like a light. And at this stage I should tell you about the only embarrassment I experienced in all my five months there, because in every other respect the hospitality and generosity and warm, spontaneous friendship of everybody connected with that theatre were overwhelming. Every morning I walked from my apartment to the theatre and spent the entire day there . . . as I say, just hanging about. Now Americans, apart from bums, don't hang about. When they are on a job they are a busy, business-like people. And the Guthrie Theatre folk—the actors, technicians, musicians, cleaners, photographers—they were all up to their eyes in work in preparation for the opening night. And when they paused to eat a sandwich or have a smoke they sometimes got a glimpse of a lean, rather furtive-looking man flitting about in the gloom of the auditorium or drifting silently back-stage.

Finally they cornered this phantom of the opera and demanded of him, "Are you a pressman?" "No, no, I'm not"—when I feel I'm being trapped my Derry accent gets ten times worse—"From the TV studios?" "No, no,—aha—no". "A producer?" "Me? Have a bit of sense!" "A designer? A prop man? An understudy?"—and so it went on and on, my face blazing, my false grin turning from obsequiousness to misery, until the janitor joined the group—Stewart was his name and he was known as Stew. And Stew took one look at me and said, "Yeah. I know this guy. He's an Irishman. He's an observer here. Right, Mr. Friel?" Brave, brawny, brilliant Stew. You rescued me from Limbo; you gave me an identity; you christened me An Observer, and from that happy day I observed unashamedly like one man.

I saw three plays being got ready—*Hamlet*, *The Miser*, and *The Three Sisters*. The Shakespeare and Chekhov were produced—or directed, as the Americans put it—by Sir Tyrone Guthrie, and *The Miser* was done by the assistant artistic director, Douglas Campbell. Now, before I talk about Guthrie's work—and when I do, I'm liable to use what may seem to be extravagant language because to me he is by far the greatest living producer—but before I slip into the superlatives, you must know what he looks like: he is six feet five inches tall, in his middle sixties, and has in his blood a mixture of English reserve, Irish exuberance, and Scottish astuteness. He came to rehearsals usually in a shirt, baggy flannels, and navy tennis shoes. Because his stomach is more than slightly wayward he was constantly tugging at his trousers to keep them decently hoisted, and this tussle invariably undid the bottom button of his shirt, with the result that by the time work was well under way the actors found themselves being peeped at by his navel—and for smaller actors whose eyes were about the same level as his stomach, this must have been a disquieting experience, like being spied on by a baby Cyclops. His eyes are clean and alert. He has a military moustache. His hair is close-cropped and greying, and occasionally—and this is something I have never seen anyone else do—he scratches it with both hands at the same time.

Well, rehearsals were not carried out at white-hot heat. As in all creation there were ninety-nine minutes of perspiration for every minute of inspiration, and during the hours of routine toil Guthrie wandered around the empty seats, for the most part just listening, and encouraging, occasionally pulling an actor up for a gauche movement or a faulty pronunciation, or to ask him to stress a key word in a line. But then the hour of inspiration would come, lasting maybe twenty minutes, maybe five, and at those moments—perhaps at the closet scene or the nunnery scene—he radiated his infectious excitement so that the actors caught it, responded to it, excited him in turn. Then, in those precious times of action and reaction, director and cast worked in such intimate communication, so intensely, so vibrantly, so fluidly, that the distinction between director and directed seemed to disappear. They were in perfect harmony, conductor and orchestra, inspiring and complementing each other, informing and being informed, so that the scene suddenly blossomed and matured in meaning and significance and beauty.

But they were not altogether haphazard, these brief sequences. At times they *did* strike, like lightning. At other times they were induced by the exuberance of the Irishman and—until the actors responded naturally—sustained by the astuteness of the Scotsman. But always, always he was responsible for the atmosphere in which this inspired coordination could take place—by his endless good humour; by the gentleness of his rebukes; by keeping his actors busy; by making the least important court extra feel that the action depended entirely on him alone; by his generous encouragement; and, if all else failed, by his towering four-letter rage. With such a variety of ruses at his command rehearsals were never dull, often electrifying, and always interesting.

Well now, what else did I observe? Oh, yes, the dedication and industry of the actors. Their whole lives were geared to their art. When they were rehearsing they worked like beavers, and during their free time they read or listened to music or visited galleries and museums or gave lectures in schools and colleges throughout the state. Many of them had tossed aside fat television and film offers in favour of Minneapolis. Many of them were living in not-too-elegant apartments and rooming houses. But like actors everywhere they were gay and generous and vain and volatile—and the salt of the earth.

When I came home, people asked me: What did you learn out there? Did you pick up a lot of expertise? And I found myself replying elusively, "Oh, yes, yes . . . yes, indeed", nervous that someone some day would pin me with the direct question: "What exactly did you learn?" Because, of course, I acquired no exact knowledge; I came away with no inside secrets and no special information that could be marshalled like a financial statement. And what I did learn has nothing to do with props and curtain-lines and entrances and exits but with the whole meaning of theatre, this strange ritual of make-believe that people from time immemorial want to take part in either as actors or as audience. I learned, in Guthrie's own words, that theatre is an attempt to create something which will, if only for a brief moment, transport a few fellow travellers on our strange, amusing, perilous journey—a lift, but not, I hope, an uplift. I learned that the playwright's first function is to entertain, to have audiences enjoy themselves, to move them emotionally, to make them laugh and cry and gasp and hold their breath and sit on the edge of their seats and—again to quote the great man himself—"to participate in lavish and luxurious goings-on". And I made the startling and humiliating discovery that the few plays I had written were not the masterpieces I had thought them to be, but were, in sad truth, tedious and tendentious and terribly boring. And that intelligence I consider to be the beginnings of wisdom for a writer.

The day before I flew back to New York I said goodbye to Stew, the janitor.

"You leaving us?" he said.

"I've got to go home," I answered.

He paused: "Well, I guess you'll be glad to get back to Ireland. I never been there but I'm told Edinburgh's sure a fine city."

His geography may not have been altogether accurate, but I'll always remember him as the man who led me from the shadows and bestowed on me the most impressive title I've ever carried—Observer.

Philadelphia, Here the Author Comes!

Brian Friel / 1966

During the time he spent observing Tyrone Guthrie at work in Minneapolis, Friel encountered a view of theater that was at once more frivolous and more serious than he had considered. Guthrie was "firmly opposed to the hushed, awed, sacrosanct approach to theater" found in "playhouses whose directors have a solemn purpose to renew the face of the earth." Ironically, given Guthrie's "frivolous intent . . . to have audiences enjoy themselves," Friel found that "the plays best suited to his genius" were "oddly enough, the classics: Shakespeare, Jonson, Molière, Congreve, Sheridan—men whose frivolous intent was also to entertain." While making audiences "laugh and cry and gasp and hold their breath and sit on the edge of their seats," Guthrie held that the purpose of such frivolous goings-on was nothing less than "to show mankind to himself, and thereby to show to man God's image." "At such a figure," Friel says, "one can only gape." It is easy to imagine that the Derry ex-school-teacher gaping in the gloom of the Guthrie auditorium during months of rehearsals must have wondered if his own plays would make audiences laugh and cry and gasp and hold their breath and sit on the edge of their seats. Friel's next play, *Philadelphia, Here I Come!* was a quantum leap beyond his previous work. The play received rapturous responses in Dublin both in 1964 and in a 1965 revival. Following publication of the text, Sir Tyrone Guthrie himself reviewed the play for the

Transmitted on the BBC Northern Ireland Home Service, 21 July 1966 (recorded 15 June 1966).

BBC and referred to "young," "inexperienced" Friel as "a born playwright." "Meaning is implicit 'between the lines' of his text," Guthrie explained, "in silences, in what people are thinking and doing far more than in what they are saying; in the music as much as in the meaning of a phrase." Guthrie concluded: "I think perhaps we have an important dramatist on our hands. Watch out for Brian Friel of Derry." Still, as gratifying as Guthrie's words must have been, what Friel had learned from his mentor was that what mattered most was the response of the audience. It was with a keen sense of trepidation that Friel set off like Gar O'Donnell to see if his dreams would be realized in Philadelphia—and, in Friel's case, on Broadway. Back in Ireland after his trip to America had ended in triumph, Friel implicitly compared himself to Gar in a BBC talk titled "Philadelphia, Here the Author Comes!" He talked about whether to translate his Northern Irish vernacular for Yankee ears, imitated an American twang when he told his BBC listeners about American actors needing "to verbalize about their blockage," and marvelled at the bizarre comments of American theatergoers during intermission. But the young playwright who reports the responses of the opening night Broadway audience reveals just how much he had learned from Tyrone Guthrie about theater. The lean figure skulking about in the gloom of the Guthrie auditorium less than three years earlier now stood at the back of a Broadway theatre knowing something of what it must feel like to accomplish the frivolous intent of a Shakespeare, Jonson, Molière, Congreve or Sheridan.

On Monday, December 27th last, in the snow, six of us set out from Dublin Airport, headed for New York. Our simple ambition was to present my play, *Philadelphia, Here I Come!*, on Broadway. The six consisted of the director, four principals, and myself.

We had done the play twice before in Dublin, in 1964 and 1965; and it was during the second run that Mr. David Merrick, Broadway's biggest impresario, came over for a night, saw it, and wanted it. And in case you now have a mental image of a flamboyant, cigar-smoking, wheeler-dealer theatrical figure shattering the relative calm of Dublin's Gate Theatre with great shouts of "I've gotta get that play, no matter what it costs", I should tell you that Mr. Merrick is a soft-spoken gentleman who wears judicious Savile Row clothes, that he doesn't smoke, and that he made only one comment to me after he had seen the play. What he said, in cool Alastair Cook style, was "Good night". And at this stage, too, it might be a good idea to define my terms before I come to the hazards and anxieties and frustrations and delights of bringing a play to America.

Definitions first, and then for convenience I'll stick to American parlance. The producer in the United States is the man who sets the play up, engages the actors, books the theatres, hires a publicity firm, organizes the tour. And the director over there is, in our language, the producer. So that in the case of *Philadelphia, Here I Come!* David Merrick was the producer and Hilton Edwards the director.

A further set of distinctions before I go back to my story. You may bring a play to Broadway but you never in fact get there. Because Broadway, strictly speaking, is a long, wide boulevard which boasts a great variety of dirty-book stores, eating places, record shops, joke stores—but not one theatre. The actual Broadway theatres hide modestly in the streets which run east and west off Broadway. And just to confuse you completely, those theatres are not to be confused with the theatres which are specifically known as off-Broadway theatres which are small places operating anywhere they can get a foothold in the length and breadth of Manhattan. One last detail: before you finally hack your way into the Broadway jungle, you are sent touring a well-beaten path which passes through Boston and New Haven and Washington and other lesser known cultural centres, which are all classified with the superb arrogance of a metropolis as "out of town".

Over nine weeks elapsed between Mr. Merrick's 'Good-night' and our departure from Dublin Airport. They were punctuated by long letters and telephone calls and transatlantic cables—all the drama that the peripheral people in the theatre invest their business lives with. The jargon of this world has a fascination. A typical example would read: "Merrick very keen on property. Stop. Advises early U.S. opening. Stop. Would you consent travel to New York tonight to discuss. Stop. Please advise." And eventually, as a result of all the negotiations and alarums and excursions—or maybe in spite of them—it was settled that we would fly to the United States immediately after Christmas and go to work.

So, for three weeks we rehearsed in New York. This was necessary because we had recruited over there nine new actors to our cast. They were pleasant people and competent actors and things went smoothly. I had very little to do. In fact, before I had left home I cut the play by fifteen minutes because Americans, according to the market-researchers who were fed into computers, are quite content to sit in a theatre for two hours and seven-and-a-half minutes, but are liable to riot if that limit is exceeded. So there was no on-the-spot cutting problem. But there was another problem. At the very outset we were faced with language difficulty. What in heaven's name were we to do about fine Northern Irish words like *get* and *stirk* and *pandy* and *thick* which meant nothing to Yankee ears? Should we literally translate a line like "He's a thick bloody get, yon fella" into "He is an insensitive, block-headed, misbegotten person", so that every word would be intelligible to foreigners? Well, of course, we couldn't. And we made a policy decision on that at the beginning and we hoped that the context would convey the meaning.

I myself had one other smaller problem with a few of the American actors. When they had a difficulty with their parts, occasionally at the beginning they would come to me—as they put it—"to verbalize about their blockage". I found this quite terrifying. Of course, what I should have done was send them to the director but they were so earnest and so honest that dismissal would have been cruel, and the result was that I found myself—with equal earnestness and honesty—explaining these tiny difficulties in characterization by delivering a lecture on the social history of Ireland, beginning with the Norman Invasion. I found this typically Irish solution to the Americans' problems very satisfactory. I was soon left alone.

We opened in Philadelphia on January 17th. The performance was mediocre, the audience tepid, the critics timid. Lots of enthusiasts came backstage afterwards and cried on our shoulders and said, "Gawd, what a play! What a play!" and then went on to ask did young Gareth O'Donnell really emigrate from the old country—which was, of course, the whole point of the story. But what I liked about Philadelphia—and indeed about Boston and New York—was that I was able to prowl around without being recognized during the intermissions and listen to the comments of the audience. They were, and I put it very mildly, bizarre; but then eavesdroppers seldom hear good of themselves. One corpulent, silver-haired lady exploded into her husband's face, "So he's coming to Philadelphia! So what the hell's he crying about!" Another little wasp of a woman battled her way towards the exit: "If that's Irish drama you can keep it!" And a third, eighty if she were a day, with a sweet Madonna face and chaste blue eyes, said, "Mark my words, Harmon: the housekeeper's the father's mistress, and Gareth is their illegitimate son, and *he's* having an affair with the doctor's wife. My goodness, real shanty Irish!"

We were driven to City Hall and introduced to the mayor and presented with trinkets. We were invited to luncheon parties, dinner parties, and after-theatre parties. Even the taciturn Mr. Merrick threw a party on opening night and on his lapel sported a green flag that bore the legend Erin Go Brath. Fan mail began to pour in—complimentary letters, abusive letters, and begging letters. And after two weeks and in fifteen feet of snow, we set out for Boston with the assurance that really wasn't very assuring that "Anyone that gets past the Philadelphian critics is okay".

Anyhow, we opened in Boston on the last day of January. The performance was brilliant, the audience wooden, and the critics—as ever— timid. Again the round of parties, and the press and radio and television interviews, and a tightening of the nerves because Broadway was now only two weeks away. Then the director went down with pneumonia. Snow was forecast. The Boston Strangler struck again. Messengers from New York brought the news that five shows had folded, that the season was in a shambles, and that Merrick was so defeatist about our chances that he had gone off to Paraguay to see about setting up *Hello, Dolly!* out there. And we were tired. We wondered would we ever again receive the rapturous responses we had got in Dublin. We began to count our halfpennies and eat in automats and badly-lit foreign restaurants. Rumours spread widely: that our packed houses were made up of Irish people; that no one understood a word of the play; that it was too long, it was too short; it was too slow, too fast. And we listened avidly to each rumour and reacted desperately. It was no consolation to be told that anyone that gets past the Boston critics is okay. And on Sunday, February 13th, we travelled down to New York in a deluge of rain, and scattered to our various hotels and rooming-houses. I don't think any of us had the heart to unpack.

Before the official opening—which was on the following Wednesday—we were to have two preview performances on the Monday and the Tuesday. Well, the Monday performance was good, the audience was good—and of course there were no critics. The Tuesday night performance was cancelled because of a row between Mr. Merrick and Stanley Kauffmann, the drama critic of the *New York Times;* but that's a story in itself.[1] And on Wednesday, February 16th, at 7.30, we opened, officially,

---

1. The night before *Philadelphia, Here I Come!* opened on Broadway the marquee lights of the Helen Hayes Theatre never came on, and hundreds of theatergoers—tickets in hand—were turned away with the explanation that the final preview performance had been cancelled due to "technical difficulties." Friel acknowledges—in this BBC talk given four months later—that the reason for the cancellation was a dispute between the show's producer, David Merrick, and Stanley Kauffmann, the drama critic of *The New York Times.* Kauffmann's press tickets to the preview performance came in the mail with a note from Merrick that said "At your peril." Merrick objected to Kauffmann's custom of reviewing a preview performance rather than that of opening night. Kauffmann had adopted the practice—objected to by the Dramatists Guild, by Actors Equity, and by the Society of Stage Directors and Choreographers—in order to have an additional day to write his review prior to publication the morning after the premiere. In the event, Kauffmann had to attend the opening night performance of *Philadelphia,* and his tepid review the next morning said Edwards's direction was "workmanlike" but "a disappointment" and that "it is Mr. Friel who lets us down" with a play that is "amiable and appealing enough but unexciting." Other

in the beautiful white Helen Hayes Theatre, just off Times Square in the very heart of Manhattan.

When the curtain came down, that tiny fraction of my mind which was still perceptive knew that all was well. It probably knew five minutes after the curtain rose because the actors were good and the audience— the audience was marvellous. One writes for the audience, for a group of people of all ages and types who become an entity for a period of something over two hours; and you expect, you hope, you pray for certain reactions from that entity. And that night the audience was perfect. They laughed and cried when we wanted them to laugh and cry. They gave us their attention and then their minds and then their emotions. And when the curtain fell, after that second of mental adjustment, they clapped and cheered and called "Bravo". And standing limp at the back of the auditorium I didn't give a damn what the critics would say. Happily they were rapturous next day. They paid us the highest compliment they knew: they said briefly that we were a hit. Some of them, notably Walter Kerr of the *Tribune,* wrote carefully worded analyses that were very flattering. Queues formed outside the box-office. We had a grand celebration lunch in the grand Algonquin Hotel. And Mr. Edwards told the press that we always knew the play was a success; what worried us was—would the critics be a success. Overnight we had become cheeky.

That was Thursday. On the following Sunday I took a taxi to Kennedy Airport and I flew home. Since then I have tried to assess what a Broadway hit means. And for the benefit of anyone who has aspirations, these are my findings. The fact that a play is successful on Broadway doesn't mean that the play is a good play; nor does it mean that the play is a bad play. All it means is that on a particular night the majority of the critics liked what they saw on stage, and told their readers; and the readers in turn said to themselves, "Ah! Howard Blinks says this is a good play, honey. We must go and see it because this is a good play." And success breeds success. The agencies take block bookings. Various theatre guilds buy seats for their members. A ticket, as they say, becomes hot. And you're in for a long, long run.

What makes the critics over there like you is another problem. This season they liked Osborne's *Inadmissable Evidence* but not Tennessee Williams' *Slapstick Tragedy.* They praised *Marat/Sade* and panned *Where's Daddy?,* William Inge's new play. In fact this season the critics killed something like twenty new plays, some of them surviving for only two

reviewers shared the opening night audience's sense of excitement about the play; the Variety annual poll selected Friel as the most promising playwright of the Broadway season, and *Philadelphia* played to packed houses for months. *Ed.*

weeks, some of them closing after two or three performances. The odds against your succeeding are about ten to one.

Now, you may ask me a question: would I like to have another play on Broadway? Of course I would. But the second time wouldn't be the same. One's professional life is a series of challenges and ambitions. Once you have built a house, you want to build a factory and then a church and then an airport and then a cathedral. And once you have built the cathedral I imagine you become suddenly interested in a house again; but a special kind of house this time; a very special kind of house . . .

At the moment I'm working on a new play.

After *Philadelphia*

John Fairleigh / 1966

Brian Friel's play *The Loves of Cass McGuire* was broadcast on the BBC Third Programme on 9 August 1966, the same day the play went into rehearsals in New York for a production that would open on Broadway while *Philadelphia, Here I Come!* was still running. On the same day, the *Belfast Telegraph* published John Fairleigh's interview with Friel, which had taken place during the preparation of the BBC radio production. Although *The Loves of Cass McGuire* would not fare well on Broadway, closing after twenty performances, a subsequent production at the Abbey Theatre in Dublin was regarded by at least one reviewer as "immeasurably better" than the New York version. Even before the play had opened, Friel expressed to Fairleigh both the frustration of having to travel away from home and the frustration of being at home "in the North" where he was a member of the minority. Within less than a year Friel would move from Derry into Donegal. In building a new home in Muff, Friel was only five miles from Derry, but the move meant that he would be living in the Republic of Ireland rather than under the Stormont government.

"I always find it best to do whatever these people tell you," Brian Friel advised mildly. Having settled into comfortable conversation in a quiet BBC studio, we had been beckoned out and led to another room where the thudding of an unseen demolition team battered the communication between thought and expression.

Since his fourth play *Philadelphia, Here I Come!* set off on its run of

---

From the *Belfast Telegraph*, 9 August 1966, p. 6.

success at the Dublin Theatre Festival in October, 1964, it seems that
Brian Friel has come to accept the organising of other people in his life.

As *Philadelphia* and the backers' negotiations moved through the
initial Festival production to a revival in Dublin the following year and
eventually to a first night on Broadway some six months ago now, he was
more and more drawn from his writing to play the role of author in
rehearsals, promotions and business arrangements.

Obviously he is grateful for his success. *Philadelphia*, still running,
received excellent reviews and was runner-up for the critics' award for
the best play on Broadway. But there is, too, some resentment of the dis-
traction it has been to his work.

"All this flying backwards and forwards across the Atlantic and sitting about in hotel lobbies was bound to be fatal. I have not made much
progress with anything for the past year.

"But I suppose that at some stage every writer has to live on his
hump and I am just living on mine now."

Thirty-seven-years old, this former schoolmaster has nourished a
considerable hump of achievement to live off since he gave up his teaching post in Derry in 1960.

At first he turned most of his attention to the short stories he was
already writing successfully in his free time out of school. These beautifully observed parables on life which he set in rural Ireland he sold to
various American magazines. And eventually the *New Yorker* became so
interested in him that they offered a special contract in return for an
option on whatever stories he wrote.

"At this stage, I never thought of plays as a means of making money."
But he wrote them nonetheless.

The first, a comedy about the arrival of a French Count in an Ulster
town, was put on by the old Group company in 1960. "I want to forget
it—dreadful play. Shortly after doing it the company disbanded. The two
events are not necessarily unconnected."

Then followed *The Blind Mice*, the reaction of a family and small
town to the return of a priest, Communist brainwashed to renounce his
faith, and *The Enemy Within*, the struggle of the 6th-century St. Columba
to sever his ties of loyalty to his family. Both of these were presented in
Dublin and attracted interested reaction.

But *Philadelphia* was different. From the first night the word went
around that here was an exciting play of exceptional sensitivity, and mur-
murings were heard of a successor to Synge and O'Casey.

It expounds the dilemma of a young man anxious to break away from his Donegal village home, yet strangely unable to break the bonds with his unresponsive father and the rest of his environment. The play is written with real poetry and sympathetic humour and achieves great pathos without sentimentality.

"At first it was being billed in America as a comedy, and I spoke to the promoters several times before it was changed. I suppose they thought that a comedy would be better box-office.

"There is a lot of comedy in it. But it is according to Behan's technique of making the audience laugh and then saying something serious when they are thoroughly disarmed. And before they became morose start them laughing again."

His new play, which went into rehearsal on Broadway to-day and can be heard on the BBC Third Programme at 8-30 this evening, is in the same tradition with personal tragedy balanced and even accentuated by humour.

The Loves of Cass McGuire, it tells through a first-hand account and a series of flashbacks of an ageing Irish-American's return to what is left of her family. At first brittle and wholly in touch with reality, she gradually retreats into a world of fantasy.

"All my characters are the stock ones of Irish plays. If an American television team came over, my characters are the people they would look for. Tennessee Williams starts off with unbelievable characters and then sets out to make them credible. I use the stock people and then have to make something of them."

Indeed, superficially, many of the individuals he presents are the predictable ones. But he cracks them one by one to reveal in each of them some great personal deception or disillusionment.

"It's just the Irish gloom, I suppose—but it is partly a dramatic technique as well.

"I always write about Irish people. It's not by choice—they are the only people I know. It's a good thing to get away from Ireland from time to time to get a clear perspective, but I find when I have been away for a while I want to get back.

"Of course I feel the frustration and the resentment of a Catholic in the North of Ireland and sometimes get very angry and can't think calmly about the country at all. But I am committed to it, for good or evil. Whatever you flee from in one place, you'll probably find the same things somewhere else."

With Cass McGuire set to go through the same detailed preparation and initiation as *Philadelphia* before it makes its Broadway first night, it seems that it will be some time again before Brian Friel can settle down in Londonderry with his wife and three daughters and get on with his writing.

An extremely modest and intellectually honest man, he is not to be destroyed by success. As soon as he can he will be back to his regular nine-to-five day at his desk.

"This time I am trying to work on an idyllic love story. But I may have thought about it too long. It hasn't got a title yet. I don't know if it will ever come to anything."

Interview with Brian Friel

Lewis Funke / 1968

Friel came to New York in mid-September 1968 to see *Lovers*, his pair of one-acts that balances the lyrical *Winners* with the farcical *Losers*. Starring American actor Art Carney with three members of the original Dublin cast, *Lovers* had opened in New York on 25 July, but Friel had been unable to attend rehearsals or opening night because of the birth of his fourth daughter. Carney's return to the stage—after having abruptly left the cast of *The Odd Couple* with a nervous breakdown amid the breakup of his marriage and legendary conflicts with Walter Matthau— was greeted by critics as "superb," "incomparable," and "merely immortal." But Friel's plays were termed merely "pleasant," "B- plus," "a little too familiar." Two months into the run Friel was supposed to boost the plays' box office with a series of interviews. After a full day of television interviews but before departing for the evening performance of *Lovers* and a post-performance party in his honor, Friel met Lewis Funke in the cramped quarters of a small room in the Algonquin Hotel. Friel took off his jacket and tie and sprawled on the bed; Funke sat on the bed and had difficulty placing the tape recorder; the traffic outside was heavy; barking dogs competed with clanging fire engines to drown out Friel's soft-spoken replies. "It wasn't the most felicitous environment" for an interview, Funke reports with wry understatement. But what transpired under those circumstances was one of the most extensive interviews of Friel's career. It did not get off to a promising start. Funke says that when he began by asking why he wrote, Friel "nearly

From *Playwrights Talk about Writing: 12 Interviews with Lewis Funke* (Chicago: Dramatic Publishing Co., 1975), pp. 111–33.

knocked the tea off the tray as he observed that that was the lousiest first question he'd ever had to field." Funke had been warned by press agents for *Lovers* that Friel's answers might be monosyllabic, and at times throughout the interview Friel's impatience seems almost palpable even on the written page. Nevertheless, Friel provided a forthcoming account of his problems with theatrical form both in *Lovers* and *Philadelphia, Here I Come!,* offered some of his most telling insights into the way he sees *Philadelphia* as something more than an emigrant play, and talked about the differences in the New York and Dublin productions of *The Loves of Cass McGuire.*

FUNKE: Why do you write?

FRIEL: (*laughter*) That is the lousiest first question I have ever heard.

FUNKE: Well, what made you become a writer? What is the pleasure for you in writing?

FRIEL: At 39—at this stage in life—I don't know what the pleasure is. It is a mixture between a compulsion and an indulgence. I don't know why I write, really.

FUNKE: You started out as a teacher. What was your subject? Was it general teaching?

FRIEL: General teaching; at times I taught in higher grade schools and moved about.

FUNKE: What was it that impelled you to turn to writing?

FRIEL: For a period of ten years I taught school, and during that period I did a lot of writing. Leaving esthetics aside, the practical reason that I became a full-time writer was that I got one of those contracts with the *New Yorker*—reading agreements, as they call them. This, not so much in what it financially gave me, represented a sort of act of confidence that I think was very useful at that particular stage. It didn't necessarily mean that they were going to publish every story I wrote, but it meant that they had a certain confidence in the kind of thing I might turn out. When this arose, I thought, I will try it for the time being and even if I don't make a living, I can go back to teaching.

FUNKE: You actually started writing short stories first. Did you write any poetry?

FRIEL: No.

FUNKE: What gave you the notion that you could write fiction? What was an impelling motive, or was it something that you had always had in the back of your mind?

FRIEL: You are using this word, compulsion, and it is a word that I'm sort of nervous of.

FUNKE: If you feel I'm using the incorrect word . . .

FRIEL: No. It's just a word that I'm sort of weary of. People talk of the artistic compulsion and the necessity to write. All I can say is that it's something I want to do very much, and I enjoy doing it very much, and it's good for me. On the other hand, if a set of circumstances could foreseeably arise where writing interfered with something that I hold very dear in life—and don't ask me what that could be—I would sacrifice writing for this other thing. "Compulsion" may be slightly stronger than I would choose to put it myself.

FUNKE: Do you like writing?

FRIEL: The specific writing, I like very much; the actual job of sitting down writing is actually hell.

FUNKE: I was going to ask you, what is the most pleasurable part of writing? Some people find that once they are writing and the thing is moving, there is a great joy in the writing itself. Other people are bleeders and the very act of writing is a dreaded thing. Which way is it for you?

FRIEL: I dislike sitting down to work, for a start. When things are going well, I do get a lot of gratification or satisfaction, or something like that, out of it. I think, perhaps, the best moment, or the best time, is immediately when you have finished something. You then have a sense of completion and satisfaction; a job is done. It's just before the period of reassessment when you realize it's not really as good as it ought to be.

FUNKE: What was it that turned you to playwriting?

FRIEL: I came to playwriting in a very obtuse and indirect sort of way. I had done one or two radio plays in Ireland for the BBC and the producer gave me lovely encouragement and asked me to do some more. This I did, and then I progressed from radio plays into theatre. I think what the radio plays did for me was show me I could write dialogue. But the whole tedious business of learning the craft of the theatre is something that came to me very slowly.

FUNKE: How do you set about learning the craft?

FRIEL: I think there is a lot of rubbish talked about this. The craft of theatre is basically plain sense. I think one can learn something more about the formal theatre from watching good plays, and I had a good opportunity in doing this in Minnesota at the Guthrie Theatre. I spent six months out there. A season.

FUNKE: Were you a resident playwright?

FRIEL: No, I had no official function at all. Tyrone Guthrie was a neighbor of mine, and when he opened the theatre out there, he suggested if I were going into theatre, it would be a good idea to watch it, survey it, study it and so on.

FUNKE: When you really felt that you were ready to try the theatre, did you begin to do a lot of reading of plays or go to the theatre a great deal?

FRIEL: No, I didn't go to the theatre because I had no theatre to go to. So I did a lot of reading of plays, but at this point in time, I went out to the Guthrie Theatre. I had no function; I was simply a hanger-on. It was a very exciting time for the theatre itself because the new building had just opened and there were excellent actors.

FUNKE: Guthrie is one of the most exciting men in the theatre that I have ever had the pleasure of meeting.

FRIEL: A great man.

FUNKE: Would you be able to identify any influence on you as a playwright?

FRIEL: I don't think I could. There are many people that I admire very much and perhaps they influence me. I just don't know.

FUNKE: Before you turned to playwriting, had you read Chekhov or Strindberg or Ibsen?

FRIEL: Yes.

FUNKE: Did you feel that they had any kind of effect on structure for you?

FRIEL: No, I don't think so. I think Tony Guthrie must have had an influence on me. I can't see in what way it has manifested itself since he is a director, you know. I don't write great big Tony Guthrie plays with pageantry and splendor and so on.

FUNKE: Well, what was it that you got out of being at the Guthrie Theatre?

FRIEL: I don't know the answer to this. I'm sorry. All I know is that it was a marvelous time and that I was absolutely thrilled and awed by it. Watching Guthrie work was just an education.

FUNKE: I suppose, aside from reading a great many plays, this was really your basic education as a playwright.

FRIEL: Yes. The number of professional performances that I have seen to the present time are minimum, practically.

FUNKE: You don't get down to London very much.

FRIEL: I'm in New York more often than I am in London. I am in London maybe once a year, at the most.

FUNKE: Then the construction of your plays is strictly of your own invention. You have no formal guide. You are not cluttered with rules of what you are not supposed to do or what you are supposed to do.

FRIEL: I suppose that's true. I think the best way to answer that is that people sometimes say to me, "Will you not be directing a play of your own?" Well, I think I couldn't even begin to put five actors on a stage. I am quite sure that there are many technicalities that I am totally unaware of. But I don't think these are important.

FUNKE: What do you think the relationship between a playwright and a director should be? Should a director have a great deal of control or do you feel your ideas should carry?

FRIEL: I'm afraid I'm very arrogant about this. This reveals my attitude to the whole profession of playwriting and the theatre. My belief is absolutely and totally in the printed word, and that this must be interpreted precisely and exactly as the author intended. The ideal relationship between the writer and the director is one where the director interprets to the best of his ability what the author intends, and only this.

FUNKE: Then I would presume that you have many conferences with the director before you go into rehearsal, and that you are a daily attendant at your rehearsals.

FRIEL: Oh, yes. For the first production of a play, and this is the only one that is so really important to me. Hilton Edwards and I have worked together for three or four plays and we understand one another. We've got to a stage where we don't really have to sit down and discuss in great detail the character, because he knows what I am doing. In fact, he usually works alone the first week but then I come in and work with him for the last two weeks.

FUNKE: How are you in terms of receptivity to suggestions that he may make? If he says, "Well, you know, Brian, this isn't quite working. I think you ought to change it," what is your reaction generally?

FRIEL: I think my instinctive reaction is, "This is your job—make it work." This is very un-American, I think. Here, the whole situation is much more fluid. An analogy I use in this case is: the script of a play is like a musical score, and you present the score to your musicians and you say, "Play this." And if the second violinist says, "This passage is far too long," you say, "Play it, Jack, that's your job." It's another matter when he says, "Were you drunk when you wrote that, because this is written in a different key; the main passage is A minor and you have written this in B flat." You say, "Well, oh gosh, I forgot that!" But generally you say, "There's the script, there's the text. Go out and interpret it."

FUNKE: You would never undertake at this point or ever, you think, directing your own play?

FRIEL: No.

FUNKE: What do you think is the disadvantage for a playwright in directing his own play?

FRIEL: I can't speak in general on this. All I know is that I can't talk to actors very well. I find I don't have the temperament; I don't have the manner for this. They are a special sort of people and they need a special sort of approach and a special sort of language. In fact, there is a sort of private language that is spoken between directors and actors. You jump up and you say, "Darling, that was absolutely beautiful, but . . ." This is the sort of language that I can't tolerate, and I don't think I'm ever going to learn it, so I can't see myself having this job.

FUNKE: What have you found the most difficult part of writing? Do you find the characters difficult, or plot, or just sitting down to write, as we mentioned before?

FRIEL: By far, and far the most difficult thing for me, has always been finding the correct form for this particular theme. This has always been my trouble and I find, as years go on, I get more and more, as Americans say, "hung up" on this business.

FUNKE: In *Philadelphia, Here I Come!,* what was it that motivated the idea of having the alter-ego on the stage?

FRIEL: I think it was necessity, in that case.

FUNKE: This was part of the problem, wasn't it?

FRIEL: This was the big problem. How to interpret or how to reveal this young boy; how he felt, his thoughts, his emotions on this particular night of his life. How to reveal this without having to stop, freeze the action and talk in asides. When I used the second actor to play his alter-ego, I had no idea in the world that this would work. Had I been a very first-class theatre technician, I'm sure I would have known instantly that it would have worked.

FUNKE: It worked beautifully, actually.

FRIEL: Yes. But I consider this sort of a happy accident. I didn't know whether this would work, or not.

FUNKE: That is very interesting, and then that would apply to both "Winners" and "Losers" of the collective play *Lovers.* Where did that idea come from: the idea of the drowning and telling it in retrospect? Was this, let us say, from a newspaper clipping about two young people?

FRIEL: I just don't remember how it originated.

FUNKE: In other words, you have no particular source for the ideas.

FRIEL: No, but the form of that play gave me hell, too. I wrote that play five times before I got this form. I wrote it simply with two young people on the stage telling their story, and then I was caught again with the situation of the death which was partly real and partly symbolic. Eventually, I got on this idea.

FUNKE: Well, it works, of course, which is the most important thing. The length of the speeches that each one makes interested me. It is almost their subconscious speaking, and yet, they are not just spouting. Well, in a sense, possibly she is, talking everything that's in her mind, but that's the kind of girl she is. I would think that a playwright would be concerned over the long monologues that are not really dialogue, strictly speaking. What gave you the confidence that this would work on the stage?

FRIEL: I think a lot of credit is due to a good actress. A less than excellent actress would have lost her audience or the audience would have lost her long ago. On the other hand, I don't think it is altogether relevant when you look at the way Osborne writes. You know, he writes pages of monologues.

FUNKE: That's right.

FRIEL: And succeeds. From the point of view of daring, I have nothing on Osborne in long speeches.

FUNKE: You do, both of you, have a gift of making this kind of long speech so vitally interesting that people's attentions are held.

FRIEL: Perhaps this is an intuitive sort of thing.

FUNKE: I'm sure it is.

FRIEL: I don't think it's something you can learn. Some people are, maybe, tone deaf and color blind, and I think I have this little, little, tiny gift of knowing how long a speech may hold and being able to write this kind of dialogue.

FUNKE: That's interesting.

FRIEL: It's not something I'm particularly proud of. I think, there it is. I'm left-handed, you know. I think this is an accident of fate. I can do this with dialogue, so I think—there it is.

FUNKE: All writers, at some time or another, encounter blocks and then they are forced to put the script aside and go for a walk, or something. What is your approach? Do you run into blocks once you start writing?

FRIEL: Oh, I do, all the time. I just drink a lot of tea.

FUNKE: You don't put a script aside?

FRIEL: No, I stick with it to the end.

FUNKE: You do?

FRIEL: Yes. I haven't this gift that some writers have of handling two or three plays at one time. When I'm with one, I'm married to it, and that's it.

FUNKE: Is it a hair-pulling time for you?

FRIEL: It's a rotten time.

FUNKE: Was there any particular thing that gave you the most difficulty with *Philadelphia, Here I Come?*

FRIEL: I think always my difficulty is before I write anything. Someone said of architecture that form is everything, and I find that in playwriting it's becoming almost the same thing for me; form is everything. Well, that's exaggeration, of course, but it's getting more and more important to me that the form should be the knit or extension or part of the content. In the case of *Philadelphia,* I had no problem at all with the characterization, no bother at all with dialogue. These people were all ready to go if I could just have got the situation right for them.

FUNKE: How long is the gestation period? How long do you take before you really are ready? Sometimes, people carry around an idea in their heads for a year before they actually go to work. Was this the case with *Philadelphia* and *Loves of Cass McGuire?*

FRIEL: This period of gestation is becoming longer with me, I find. It's certainly a year now.

FUNKE: During that gestation period, are you thinking all the time about the play?

FRIEL: Consciously thinking of it—sitting at a desk with a sheet of paper and a pencil and working on it, I spend maybe four or five hours every day. Then during relaxation periods, I keep going back to it and I'm worried about it and it's needling me all the time.

FUNKE: Well, that's when you've begun to work on it. Do I understand you correctly?

FRIEL: No, no.

FUNKE: This is the preliminary period.

FRIEL: My experience is that once I start working, once I know where everything is, then I've got to go at it very rapidly.

FUNKE: What is your approach when you say that you're working on this preliminary and you work at it four or five hours? What are you actually doing? You're not writing the play.

FRIEL: Let's take the case of *Lovers.* I consider, of course, the gestation period and the actual writing period of the script, what turned out to be a script, all one ultimately. It is the time that you spend on this play. In the case of the first play, *Winners,* I spent months and months writing about this boy, this young boy.

FUNKE: That's what I wanted to ask you. Do you sit down and write as much as you know about each one of your characters?

FRIEL: I did that in this case and I did it with *Philadelphia,* too. I think maybe I'm getting into this bad habit; I think that's what it is.

FUNKE: In other words, you write down about everything that you can think of in terms of who he is, where he came from, what he is about.

FRIEL: Whether this is becoming my method or not, I don't know, but I know I have done it the past two or three plays.

FUNKE: Then once you have acquainted yourself with all your characters, or the people you're going to have, and you have worked out in rough the outline of the action, do you write a scenario for yourself?

FRIEL: No.

FUNKE: You go right to work in the structuring of the play?

FRIEL: Again, coming back to the most recent play, which was *Lovers,* I did sort of geometrical drawings of the play, of the form of this play. In the case of *Winners,* for example, I knew that this was going to be the shape of a rectangle. This was going to be total shape of the play and half of it was going to be Mag, the girl, with Joe contributing occasional bits of conversation. The other part of the play was going to be the boy. That was simply the geometric shape of that play.

FUNKE: Did you ever teach math?

FRIEL: I did for a period.

FUNKE: Then you would think geometrically. That's a very interesting procedure.

FRIEL: I've never done this before. I did it with this play, though.

FUNKE: About how many drafts would you write? Ibsen frequently wrote at least three drafts and each time he got to know what he was doing better in terms of the people and their relationships, etc.

FRIEL: This isn't my experience at all. From the moment I'm ready to go, I'm engulfed. I know exactly everything about them. I know precisely what they are going to do at any given moment, thrown into any circumstance at all. The only reason I ever have to rewrite is because this is a particularly fascinating character that I haven't developed sufficiently or because the shape of the play has become obese at this point, or too lean at this point.

FUNKE: Are you your own critic and your own editor? You don't show the play to anybody at this point?

FRIEL: Never, no.

FUNKE: When you finish a draft, you don't show it to anyone?

FRIEL: No, no.

FUNKE: Some playwrights might show it to close friends or have a reading for friends.

FRIEL: No.

FUNKE: Do you read widely—fiction and non-fiction, history, biography?

FRIEL: I'm just an indiscriminate reader. I think what I read was dictated by the time I grew up in. I was born in 1929, and I sort of passed through the immediate post–Scott Fitzgerald period and the Hemingway time, and then came the Graham Greene time, you know, and one rushed along with the fashion and read everything that these people wrote at these particular times. I just read recklessly and stupidly, I think.

FUNKE: The reason I asked that is that a playwright presumably should be deepening and broadening his knowledge of people and the time in which he lives. I wonder whether you gave yourself that kind of education.

FRIEL: Not consciously. I never sit around and read a book because this is something that a playwright should know about, even though he is never going to use it.

FUNKE: Well, what about Freud in terms of a playwright?

FRIEL: No.

FUNKE: You have nothing to do with Freud, either. Then, in other words, you write strictly out of your own observation of the motivation and psychology of the characters with whom you are working.

FRIEL: Yes. I have read some Freud and I like Jung, but I don't read these people to give me an insight into psychology or the process of the mind or anything like this. I just read them because of curiosity. I don't read professionally. That's what I want to say.

FUNKE: As a writer who observes people, are you constantly watching people in their reactions and listening to people talk about their problems?

FRIEL: Again, not indiscriminately. I find that you develop a sense of when to listen and when to tune off and what sort of situations to record mentally, and what not to. It's a sort of private process, I think, that works automatically.

FUNKE: Do you have a notebook?

FRIEL: Yes. It's a very tiny little book and I just write nothing more than six words at a time. Two or three lines is the most I ever write. I look over this book maybe once or twice a week, but if I leave it longer than that, I've forgotten what the reference was, very often.

FUNKE: You're very unorthodox about this, obviously. You're not like Chekhov's Trigorin who, every moment, is making a notation and is so systematic. If he sees a cloud passing overhead, it has a certain shape.

FRIEL: No, I think the writer, at least in this aspect, is something like a water diviner. He has the diviner's twig in his hand all the time. When he's moving across a spring, suddenly the twig will twitch for him—the Geiger counter will go for him.

FUNKE: We talked about the source of ideas and you said that you don't read newspapers and look for particular incidents, and so forth. Well, where did the idea for *Philadelphia* come? Now, I know that the situation in *Philadelphia* is quite a national problem in Ireland.[1]

FRIEL: Yes—it's a part of the planet, you know. In fact, the idea is so old-hat in Ireland, that it was almost courageous to tackle it again. Everybody has tried an emigrant play. But then again, I don't think it was altogether an emigrant play—about emigrants. It was as much about a boy, belatedly becoming a man; a relationship between a father and son not coming to fruition; and a love affair that never flowered simply because of incoherence or shyness or whatever. I think it as much about these things as emigration, and the emigration was really the scaffolding around which one built all these other things.

FUNKE: There is no need to apologize for it—in terms of old-hat. How many original situations are there in the world? It's what the playwright does with the situation and what his own individuality and sensitivity bring to it that make it valid. You have been a teacher and you are a writer. Do you think there is any value for a man or a woman who wants to be a writer to take lessons or courses in writing?

FRIEL: No. It's the sort of thing I hate pontificating about. All I can say is that I just couldn't; it wouldn't be for me at all. If I had a son who wanted to do it, I would say, "Have sense, child."

FUNKE: What would you recommend that your son do? You, in a sense, wandered into it, didn't you? You did not set out early in life with the idea that some day you were going to be a playwright.

FRIEL: I hoped I would be.

FUNKE: Oh, you did have those hopes.

FRIEL: Yes, I hoped to be a writer, either in short stories or in theatre. Otherwise, I wouldn't have attempted either. You had talked about this "compulsion," and the word made me slightly nervous.

FUNKE: Then, if your son indicated that he wanted to be a writer, how would you advise him to proceed in contrast with what had been your own procedure?

FRIEL: If he wanted to write for theatre? I think that being in theatres or messing about in a theatre workshop isn't all that important. I don't see how there is any great relevance. I think if he has a certain

---

1. The departure of the young people from Ireland for greater opportunity available elsewhere.

insight, if he has a certain awareness and a certain perception, he can learn these other things quite simply. Two hours will teach him all these other things.

FUNKE: How exactly can he learn? By simply going to a play and seeing what the theatre is about?

FRIEL: I think he would, yes.

FUNKE: In other words, you wouldn't recommend that, if he went to the University, he concentrate on courses in drama?

FRIEL: In fact, if he wanted to be a dramatist, I would say to him, "If you have a choice between doing a drama course and a course in some of the humanities, or doing Greek or Latin or something, do Greek and Latin."

FUNKE: What do you think your son . . .

FRIEL: He's mythical, by the way. I have four daughters.

FUNKE: Well, who knows, one of them may want to be a playwright—or all four. Aside from knowing the rudiments of drama, what do you think a writer requires in terms of equipment?

FRIEL: Mental equipment, you mean?

FUNKE: Mental equipment, and temperamental.

FRIEL: I think if he has a great social commitment and a certain dramatic skill, he's a lucky man. He'll then be Sean O'Casey, Brecht or somebody like this. He'll feel sort of a Messianic urge to do something about the condition in which he finds himself. If he hasn't got this, he is still well-equipped, I think, if he is in sympathy with people. If he is interested in people and he reacts to people.

FUNKE: The social commitment that you mentioned, that's very interesting because, as far as I can determine, you don't have a social commitment. I don't feel something that you are committed to, that you are trying to let an audience know. Am I wrong in that sense?

FRIEL: No, let's put it this way. There are many social things that I am frankly interested in. For example, there was a period in my life when I was a violent Nationalist, an Irish Nationalist. Now this is something that has never appeared in the work I have done. There are other areas of my life that made very deep and—the popular word is "traumatic"—influences that have never appeared in what I have done.

FUNKE: I understand entirely what you're saying; at least, I feel I do. It seems to me, you are illuminating individuals, but not necessarily in relationship to the social climate—which I take to mean, social commitment.

FRIEL: Fine, yes.

FUNKE: Is there any reason why you haven't yet developed that, or is that something you will come to?

FRIEL: I don't think it's something I'll come to because I'm very uneasy about using the theatre for a political or a social purpose. As a matter of fact . . . I'll tell you, perhaps I couldn't do it. It's something perhaps I couldn't do.

FUNKE: Because of your own nature?

FRIEL: I suppose so. I think so.

FUNKE: But you said before of a hypothetical young son, you would feel he was a very lucky young man if he had both social commitment and a sympathy with people. Were you trying to tell me that . . . although you don't care to do it—you would like to see a young playwright realize the social function of the playwright in terms of the theatre and in terms of society?

FRIEL: No, I think that the playwright can be lucky if he has the social commitment or if he has this sympathy with people. I think on either of these two levels, he can function in the theatre.

FUNKE: But if he had both, he would be . . .

FRIEL: He would be blessed.

FUNKE: What do you feel is the function of the playwright, broadly speaking? Do you think that the playwright should be associating himself with causes and espousing causes in the theatre?

FRIEL: I can't do this; that's all I know. I tell you, I would like to do a satire or a farce preferably on contemporary Ireland because the situation is absolutely ready for it, but I'm afraid I won't be able to do it. In fact, I'm working on it but I don't think I'll be able to get the job done.

FUNKE: Well, your bent is more comedic than comment in a sense, is it not? You don't write straight drama—the heavy Strindberg type of drama. You're in a lighter vein. You feel that this is your milieu.

FRIEL: Yes, that's what it is.

FUNKE: In other words, you don't aspire to write the so-called social play, the Arthur Miller play or the Clifford Odets play.

FRIEL: Right. I think the tragedy of theatre is that one assumes that if you laugh, you're being silly.

FUNKE: I'd like you to tell me a little bit more about that. There is a tendency to downgrade a playwright like Neil Simon in intellectual circles and yet comedy does have a very basic value in the theatre. Through comedy, you can say much. Is this your feeling?

FRIEL: Oh, very strongly. The point is, I know I am deadly serious all the time.

FUNKE: I know you have called yourself a "black Irishman."

FRIEL: Yes, and deadly serious all the time when I'm writing. If people want to read me as a comic writer, well, fair enough. This is not how I feel.

FUNKE: The reason I said "comic" was that there's a good deal of laughter in your plays. I mean, the relationship between the two young people,[2] the boy and the girl, has many comic overtones and people burst out laughing. Underneath there is a poignancy, but there isn't that much poignancy in the second play—because you have got this wild situation of the mother upstairs who's trying to interfere with their relationship. That was a comic situation for you, was it not?

FRIEL: Yes, of course, but it's a very serious situation, too. I think it's tragic really.

FUNKE: In what sense?

FRIEL: I think it is tragic to see lives blighted as were these two middle-aged lovers—blighted in the name of God or for some obscure reason like that. I think this is tragic, but I think if I were to present this in tragic terms, people wouldn't listen to me or people would be bored by it. You present it in a very different light and I think you make your point equally well.

FUNKE: Yes. You make a habit of sitting down at a typewriter or with a pencil, regardless of whether you feel like working or not?

FRIEL: I do this.

FUNKE: Do you sometimes just start writing without any idea in mind, just free association writing?

FRIEL: No, I don't.

FUNKE: What are your working habits when you are writing a play? How many hours a day do you work?

FRIEL: From say 9:30 in the morning until one o'clock with many, many breaks for tea and from nearly two o'clock to until, say 3:30—and that's it.

FUNKE: And what do you do for relaxation?

FRIEL: The following morning I go up, rework what I've done the previous day and then start off again. For relaxation, I garden a bit, do some trout fishing.

FUNKE: Do you have any particular regimen, I mean in terms of keeping yourself physically fit and alert?

FRIEL: No.

FUNKE: Where do you work?

---

2. *Lovers*

FRIEL: I work in a room upstairs in my own house. It's out in the country—very quiet.

FUNKE: You couldn't work in the city, I presume.

FRIEL: No. I lived in the city until a few years ago, but I worked again in a very quiet room upstairs. I couldn't work in an hotel bedroom.

FUNKE: Do you work every day, regardless of whether you have anything to write or not?

FRIEL: I do, yes. But again, it should be qualified. If I say to you, "Do you work every day?" you say, "Yes, of course I do." But there are days when you don't go to the office—when you have a good excuse for not going. I find I constantly make excuses for myself—I'm getting better as the years go on—but I still do a lot of hours every day.

FUNKE: And when you are not working on a play, are you working on short stories?

FRIEL: Not in recent years. I'm either working on a play or else I'm just not working.

FUNKE: You mean you're not working on anything specific, but you are trying.

FRIEL: Oh, yes.

FUNKE: Do you have many ideas floating around all the time, and then you make a selection of these ideas and say "I'm going to work on this"?

FRIEL: I have my notebooks and other sheets of paper where I jot down ideas that perhaps I might do some work on. As I mentioned earlier, I'm very anxious to do a satire on present-day Ireland. I probably know that I'm not going to get this thing done, but I have been working on this for six months and I'm afraid it's going to get me nowhere, you know. This is going to be a period of time where there is nothing to mind.

FUNKE: Was writing a two-character play extremely difficult?

FRIEL: You are talking about *Winners* now?

FUNKE: Yes; I mean, knowing you are just going to have two people on the stage.

FRIEL: No, I don't think so. No, I find that my one problem was a form problem. The other things don't present problems to me.

FUNKE: You don't have any problem with character?

FRIEL: No, not at all.

FUNKE: Do the people in your plays come out of people whom you've known?

FRIEL: They probably begin with someone I have known. I certainly don't transport. One can't transport people from the street to the stage.

FUNKE: Actors have told me that frequently in interpreting a part they will remember some mental note they made of a person reacting in a situation of stress, for instance, in a certain way. I was wondering how much that figures in a playwright's technique.

FRIEL: It could happen. This raw material could be fed through your head but it comes out in a different shape.

FUNKE: In other words, you didn't actually know a boy such as the one in *Philadelphia.*

FRIEL: No. I'm sure I knew ten boys, bits of whom made up this one boy.

FUNKE: You have been praised for having a great ear for Irish speech. How does a writer train his ear for the speech of a people? What kind of guidance could you give a playwright on that?

FRIEL: I don't think I could give any guidance. I think this is an intuitive thing. I think it's like being musical. You hear a tune on TV and you can repeat it. You can sing it again.

FUNKE: You don't think it can be learned?

FRIEL: Perhaps it could be. I could, I think, give a thoroughly good imitation of Jewish dialogue. Here is an example now. I was out last night at *The Happy Time,* which was set in French Canada, and I said in the middle of the first act, "It's funny but the humor in this strikes me as being Jewish." The person with me said, "Well, it should be because the man who wrote this writes Jewish humor." I think this is something I could learn if I set out to do it. I just couldn't do it tomorrow or next week, but if I wanted to learn Jewish humor dialogue, I think I could learn it and do it fairly well.

FUNKE: Then, you feel you have a natural ear for speech?

FRIEL: I suppose this is true.

FUNKE: There is no way that one can train himself to catch the tone and the inflection? One has to have this gift?

FRIEL: I suppose so.

FUNKE: I'm asking you questions that probably haven't occurred to you before.

FRIEL: No, they haven't occurred.

FUNKE: Which of the plays you have written is your favorite?

FRIEL: When I answer that, it is the one I have just finished. This sounds like a smart answer, but the reason always is that it is at the stage where it hasn't been exposed to any sort of brutality or any sort of savagery and if it were done ideally, as I would like it to be done, I think it could be very good. I look back on the other plays that I have done,

Philadelphia, Cass McGuire and *Lovers,* and I'm not ashamed of them—
let's put it that way.

FUNKE: Have you ever felt the urge to say, "Maybe, if I had done it
this way, it would have been better or stronger, or more effective," and to
go back to rewrite a play even after it has been produced? Tennessee
Williams does that. Have you ever had that experience with any of your
plays?

FRIEL: No. Occasionally there may be tiny little areas where I think I
should have done it that way, but this really doesn't bother me. I look at
the whole shape of the play and I think I really wouldn't do that whole
play in that whole way again. I don't want to sit down and rewrite it. I'm
bored with them all—they are finished.

FUNKE: It must have been a very satisfying experience for you with
The Loves of Cass McGuire. After the failure here in New York, you saw it
done in Dublin, and done properly, so that it became such a major hit.

FRIEL: Well, I don't measure failure or success. I had no doubt that
the play could have been done well. I was terribly worried and terribly
upset by all this and the carry-on when it didn't do well, but the play was
the play all the time and I had faith in it.

FUNKE: Were you here when *Cass* was being done?

FRIEL: I was here.

FUNKE: Did you feel it was going in the right direction during the
rehearsals? What was it that gave you the nerve on the basis of its bad
luck here to proceed with it for a Dublin production? Did you feel it
hadn't been done properly?

FRIEL: I was quite happy about the script always, and the fighting we
had here was over the script, and of course, on the casting, too. But that's
another story.

FUNKE: Your social life, I gather, is rather isolated. You don't mingle
with theatre people.

FRIEL: There's no theatre group within 150 miles of me.

FUNKE: Well, do you think this is good, or do you think a playwright
should be part of the so-called trade—associate with theatre people?

FRIEL: I don't know. I'm not an isolationist by design. I just happen
to live in this part of the country and I happen to like it and I'm not a
very gregarious sort of a person by inclination. I like theatre people but
I don't constantly want to go out with them or seek their sort of company.

FUNKE: Then, you don't miss it?

FRIEL: No, not at all.

FUNKE: You don't feel any compelling need to be familiar with everything that is happening in the Dublin theatre or in the London theatre?

FRIEL: No interest at all, really.

FUNKE: In terms of giving a young playwright advice on the development of character, is there any clue that you can give him? With you, it's all pretty much of an intuitive process all the way.

FRIEL: An intuitive process with a great certainty at the same time. That's a priggish thing to say, isn't it? But I think this is what the craft is, you know. It is an intuitive process, but you know, by God, that you're right.

FUNKE: I wonder how young drama students are going to react when they are told in so many instances that they can't really learn those things. They have got to have it or they don't have it. I think, basically, that is your reaction to the whole business of writing.

FRIEL: I think maybe it is—or let's put it another way. I think these workshops, theatre workshops and writing classes and so on can take you so far, but I think also you have got to have this other thing and that is what carries you the important inch further.

FUNKE: You indicated how important timing was in the theatre. You feel that you can hold a line of monologue only so long. Now this again is instinctive, isn't it? This is something that you don't learn.

FRIEL: This is instinctive, but it is a very easy instinct. If you are sitting with four people in a room and you are telling them a story, a funny story, you know instinctively if you are losing one of them or two of them or three of them, isn't that right? This is a very simple matter and even though I'm sitting at a desk in a top room in the country, I can envisage the situation on the stage. I know whether this girl in this monologue can hold these people past this point or not, providing she's a first-class actress. We are inclined to make a sort of mystique out of this business, you know. I don't think there's much mystique in it, I think it is something one knows.

FUNKE: Well, of course, one of the great problems for writers in various areas of writing, whether it be in the short story or the novel or the theatre, is to edit themselves. Now this is a great problem and there is no way, I suppose, other than having a sense of where to end.

FRIEL: You mean editing themselves in their own workroom?

FUNKE: That's right.

FRIEL: But I think once they leave the workroom if they let their script pass into the hands of producers, directors or actors, God forbid, who will then edit the script, they are finished. Back again to Beethoven's Fifth Symphony. There's the score—play it.

FUNKE: When you are writing a play, you are always conscious of the audience. Are you conscious of the critics?

FRIEL: Not at all. I think one has to develop an attitude towards critics, isn't that right?

FUNKE: Well, yes.

FRIEL: I mean, everybody who is involved in the art forms must have some answer to this. Well, mine is, if I dismiss the critics because they are hostile to me, then I can't accept their praise. That's not very logical. So I'm not flattered when they praise me and I'm not hurt when they slay me.

FUNKE: This takes a great independence of mind, doesn't it?

FRIEL: Let me qualify this further. The praise of critics just washes over me but very often the hurt that they inflict will stay.

FUNKE: In other words, then, you are not insensitive to what . . .

FRIEL: No. Not totally insensitive. Not at all. Damn it all. We are always susceptible.

FUNKE: But when you are writing, you are not thinking in terms of "Will the critics like this?"

FRIEL: No, this has nothing to do with theatre.

FUNKE: One of the wonderful things about *Lovers* is that in a period where a great deal of avant-garde theatre is being done, what has been called the "theatre of now," here are two plays which have no thought other than being plays. What is your feeling about what is going on in the contemporary theatre?

FRIEL: So many people ask me this question. To use their own terminology, I think all one can do is do your own thing. I think there has been great obsession—particularly in America, and certainly in New York—with what is contemporary. Are you writing in an "in" mode? Are your forms of 1968? Playwrights aren't fashion designers, you know.

FUNKE: Walter Kerr had a very interesting piece last Sunday in which he said we are getting too much of this "theatre of now." A lot of young people are saying the March[3]—the Demonstration—this is a play in itself. Kerr has begun to object to this on the grounds that that is not the function of the theatre. What Kerr is saying is that—sure, the theatre should do with "now," but the playwright must distance himself to interpret the "now." Is there much of this avant-garde in Dublin?

FRIEL: Absolutely not. I am thirty-nine years of age. If I were an

---

3. A fifty-mile march by hundreds of people, in 1965, from Selma, Alabama, to Montgomery, Alabama, to demonstrate Negro protests against Civil Rights violations.

American man of thirty-nine years of age, I'd think I must be writing about this particular time and the people of my time. But why must I be so obsessed with writing about this morning's newspaper headlines? This seems to be their concern. You know, Selma[4] is as far back in American history as the Gettysburg Address, isn't it? And that was only a few years ago. An obsession with this morning's headlines is really what it is, and there's nothing as dated as this morning's headline.

FUNKE: But the relationships between people . . .

FRIEL: Well, if I am an American dramatist living in New York at the present time, these current events are making me the type of man I am. So if I write about the people in the apartment above me or if I wrote about LBJ[5] or if I write about the Green Berets[6] or whatever—I'm writing as a contemporary man living in present-day New York and I shouldn't be so obsessed with making my theatre or my plan an editorial, a newspaper editorial. Are you with me there?

FUNKE: Yes, I'm with you. I think that what we are trying to arrive at is a definition of what really the playwright's function is as a playwright. What should the playwright be doing for an audience? Should he be trying to recreate events that have just happened or should he be looking at the events and trying to figure out why they happened?

FRIEL: There is no point at all in recreating events. I don't think this has anything to do with art at all or the art of theatre. I think his job is to interpret them. This is the function of the artist—to select the significant details and arrange them into a significant pattern. Then people will look at the significant pattern and say, "Of course, this is what it is all about." And in this way, the dramatist then hopefully changes the face of the earth.

FUNKE: There is a tendency among the young playwrights today to feel that the interpretations that playwrights have been using are not the truth and that the only way to get at people is through showing them events. But this is not the function of the theatre.

FRIEL: I don't think so and I think it's very boring.

FUNKE: Have you made any conscious effort to grow as a playwright? Is there anything that you do to grow as a playwright in depth and perception?

FRIEL: In my writing techniques, you mean, or as a person?

---

4. Alabama city, where, in 1965, organized campaigns to end discriminations in voter registrations began.

5. Lyndon Baines Johnson, thirty-sixth president of the United States.

6. Special Forces Unit of U.S. Army, distinguished by a distinctive emblem—the green beret.

FUNKE: As a person. Or are you what you are and you accept that. You don't go beyond that.

FRIEL: Again, this is kind of unconsciously seeking experience. This is what you are asking me, isn't it?

FUNKE: Yes.

FRIEL: Whether it is through reading, travel or meeting people, I doubt if one can. Think of Jane Austen and the Brontës and people like this. The intensity of your feelings is much more important than the range of it.

FUNKE: The intensity is more important than the range of it. There is a feeling in America—I don't know how true this is in Ireland, but I guess it's true to a certain extent in England—that the young people are supposed to have been lost to the theatre. Have you been conscious of that? What do you think should be, or can be, done about it? Why do you feel young people have been alienated from the theatre?

FRIEL: I'm not even aware that they are. I just don't know.

FUNKE: What is your feeling about the theatre of the absurd, the theatre of Beckett and Ionesco?

FRIEL: Just generally about them?

FUNKE: Yes.

FRIEL: Well, you see, again, I admire them all. I admire Beckett immensely. This is not my instrument.

FUNKE: In other words, you don't think that a playwright should try to adopt or adapt to anyone else's form or style?

FRIEL: I think he is his own man. He has his own truth. He has his own method of presenting his own truth. And the more honest he is in doing this, the better playwright he'll be.

Frank Talk from Friel

Alan N. Bunce / 1968

Throughout most of his career Brian Friel would insist that he was indifferent to what Broadway critics had to say about his work—whether of praise or blame. Friel had lots of experience of both. The Broadway success of *Philadelphia, Here I Come!* (1964) was followed by the disappointing reception of *The Loves of Cass McGuire* (1966). The strong run of *Lovers* (1967) was followed by scant enthusiasm in New York for *The Mundy Scheme* (1969), *Crystal and Fox* (1973), and *The Freedom of the City* (1974). Decades later, the same pattern would be repeated. Following the staggering success of *Dancing at Lughnasa* (1991), expectations were once again at fever pitch for Friel's next work. But when *Wonderful Tennessee* (1993) arrived on Broadway, its closing was announced just two days after its opening. A reporter who encountered Friel and his wife sipping tea at Shannon Airport during a compulsory stopover on their flight home recounted him saying: "Sure, I've had more flops on Broadway than I've had hot dinners. I'm immune. Well, I'm not quite immune, but you just have to get on with it." Although Friel might declare his immunity, he sometimes seemed more susceptible than he let on. The enthusiastic, if belated, reception of *Aristocrats* (which did not go to New York for a full decade after its 1979 Dublin opening) was one impetus for the writing of *Dancing at Lughnasa*. But with Alan N. Bunce in 1968, Friel's "frank talk" revealed more clearly than any other interview in his career that he had suffered from the stinging words of critics. Although Friel says he could never

From the *Christian Science Monitor,* 27 November 1968, p. 13.

direct his plays, he would eventually direct *Molly Sweeney* (1994)
in Dublin, London and New York and *Give Me Your Answer, Do!*
(1997) in Dublin.

It's easy to be fooled by Brian Friel's face. It fairly twinkles with self-deprecating glee. But the seriousness of his statements belies the leprechaun
smile.

Sitting on the bed in his room at the Algonquin Hotel during a
recent visit from his native Ireland, the author of Broadway's *Lovers*
spoke of playwriting, the theater, and his own art with a refreshing disre-
gard of current fashion.

About the success here of *Lovers,* and three seasons ago of *Philadelphia, Here I Come!* he says: "It's the part of you that's least important that
blossoms under this sort of situation, isn't it? What's really important in
yourself isn't ultimately affected by these things.

"But the hurt one suffers [from bad notices] is a more permanent
thing. I'm sure I suffered more over *Cass McGuire* than I expanded or
enjoyed myself with *Philadelphia, Here I Come!*"

The Loves of Cass McGuire, produced here two seasons ago, received
disappointing reviews. Mr. Friel has his own view of this:

"American audiences are more attentive than in Ireland, but I think
they're terribly influenced by what critics tell them. Critics don't count in
Ireland at all really. Nobody in Dublin can tell you what the critics said.

"But I can't talk with any honesty about critics. We build certain
defenses. Mine is this: If you believe them when they praise you, you
must believe them when they kick you, and vice versa. I don't believe any
of them, and I don't allow them to influence me."

Lovers originally opened here at Lincoln Center's Vivian Beaumont
Theater, with Art Carney starring. Moving to the Music Box Theater on
Broadway was considered a sign of success, especially after it was
announced the play would become a movie soon. But once again, Mr.
Friel takes exception:

"A thing of nothing is Broadway, isn't it? This is where all the low sus-
ceptibilities are touched. One is flattered by the fact that it's going to
move to Broadway. But I was looking through the Broadway listings in a
magazine, and there's nothing you'd want to see. Yet one is always
impressed by American acting."

Mr. Carney has temporarily stepped out of the show to fulfill long-
standing television obligations with Jackie Gleason in Florida. Meanwhile, his role—which ranges from near-burlesque comedy to documentary incisiveness—has been taken over by Peter Lind Hayes. When Mr.

Carney returns to the production in early February, it will begin a national tour that starts in Los Angeles and lists 10 cities on its itinerary.

Both *Lovers* and *Philadelphia, Here I Come!* were produced first at the Dublin Gate Theatre. It's a process Mr. Friel prefers. *Cass,* on the other hand, received its first staging in New York.

"This was a fatal mistake," he says. "The best theater was always done, in history, with a writer working with a director and a resident company. This is, of course, what you don't have on Broadway, and indeed what you don't have in Ireland except in the Abbey Theatre.

"Irish theater seems to be in a permanent state of senility. It isn't going to die, and it certainly isn't getting rejuvenated in any way. Ireland doesn't have the experimental theater you find here Off and Off-Off Broadway."

Whatever his reservations, Mr. Friel will be seen again on Broadway next season when his new play *Crystal and Fox* opens. Meanwhile, it is being offered at the Dublin Gate Theatre under the direction of Hilton Edwards.

One of the notable things about a Friel play is the melody of its dialogue—sparkling but unaffected, something akin to the cadences of his own lilting speech. Writing it, he says, is a bit like picking up tunes. Some people have a good ear for music. He has one for speech patterns. Style, though—which he calls the marriage of content and form—is a problem for him.

"It's something that doesn't come easily to me," said Mr. Friel. "This is where I think American dramatists are very good. They're unself-conscious about style. I find I never have much problem in content. With *Lovers* I practically wrote the play just as it was, with the boy and the girl by themselves."

Later he added a background narrative at certain points. "The content never really varied, but the way in which it was framed, or presented, the architecture, was altered a dozen times before I eventually ended up with this form."

As presented, *Lovers* is delightfully free of mannerism or sectionalism. Perhaps this is because Mr. Friel does not write for Irish audiences—or for any single group.

"I think if you write with as much truth and accuracy as you can, and if the play turns out to be a good play, it can transcend these boundaries. If it's in India, and it's written with as much truth about Indians, they're going to be people and we'll recognize them and understand what they're at."

They may be people, but as he creates them he has no idea how they should look.

"I can see all the characters moving in various directions as they speak. The only thing that's missing from all these people on stage is that none of them has any features. I write descriptions of them, but funnily enough when I see them in my mind they don't have facial expressions. Then after the first production of the play, this tends to become [for me] the definitive face for this person, which is very stupid."

Mr. Friel does not believe a playwright can be trained.

"Perhaps it can happen, but I detest theater workshops, and I detest writers' workshops. I think this is something you go and do in private and sweat and labor over by yourself. Perhaps there are a few relatively unimportant things you can learn. And probably I've never learned them yet—how many people you can have on stage at one time and how to get them off. All this sort of trivia."

"But then again I'm out of date with this," he went on. "I mean I don't understand how the Beatles' 'Sergeant Pepper' [record album] can be acclaimed a great musical work. This is something that's arrived at in a laboratory with certain sound effects. The Beatles themselves don't know how it was achieved. It can never be repeated. The Beatles couldn't come into this room and play 'Sergeant Pepper' for us.

"The same thing applies to the theater. Perhaps with four or five writers swearing at one another or discussing, one of them may produce something, but I can't see it."

Nor does he have much use for another current trend in New York, especially Off Broadway: the use of a play as merely a framework for improvisation and development.

"It has to do with this director's theater, which I'm not very much in sympathy with. They're of very new vintage in the history of the theater, and suddenly they get billing above the title practically. I can't work like this. And because I can't, I think it's wrong, which is a little ridiculous."

"I'm arrogant about this. I expect the actors to do what I want. I don't want to write for actors ever. I think their job is simply to interpret the musical score that's handed to them. If you hand a group of musicians a score and they decide to change it, it would be impossible. It's only in the theater we tolerate this. Dramatists have so prostituted themselves that they accept this.

"I don't want them to use my plays as a springboard. Let them spring off something else."

But Mr. Friel has no directorial ambitions personally.

"I could never direct my plays. I sit beside Hilton Edwards, the director, and mutter in his ear and kind of hide behind him. I don't understand the choreography of movement on the stage at all. But I'd know when it was wrong."

Mr. Friel writes in his house outside a village called Muff, five miles from Derry. "I live 150 miles from Dublin. By American standards this is nothing, but I consider it a long trip. I never see civilized society at all, never meet actors or directors."

But he already has another play ready, and if it's as good as his previous works, he'll no doubt find himself back here once more.

Press Diary:
Unsinkable Brian Friel

The Irish Times / 1969

By the 1968–69 theatrical season, the *Irish Independent* could declare that Brian Friel—the author of three plays performed on Broadway, including one that had been performed world-wide in over a dozen languages—"is undoubtedly our greatest playwright" and that "any new work bearing his name is of wide international interest." It therefore came as something of a shock when Friel reported that the Abbey, Ireland's National Theatre, had rejected his latest play. Describing *The Mundy Scheme* as a "satire on present-day political Ireland," Friel told reporters that he was "very angry" about the Abbey's rejection: "I wouldn't have given it to them except that I feel it is the kind of play which should be put on in a national theatre, as *Soldiers* should have been put on in the National Theatre in London." What *The Mundy Scheme* had in common with Rolf Hochhuth's *Soldiers*, championed in London by National Theatre dramaturg Kenneth Tynan but vetoed by his board of directors, is that both plays are political. But whereas *Soldiers* is based on history and accuses Churchill of betraying Poland to keep his alliance with Stalin, *The Mundy Scheme* is set in the future and deals with a far-fetched proposal to turn Ireland into a vast graveyard for Americans. Still, Friel felt the play raised questions that were more broadly political than his previous work. "In the past," Friel said, "I've tried to investigate individuals, but this is an indictment of the general establishment." Such an indictment extended even to the Taoiseach (pronounced "tee-

From *The Irish Times*, 11 April 1969, p. 17.

shockh"), the prime minister of the Republic of Ireland. Following the rejection by the Abbey, *The Mundy Scheme* was shifted to the Olympia Theatre. Prior to that opening, Friel describes the tone of the play as "savage." In the event, the Olympia production was greeted as "a squib" ("perfectly safe for children of all ages"), and neither of the two film projects Friel had in the works ever came to fruition.

"I have few political friends in the North of Ireland, but I'll have fewer in the South after my new play opens in Dublin", said the unsinkable Brian Friel. It has been scheduled for the Olympia Theatre in June and will be directed by Donal Donnelly, which is a new role for him. "Godfrey Quigley will take the lead and I'm hoping that T. P. McKenna and John Cowley will be free to join the cast.

"Some of the papers have described it as a comedy but it is really a savage satire on Irish politics. It has a Taoiseach in it too who is an auctioneer, and being Irish, a bachelor."

The play has an intriguing title, *The Mundy Scheme: or May We Write Your Epitaph Now, Mr. Emmet?*

"Mundy is the American name for MacCloone", says Brian with an obvious eye on Broadway. "Can you blame me," he says. "J. B. Keane seems to be the only Irish playwright who can make money out of his plays in Ireland. As for me, if I were to depend on Irish royalties I wouldn't last more than three months."

However, he doesn't need our tears on his way to the bank, for he confirmed that two of his plays *Philadelphia* and *Lovers* are being made into films. He will write the film scenario only for *Philadelphia* which is to be produced by Jane Nusbaum, an independent producer, who was associated with Peter O'Toole's and Hepburn's *The Lion in Winter.*

Columbia will make *Lovers*. He is naturally very pleased that the play has been nominated for a Tony award in America. Two members of the cast, Anna Manahan and Art Carney, have also been nominated for awards.

"Is it true that Richard Burton is considering the role of the Fox in your *Crystal and Fox* for his return to Broadway?" I asked. "Yes, but I personally feel that he might go for Shakespeare rather than for a new play. I wouldn't be surprised if he were to choose *Coriolanus* for this."

Kathleen Mavourneen, Here Comes Brian Friel

Desmond Rushe / 1970

Interviewing Brian Friel for an avowedly religious publication, Dublin drama critic Desmond Rushe plunges in at the deep end with questions about the playwright's worldview and stance toward religion. The approach evokes Friel's most explicit attempts to explain the complexities of being a "practising lapsed Catholic" as well as his most direct commentary on the Church. Although Friel may describe his own vision as bleak, he distances himself from the "complete abnegation of life" he sees in Beckett and Pinter. In his wide-ranging interview, Rushe explores the roots of Friel's Irish nationalism, prompting Friel to talk about fearing for his life as a boy in Derry. Friel discusses contemporary politics, including his participation in the Civil Rights movement, and explains his move to the Republic of Ireland, while expressing his reservations about Dublin life. But Friel ends the interview talking about the importance of his wife and family, which might have given rise to the article's title. *Mavourneen* is Irish for *darling* or *darling dearest.* "Kathleen, Mavourneen" is a nineteenth-century ballad sung by one who is emigrating from Ireland, much like the protagonist of *Philadelphia, Here I Come!*

In most of your plays, Philadelphia, Here I Come!, *and* Lovers, *for instance, which have been performed in many countries, there is a lot of comedy and a great deal of human sorrow and misery. Is this how you see life in general?*

From *The Word: An International Catholic Pictorial Magazine* (Divine Word Missionaries, formerly of St. Richard's College, Hadzor, Droitwich, Worcestershire, England; now published at Donamon, Co. Roscommon, Ireland), February 1970, pp. 12–15.

By nature I'm a bleak sort of person, and whatever comedy there is is the absurd sort. The only type of comic situation I see in life is a distortion of normality—which is a sort of definition of comedy.

Have you always been like this—bleak?

I don't think I'm getting bleaker as the years go on, but my view of life isn't very generous, isn't very tolerant.

What have you seen in life to make you bleak and ungenerous?

Now we're sort of dipping our toes into an area of philosophy in which I'm not expert at all. We all have such a brief period here in life, and the great portion of this time is spent either in working or crying. This general gloom is relieved only very seldom by periods of some kind of levity. I think this has got to be portrayed on the stage.

Are you a pessimist, then?

I don't know. Maybe I am.

But do you not see something marvelous for the human being at the end of everything?

You're talking in religious terms now?

I'm talking in general terms. Can you really separate them?

From the religious point of view, I'm a very confused man. The only thing I think that is of absolute importance is life—being alive and holding on to this condition of existence—but this in itself isn't really a cause for joy.

Doesn't religion teach differently? That everything really worth anything is beyond life?

This is heretical religion. And especially the Irish Church, which teaches that the only thing worth living for is the after life—this is total heresy. If there is an after life, the only way one can merit it is by being totally involved in the here-and-now.

Is there an after life?

I have no answer to this. At the moment I don't know. As soon as I make a ponderous statement, I'm usually embarrassed by it the following week.

What is your attitude to God—believer, agnostic or atheist?

Oh, I'm not an atheist. I'm probably closer to agnosticism. This is a very searching and groping sort of area where one can't have any sort of scientific truth. You can't prove to me that there is an after life, and I can't disprove that there isn't. So it really is an area of speculation.

Is it an area of importance to you?

I don't think it's all that important. I am absolutely certain that if I die next week and am going to go to heaven, I don't think it's going to affect how I live here and now. I am not going to be any more charitable or uncharitable than I am now. One tries to live one's life as best one can. Let's forget about the after life for the moment, and live this one.

You were born and reared in the Irish Catholic tradition.

I suppose I'm a sort of practising lapsed Catholic. It's one of these attitudes I'm not prepared to defend, because I'm a volatile sort of person and next week I could be crawling up Croagh Patrick on my knees. And I don't see any great contradiction in this either.

What is your background, Brian?

I was born in Tyrone, outside Omagh, and lived there until I was ten. Then we came to live in Derry, where my father was a teacher.

Your background was Catholic and nationalist.

Very intensely nationalist, and in those days one's whole nationalism and religion were constantly interwoven and inextricable. The result now is that while I'm not as intensely Irish Catholic as I was, I'm still left with this very vigorous nationalism, as intense as it always was. This hasn't much to do with the Border.

It isn't just a matter of wanting a 32-county Irish Republic?

The desirability of this isn't as obvious now as it was, because the turn the Republic has taken over the past nine or ten years has been distressing, very disquieting. We have become a tenth-rate image of America—a disaster for any country.

What form does your nationalism take?

There are certain values in this country which were very dominant 50 or 60 years ago and are well worth preserving. What we accepted as our cultural identity is certainly worth preserving.

Do you want Ireland to get back to the old culture?

One can never go back to the old culture, but it could extend to the present day. Our country should be as distinctive and individualistic as Belgium and Holland—I'm talking of small countries. Instead of that we're becoming more and more Madison Avenue–ish and slicker in a very shabby sort of way.

What can you do about it? We are wide open to American influence, much more so than Holland or Belgium.

I think, for instance, Ireland is politically sitting in the lap of America. We have never taken a stand on issues that were certainly moral—issues at the UN where Aiken should have taken a stand and didn't. But to go back to what is going wrong, I think the emphasis is on having at least one car and preferably two. One has only to go into any of the posh Dublin hotels and one can see the new Ireland sprawled around in the lounges. This development is terrifying.

Is this not an inevitable part of increasing prosperity?

I don't see that it has any relationship with prosperity. One can have all the riches of the world and still have a very clean mind. It is sullied in Ireland at the moment.

How would you go about cleaning it?

One of the big problems is that there are two societies, and I feel very strongly about this. There is the Dublin society in the Dublin environs, and then there is the rest. This is not quite the same as purely urban-rural. You have an intensely urban society in Dublin, the cultural and political vanguard of everything that's thought and done; and you have the rest of the country living in complete isolation. The result is that instead of the rural and urban societies complementing one another and acting as a mutual balance, you have two distinct societies, one literally wilting away and the other forging ahead without this very necessary balance. A much closer link with rural roots is necessary.

As a Catholic did you have problems growing up?

Of course. As a young boy in Derry there were certain areas one didn't go into. I remember bringing shoes to the shoemaker's shop at the end of the street. This was a terrifying experience, because if the Protestant boys caught you in this kind of no-man's-land, they'd kill you. I have vivid memories when I was 12 or so of standing at my own front door and hoping the coast would be clear so I could dive over to the shop; and then, when I'd left the shoes in, waiting to see was the coast clear again. If you were caught, you were finished. It was absolutely terrifying. That sort of thing leaves scars for the rest of one's life.

What do you think of politics?

I try not to be cynical.

Do you succeed?

At the level of Irish politics I've succeeded, but looking at international politics, I think I fail.

You took part in Civil Rights demonstrations in Derry. Did the situation there offend you?

Until October 5, 1968, which was a red letter day, I thought that society was absolutely dead. Then suddenly five young men, who had nothing to gain in temporal terms, organised a very shabby rally. The parallel is not accurate, but suddenly the whole thing was dignified, as in 1916. The police beat hell out of these fellows. And suddenly the conscience of Derry was aroused.

You feel the Civil Rights Movement will succeed?

What people are looking for is human rights at a very basic level, and I think they will possibly achieve this. But the danger is that they are losing something very important—their orientation towards an Irish Republic.

You built yourself a house in Muff, Co. Donegal. Did you cross the Border deliberately?

The Border has never been relevant to me. It has been an irritation, but I've never intellectually or emotionally accepted it. We had a cottage in west Donegal, so we've moved our permanent home into Donegal.

If Muff was in the Six Counties, would you have built there?

I don't think so. I would much prefer to be under the jurisdiction of the Dublin Government. Stormont is either absurd or iniquitous, probably both.

You were, like your father, a school teacher?

I taught for ten years in various schools and liked it very much.

Before that you spent a term in Maynooth as a clerical student. Has that experience affected your life?

I don't know. It's a very disturbing thing to happen to anyone. I don't know if one ever recovers totally from an immense experience of this nature. I was two years in Maynooth.

Were they happy years?

I wasn't very happy at the time, but I was 16 or 17 and these are carefree years. If one is to have a "tragedy" in one's life, they are the best years to have it in.

What do you think of religious matters at the moment? Have you any idea what might emerge?

I've no idea, but I think this country is facing total chaos because of the complete stagnation of the hierarchy and clergy. They refuse to recognise that things are happening. Vital things are happening in the Church in Holland and America. I know quite a lot about the Catholic scene in America, where very interesting and exciting things are happening. The Irish clergy just dismiss it as just a Yankee fad, of no importance.

What do you feel about the future of the Church in Ireland?

Most likely the intellectuals will stay with it, but the mass of people will have gone. I find that the attitudes in Dublin are much more orthodox than I thought. The sermons I've heard in Dublin churches are a hundred years old. I would have regretted it some years ago, but now I don't care that much. It's a sort of spectator interest to me now. I'm not involved, except at the level of education. In my own area I see children being taught in schools that are inadequate. I blame the Church for this, because they are insisting on special schools for their own kids. It is ridiculous.

You gave up teaching to become a professional writer. What was your first published work?

It should be a red letter day in your life, but I don't remember. I'd been doing a lot of reviewing and some journalism, and I had a few stories published. But the first major breakthrough I got was with *The New Yorker,* which is the best magazine in the world. When it took my first story this was a great encouragement.

What about your plays?

My first play, *This Doubtful Paradise,* was produced in Belfast. Next there was *The Blind Mice, An Enemy Within, Philadelphia, Here I Come!, The Loves of Cass McGuire, Lovers* and *Crystal and Fox.*

You have gone over completely from the short story to play writing? They are two very different forms.

I keep seeing close relationships between them, but I hope I haven't left short story writing. It's a form I like very well. It's not as vulgar a form as the theatre, which is really a vulgar form of communication.

This is because you are communicating en masse?

Yes, and because the theatre and economics are so closely bound up—to such an extent that one is at the mercy of producers and managements. The commercial interests are immense. Not so bad in this country, which is good for a playwright. But it's awful in America. However, my experience in American theatre is only Broadway, and this isn't very fair to the country as a whole. There is very good regional theatre in America, but the Broadway theatre could not be lower. I'm not at all proud of having successes on Broadway, because I think it's of no importance whatever.

It is financially.

Financially it is of great importance, but I don't drive sports cars or have a yacht or swimming pool or these things. I'm not even fond of good food.

What play has given you most satisfaction?

I couldn't answer that. All I can say is that I think the first part of *Lovers* is probably something I remember with a certain affection.

Do you put yourself into your plays? When Eugene O'Neill finished Long Day's Journey into Night, *he said he had written it with tears and blood.*

In writing you put all you've got into it, although it may be a complete failure. Inevitably you must reveal yourself. There's a theory that actors fundamentally are very shy people and that they go into this profession because they want to hide behind the various characters they portray. I think that in much the same way a writer tries to disguise himself as best he can behind each play. In fact one is exposing oneself and at the same time hiding oneself.

Do you write about things that you feel deeply about?

These are the only things I could write about. What I would love to do in the next 18 months or so is either a farce or a brilliant satire on Dublin life. Now I don't think I'm competent to do this, but I'd like to. The very best way to treat the ills in Irish life is to satirise them.

What playwrights do you admire?

I admire Thornton Wilder immensely. He is one of the greatest dramatists of our time. For other reasons and other values, I admire people like Ibsen, O'Neill and a lot of English dramatists, Osborne, Auden and Wesker.

What about Pinter?

What I dislike about him is the complete dehydration of humanity in him. This is also something I don't like in Beckett. There is a complete abnegation of life in both these men. They're really bleak! But life is all we have, you know.

What about short story writers?

Frank O'Connor is superb. Outside Ireland, Updike, V. S. Pritchett and a Canadian-Italian writer called Vivanti.

Do you particularly admire any 20th century Irish playwright?

I admire Paul Vincent Carroll very much. And all the men, like George Shiels, who are, unhappily, going to be classified as less than great. But I'm not an O'Casey fan. This is a question of the urban versus the rural thing again. O'Casey is so intensely Dublin that I can admire him from a distance, but I'm never moved by him.

You don't like Dublin, do you?

Funny, I like coming to Dublin and I have a sort of romantic feeling—this is the capital and so forth. And very stupidly, I have a twinge of emotion when I pass the Post Office, because I admire the men of 1916.

You write at a pretty high intellectual level, but your audience is, in the mass, unintellectual. Does the problem of communication with your audience worry you as a playwright?

This is always a problem. If you deliberately write down, you court disaster. The most you can hope for is that you will hold their intelligent interest right up to the final curtain. At the end of any night's experience in the theatre all that any writer can hope for is that maybe one dozen people have been moved ever so much or ever so slightly, and that the course of their lives may be enriched or altered by a very fine degree. I don't believe for one second that a dramatist is going to change the face of the earth.

Why do you think people go to the theatre?

I don't think they're going any longer simply for entertainment. They want to be engaged mentally, and if the dramatist does this, he is succeeding. The theatre is becoming more and more an intellectual exercise.

Is the audience becoming more intellectual, then?

Mass intellect is a very different thing to individual intellect. The group of people we call an audience is something like a mob, and they're incapable of individual thought. But at the same time this mob has a different kind of attitude to the one they had 20 or 30 years ago. They are more receptive to intellectual concepts.

You said that the theme of Crystal and Fox *was that love wasn't enough. Could you clarify that.*

I feel in this age, and particularly since the Vatican Council and Pope John, that the whole emphasis in Christian doctrine is that we must love. It has been taken up by the hippy movement—love is all; make love, not war—and I find this whole emphasis to be a very watery sort of humanism, and a very shabby sort of liberalism. I don't think it's an adequate basis on which to live out one's life at all.

What do you want with it?

When we talk about life, anyway, all we mean is what are the relationships between people and between nations. Now it isn't sufficient that one orientate one's life towards a belief and love. One must also live one's life on the basis of duty and what we call charity, dedication and the sterner sort of virtues.

But if you really have love, do not these spring from it?

All I'm saying is that I don't believe in the uniqueness or absolute validity of love. In fact I don't believe that if you are in love life is going to be made so much happier or easier. One still has got to bring these other sterner qualities to existence on any level.

What do you place first among the sterner qualities?

Probably some sort of altruism. Generosity of spirit is the quality we need most now.

What type of life do you lead at Muff?

I try to do about three hours' work at my desk every day, messing around with new ideas or working on a specific play or answering letters. I've got to take the kids to school and back. Then we have friends in at night, or we go out.

Do you watch television?

No, we haven't got television. I think all television—using the term accurately—is a vulgar thing.

What do you like to do at night?

Read, or listen to music. Wagner is my favourite. I suppose this is symptomatic of something, but I don't know what.

What do you think of modern pop music?

I don't think it's of any importance whatever. I think the Beatles, for instance, are totally insignificant.

What of modern composers of serious music . . .

I don't understand them. I haven't learned the grammar of these men yet, and it's something one should do. A lot of modern music is like a lot of modern poetry—it has become intensely personal, and communication is diminished by this. A lot of these men aren't communicating with us any more.

You have four daughters. What legacy would you like to leave them?

I would hope they will find themselves jobs in which they will be happy and realise themselves. I would like to see their capabilities utilised and expanded.

Are you yourself happy? You look very content.

I'm told I look a lot of things—content, serene, placid, self-contained. But I'm not at all. I'm very jittery, vain, anxiety-ridden, worried and very uneasy. Am I happy? I don't know what happiness is. One has periods of contentment. I think we're all in a period of spiritual and political eclipse at the moment. We are all acutely conscious of this unrest and unease.

Do you think something decent may emerge in the end?

Maybe. Or it may end up in total obliteration. This is an equally possible conclusion; it's quite a proximate possibility. On the other hand, it may end up in a period of sunshine. I wouldn't know. I'm not too optimistic.

Are you easily hurt?

Yes. For instance, the critics can hurt you, but they can't flatter you. The flattery of critics washes off. Lack of loyalty hurts me. Loyalty must be total.

Would you live outside Ireland?

No, I don't think so. I don't like America at all. It still has some virtues and it's a very generous country. I loved it when I went there first and I was very enamoured of it, but this left me very rapidly. Now I dislike it very much. I don't like England. It's a country I just don't feel at ease in, although I admire it a lot. The English have a lot of admirable things.

Have you any ambitions?

No overriding one. Just to write plays and another short story. That's on the professional level. On a personal level I want my children to grow up and be realised in whatever they do. I want to be in touch with them.

You have a satisfactory relationship with them?

I have at this stage. The eldest is only twelve and she still thinks I'm quite intelligent. So the generation gap has not entered into it.

Is there any person who influences you very much, whom you look up to?

I suppose my wife. She has great loyalty and courage and generosity of spirit.

Soundings

John Boyd / 1970

Despite tepid reception in Dublin as "a squib," *The Mundy Scheme* went to New York, but it closed two days after it opened when Friel's "savage" satire encountered much more savage reviews. In *The New York Times,* transplanted Englishman Clive Barnes adopted a tone of patrician British hauteur in a sweeping dismissal not just of Friel's play but of Irish pretensions to write for the theater: "While its most talented young playwright can write plays as sloppily conceived and constructed as this, Ireland's troubles will never quite be over." Back home, Friel and Hugh Leonard compared notes in an *Irish Times* symposium on what it was like to be victims of Clive Barnes. In June, Friel agreed to a wide-ranging radio interview with John Boyd in which he confesses that he feels "a bit lost at the moment and very confused." Friel had previously parried challenges to write about the Troubles in the North by saying he lacked objectivity. Talking with Boyd, Friel seems even less sure of what lies in store in his career—or of whether he should write about the Troubles. But he responds at length regarding the theme of love in his plays, explaining how four or five of his plays illuminate different facets of that overarching concern. And he offers an extensive analysis of the state of Irish theater, comparing the circumstances for dramatic production in the North, in the Republic, in England and in America.

BOYD: I'd like to ask how you began and when did you begin writing.

FRIEL: Well, I can't answer that question with any accuracy. All I

Broadcast on BBC Radio Four Northern Ireland, 2 August 1970; rebroadcast 7 November 1972 (recorded 17 June 1970).

know is that when I was about twenty years of age I'd find myself writing. Then, as the years went on, I'd find myself writing more and more and more until eventually this became a full-time job.

BOYD: And how did you start? Were you interested primarily in short stories and novels?

FRIEL: No, I have never been an organized reader or an organized man in any way. I just read indiscriminately and short stories and plays— these all were part of a very confused pattern.

BOYD: But you began publishing short stories first of all.

FRIEL: That's true.

BOYD: Your interest primarily wasn't in the short story as a form?

FRIEL: No, it was. My first interest was the short story form, and only in much later years did I get involved in theatre—and this by a kind of indirection too.

BOYD: Why do you think that Irish writers tend to write short stories, rather than novels, for example?

FRIEL: This question has been debated many times. I don't think I know the answer to it. One theory—and it's an attractive one—is that we are hundred-meter people and that we haven't got the stamina for the four miles, that our talent lies in short quick bursts but that we haven't got either the background or the mental stability for a Gothic work.

BOYD: I suppose this is true, because there are few long poems. We are primarily people who write lyrics; the tradition in poetry is lyrical poetry. For example, there's not a *Paradise Lost* or a *Faerie Queene.*

FRIEL: That's true, unless one goes much further back into Gaelic poetry, where you have got the traditionally long poems, the epic poems.

BOYD: But I was thinking in modern Irish literature it is, really, the short burst—the lyric poem or the short story rather than the novel; and the play is comparatively recent too, isn't it? The Irish only began writing good plays from the 18th century on.

FRIEL: Well, I think the explanation for the lack of theatre in the country is historical. You don't have theatre in a country unless you have the buildings and theatre productions. Well, we didn't have this in this country. But going back to the novel again, perhaps the last big novelist was George Moore, a man who produced an awful lot of work of fairly good standard. No one nowadays compares with that, I think.

BOYD: We were talking about the history of Ireland. Now you did write one historical play, isn't that right?

FRIEL: The Columba play you're thinking of? Yes, that's true.

BOYD: What drove you to that theme?

FRIEL: Well, being a Derry man by a kind of adoption, this theme attracted me—*not* because of St Columba really but because it was the first kind of venture I made, really, into an analysis of family relations. This was my reading of the Columban story, and this was my explanation for the exile. My belief was that Columba didn't exile himself in the way that, say, the Desert Fathers who were *peregrinare pro Christo* kind of people, that Columba left the country because it was politically too hot for him, for one reason. And the second reason and equally strong one was that his family were driving him up the walls, literally. But I didn't have and I don't have any great interest in the historical play as such. The theme at that time when I was writing seemed to me to be relevant to my own attitude at the time and to my feeling about the country at the time.

BOYD: Yes, if there is one theme that recurs throughout your work, perhaps it is the theme of love. Would you agree?

FRIEL: Well, it was true. That is true, yes. It's a theme that crops up again and again in the stories and in at least four plays.

BOYD: In which plays?

FRIEL: Well, it began in the play about St Columba. I followed it through with *Philadelphia, Here I Come!* (which is a kind of love story), *The Loves of Cass McGuire, Lovers,* and the final play in this kind of accidental quartet was *Crystal and Fox.*

BOYD: I'd like you to talk a little more about your exploration of this theme. In *Lovers* you have a Romeo and Juliet situation, and it is fairly straightforward—this young couple who fall in love, the girl pregnant—and you leave the ending, which is in death, you leave it inconclusive; we have to imagine what happened.

FRIEL: Well, I'm not interested in the kind of enigma that you're suggesting lies at the end of this play. From my point of view, there's no enigma at all. My concern is that it's obvious to people sitting in the theatre that this young couple cannot extend this idyllic experience that they have at the time of the play and that this idyllic experience is bound to succumb to the pressures of life and that they are not going to expand in this kind of relationship. So that, as to whether they were drowned or committed suicide or what, this doesn't really interest me. The ending is more symbolic than that, I think.

But to go back to the general theme of love again. When I say that I wrote four plays on love themes suggests that I—and I think perhaps I used the word—*pursued* this theme, whereas I think what I should say is that we have a popular concept of love. And I'm not talking about red letter or this kind of thing, but there is a popular concept of love which is partly romantic, partly Christian, partly practical indeed. And I think what I've done in these plays is prowl around this concept and view it from the way perhaps one would look at a piece of sculpture and look at it from various different angles. The last of these four plays was *Crystal and Fox,* and the vision I got then, the view rather that I had of this concept, was in a way a kind of final viewing, a last viewing. I have seen this sculpture from all these various viewpoints; I don't care to look at it again.

BOYD: And the final view is that love is not enough.

FRIEL: Well, this is a kind of pat summation. But every writer is vain enough to hope that his work will be looked at in its totality. And if we look at *Crystal and Fox* in isolation this would be a kind of bitter and savage conclusion. But I hope that if one looks at the four plays there is much more warmth and much more generosity in the concept.

BOYD: Going back to *Philadelphia,* you explore the theme there on various levels—the relationship between the father and mother, and the primary relationship: the relationship of the boy to his parents. Now would you elaborate what were the themes you had in mind in that very complex play?

FRIEL: Would I elaborate on . . . ?

BOYD: Various themes of love, the relationships.

FRIEL: Well, the central character in the play was a young man called Gar O'Donnell, who was exposed in his relationship with his father, with a mother who was dead, with a housekeeper who acted as a kind of Victorian nanny, with a girlfriend and with a schoolmaster, a parish priest and American cousins—I'm giving you a cast list here—and finally with four young friends with whom he knocked around. Each was treated very rapidly of necessity because the play only has to last two and a half hours or whatever. But I hoped in this play that there were various viewpoints expressed about his relationship to each one of these and these were all, as far as I'm concerned, love relations.

BOYD: Is there also the theme of exile, that Ireland in that horrible environment that the boy endures, that he really had to leave, that everything is unsatisfactory, emotionally and economically?

FRIEL: This is true, and perhaps I'm minimizing this element in the play because this was a fundamental one. Even *had* the relationships between Gar O'Donnell and all these various people been satisfying or satisfactory in any way, we're still left with the problem of a man's relationship with his country, which in this island is always very tenuous and very strained—difficult.

BOYD: I don't know whether you're familiar with Eliot's essay "Tradition and the Individual Talent" where his theme is, of course, that writers who appear to be experimental and original are really not, so they are just adding to a tradition. How do you see yourself in relation to the Irish dramatic tradition?

FRIEL: I don't see myself as part of any tradition, and by this I don't mean to imply for one moment that I'm a great original voice. I don't think in this *kind* of term at all. I think that I have a kind of concept of things. I'm not suggesting it's a brilliant or illuminating one or that it's dull. I'm merely saying that it's my concept of things. I try to write about this as truthfully as I can. I'm quite sure I must belong in the Irish tradition, but this isn't my job to assess it or to recognise it or to compartmentalise it. If it happens, as it must, there it is.

BOYD: But you don't overstress the Irish tradition as such. You would read plays and look at plays and be influenced by dramatists from Russia or from France or in America or elsewhere. You see yourself in a world dramatic situation.

FRIEL: Well, let me answer that in this way, that if a new play by an Irish man comes out, I'm very anxious to see it—or a new novel by an Irish man, I'm very anxious to read it. I don't have the same necessity to read a novel by a French man. But this business of seeing oneself as an Irish man writing in an Irish tradition, I would find very limiting and perhaps oppressive.

BOYD: In writing plays, do you start with a situation or with a group of characters?

FRIEL: I begin with a situation then envisage the characters within that situation and then move to an analysis of the characters.

BOYD: And does it come easily to you? I mean Shaw is reputed to have said he just sits down and starts a play with a group of characters in a situation, and he doesn't know what's going to happen next. He was an extemporiser. Do you extemporise in that sense, or have you the play more or less worked out in your head?

FRIEL: I don't believe Mr Shaw for one moment on this issue. He always thought he was God. And I'm quite sure when he was writing plays he didn't abdicate. So one begins with a complete concept of the whole situation from beginning to end. There may be minor alterations, but this is simply a question of how best to reveal the character or how best to reveal the situation.

BOYD: Although Ireland has produced some famous dramatists like Shaw and Synge and O'Casey and so on, we're not really a country which has taken to drama. What I'm saying is that drama in Ireland as in England—possibly in America, I don't know—is still a middle-class recreation.

FRIEL: This is true. We don't consider it in terms of an art form. We think of it as a kind of social pastime. And this accounts for the hundreds of amateur groups around the country just as at one period, for example, within the past three years there were something like five or six hundred—I don't know the word for them—dance band groups around the country. We're inclined to look at drama in much the same terms.

Going back to your question about there being so few major dramatists in the country, I think that you must have, perhaps, thirty or forty very good dramatists functioning all the time in a country, and hopefully out of this group you will perhaps get one or two of immense stature, and this is something we have never had in this country. We have never had this rich undercurrent. And this is also, perhaps, why we're inclined to eulogise the one or two fairly good dramatists that we have had.

BOYD: I find it sad, for instance, that in Derry there's not a theatre, a professional theatre, that a town of sixty thousand people perhaps and with a hinterland cannot afford a theatre to do serious plays.

FRIEL: Well, I think fifty or sixty thousand people isn't sufficient to supply an audience for twelve months of the year. But with the hinterland of Donegal and with the surrounding counties there is a very good possibility that a town of Derry's size could support a theatre. On the other hand, you look at a town like Belfast, which has 500,000 people— it can't support a theatre for three weeks.

BOYD: Does this suggest that the theatre in our society is very much a minority art?

FRIEL: I think it has always been a minority art form, but I think the dangerous thing that's happening in the north of Ireland at the moment is that even those few people who did support theatre in the past are for various reasons drifting away and that, if a new theatre is to be started in the north of Ireland, a new theatre audience has got to be created.

BOYD: Irish people are notorious filmgoers, both in the North and South. Now, film tells a story—and drama, theatre, tells a story too. Why is it that people will go so readily to the cinema and so less readily to a play?

FRIEL: Well, I think for many reasons and the first reason, I think, is that what is being done in the cinema is in many cases much more exciting and much more immediate and much more relevant to the lives of the people at the moment. And another reason is that mediocrity can be sold much more easily in a cinema for technical reasons than can be sold on a stage because of the personal relationship between audience and actor. But it seems to me that either we get a first-class theatre in the north of Ireland or that the theatre audience that we did have in the past is going to drift away completely, and we will then end up with a cinema audience only.

BOYD: Would you be interested in making a film?

FRIEL: I would be very interested in making a film if I can write it, direct it, shoot it, and play in it myself. And, since I'm not very competent at any of these things, the chances of making a film are remote then.

BOYD: But your work is being filmed?

FRIEL: Yes, I'm involved at the moment in a film script of *Philadelphia, Here I Come!* and I'm not all that hopeful of the outcome because my contribution will be a kind of working script, and the whole thing will be subject to everybody from a moneybags in New York to a clapperboy on a set.

BOYD: The writer is not of primary importance in a film.

FRIEL: It's reckoned that if he controls 20 percent of the artistic product, he's very, very lucky.

BOYD: Your last play, *The Mundy Scheme,* was produced—how long ago, about a year ago?

FRIEL: A year ago, in Dublin, yes.

BOYD: Where are you going from there?

FRIEL: I have no idea at all. I'm a bit lost at the moment and very confused.

BOYD: *The Mundy Scheme* was a very different play from any play you had ever written hitherto. It was, to my mind, a savage, incisive play which got far too many laughs. Whether this was the embarrassed laugh of a cannibal looking at himself in the mirror, I don't know. But it was, to my mind, a Swiftian play. It was really savage. But the Irish, apparently, didn't take it that way.

FRIEL: Well, perhaps the laughter was embarrassed laughter, I don't know. But as far as I'm concerned that's over and done with. I don't intend to write another *Mundy Scheme* or I don't intend to write another play with that kind of here-and-now relevance.

BOYD: Does that rule out your doing a political play on the Troubles in the North? You've been asked that question, I know, before.

FRIEL: Well, I don't want to rule out any possible theme. It's a likely theme, of course, and, indeed, it's in many ways an obvious theme. And it does have a kind of international relevance because of the drift to the left over the world, because of the student disturbances, and for all these good reasons. But in some strange way I shy away from it; I don't understand this.

BOYD: Your plays now are being played in America, in Europe, in

Britain, and of course in Ireland. Now do you find the Irish situation—the Irish dramatic situation—satisfactory as a playwright, from your point of view? Have you got a kind of theatre to work in, directors and actors that approach your ideal?

FRIEL: No, I don't think we have this in this country at all. I think there are some advantages for a playwright in Ireland, and the advantages are these, that a mediocre play can be mounted at a modest cost and will get a reasonable hearing. This is something that one can't get in America and has difficulty in getting in England because mounting a production is such an expensive thing that it becomes a business investment, and if the business investment doesn't pay off instantly, the play is taken off. This is something that we don't have in this country, and this is a good thing. On the other hand, in this country we don't have a corpus of first-class actors. We have a handful of excellent actors, and of necessity they have got to emigrate. So that there isn't a resident body of actors that one can draw on. As for producers, they don't have the opportunity to learn their craft. Those that stay in the country are fat in their self-satisfaction; the competent ones go away and stay away. The general theatrical scene, I think, in the country of necessity isn't very good either, because it's a tiny island, and there isn't the population for it.

BOYD: Here in Ireland, in dramatic terms, few people get an opportunity of seeing reasonably well-done world classics, and that seems to me the great lack. I don't think you as a boy or as a young man had the opportunity of seeing great plays reasonably well done. I certainly hadn't.

FRIEL: No, this is true, and this is something that I think there is an opportunity that may be developed in the North. At the moment there is a move on to establish a permanent theatre company which will do classical plays primarily, and if the Stormont government has any sense at all it seems to me they will subsidize this quite substantially.

BOYD: By classical plays you mean Molière, Shakespeare, Chekhov, Shaw?

FRIEL: Yes, Shaw and the best of modern European theatre and, hopefully, if there is a good modern Irish play that this will be added to the repertory. And this will be an opportunity for young people to see good theatre competently done. I'm not asking for the RSC; I'm not asking for the British National. But I'm asking for a competent theatre available to young people.

BOYD: That seems interesting but not extremely exciting because the essence of theatre is its immediacy, that a playwright like yourself should be interpreting life as it is today, as you see it, and that your vision can be an upsetting one. What I'm saying is the government and lively theatre do not mix.

FRIEL: Well, a government can frequently be deluded into giving substantial grants for what they consider to be classical plays because they consider that the classics are old and therefore they're safe. But, if classical plays are correctly done and competently done, they can be as revolutionary and as exciting and as immediate as last week's play in the West End. For example, the Irish censorship board has no hesitation in allowing a play which has to do with incest, regicide, homosexuality—for example, *Hamlet*—they have no objection to their schoolchildren seeing a play like this, but they draw the line at some naughty words in a work by Brendan Behan, because the belief is that it's an old play and that it's been done for four or five hundred years; therefore it's been purged by time in some way.

BOYD: It's got artistic sanctity. Are there any playwrights that you find yourself attuned to in the world's scene or, indeed, in the Irish scene? I think you are something of a loner.

FRIEL: Well, I think one admires different aspects of theatre in different places. For example, the English theatre scene, I think, is admirable because of its superb acting and, I think, because of the diversity and intensity of a whole group of, say, fifteen or twenty youngish writers in England who are all doing very good things. None of them, it seems to me, are doing brilliant things but all doing very good things. In other words, they are creating a very good general climate within which somebody really great may emerge. The Americans I admire for their . . . the American theatre I admire for its dull application. They are in many ways plodders. But they give such dedication to their theatre that I find this something admirable. The Europeans, I think, are exciting because of their experimentation. A man, for example, like Anouilh, I think, is a superb dramatist—brilliant dramatist, clever man, witty man, funny man and a serious man. I think there's nobody like him in America, certainly nobody like him in England.

BOYD: And the Germans like Weiss and Hochhuth?

FRIEL: Well, we're moving then into this kind of theatre of fact, which is something that I've very mixed feelings about, because it seems to me that if you attempt a theatre of fact play, you have all of the advantages of history and none of the responsibilities.

Self-Portrait: Brian Friel Talks about His Life and Work

Brian Friel / 1971

When Brian Friel, the private man who had always been uneasy about self-revelation, did offer an autobiographical "Self-Portrait" on the BBC, he couched the entire presentation in the framework of self-rebuke. He also took the opportunity, however, to turn the tables on his interviewers. After a cursory review of "the facts" of his life, Friel launches into a self-interview that parodies some of the interviews he had been subjected to. John Boyd of the BBC Talks Department, who served as the producer for Friel's "Self-Portrait," had begun his own interview of Friel just a year before by asking the playwright when he began writing. Friel tweaks his producer by identifying such an opening question as "the interviewer's chestnut." Yet what emerges throughout Friel's talk is the sense that his quarrel is not just with specific interviewers but with the assumption that the questions being asked have definite answers. Indeed, even beyond his distaste for self-revelation and his distrust of the interview format, Friel also makes it clear how much he distrusts the facts. Imaginative reality vies with other conceptions of reality as Friel reveals some experiences in his memory, experiences that, as it turns out, had not happened and could not

Broadcast by BBC Northern Ireland Home Service, 19 December 1971; repeated 7 November 1972 (recorded 21 October 1971). The Servite Priory in Benburb, Co. Tyrone—which had reprinted Friel's lecture "The Theatre of Hope and Despair" in *Everyman* in 1968—reprinted a somewhat edited version of his BBC talk in *Aquarius* in 1972 along with Friel's further apologies for the "talk-style" of his "Self-Portrait." The present transcription is of the talk as broadcast and is reprinted with the kind permission of Brian Friel.

have happened, which nevertheless remain just as real to him and as freighted with meaning as those possessed of greater historicity. Even his tidy summing up of autobiographical facts indicates that such markers are no more revelatory than the "puny little pies of knowledge" that constituted the education by rote that he received and that he, in his turn, inflicted on others. With a sense that an apprehension of ambiguity is the beginning of wisdom, Friel makes it crystal clear that he distrusts all that is crystal clear. Indeed, when Friel talks about an Irish writer finding his faith he is talking about the apprehension of something that exists on the other side of certainty and absolutism.

Even a fragment of autobiography—such as this is—is of necessity and by definition an exercise in exhibitionism, an exercise in exorcism, and an exercise in expiation. And of the three, the element of exhibitionism will be least. But it usually takes the form not simply of showing off but of putting a good skin on—that is, of taking our trivial achievements and our abysmal failures and of staging them in subtle lighting and in attractive costumes and hoping to God the performance comes off. The other two elements—the elements of exorcism and of expiation—are the important ones, and they are really two sides of the same coin. Because we call up our ghosts not to lay them but in the hope of having the genuine dialogue with them we didn't have when we had the opportunity.

Then there are of course what are called "the facts". And since some people value the tidiness that they seem to afford, let's have the facts first and be done with them. I was born in Omagh in Co. Tyrone in 1929. My father was the principal of a three-teacher school outside the town. He taught me. In 1939 when I was ten, we moved to Derry where I have lived since, until three or four years ago. I was at St. Columb's College for five years; St. Patrick's College, Maynooth, for two and a half years; and St. Joseph's Training College for one year. From 1950 until 1960 I taught in various schools in and around Derry. And since that time I have been writing full time.

I'm married; I have five children; I live in the country; I smoke too much; I fish a bit; I read a lot; I worry a lot; I get involved in sporadic causes and invariably regret the involvement. And I hope that between now and my death I will have acquired a religion or a philosophy or a sense of life that will make the end less frightening than it appears to me at this moment.

What other facts are there? —Ah, the interviewer's chestnut:

When did you know, Mr. Friel, that you were going to be a writer?
The answer is, I have no idea.
What other writers influenced you most strongly?
I have no idea.
Which of your plays, Mr. Friel, is your favorite?
None of them.
Which of your stories?
Most of them embarrass me.
Do you think, Mr. Friel, that the atmosphere in Ireland is hostile or friendly to the artist?
Uh, I'm thinking of my lunch.
Do you see any relationship between dwindling theatrical audiences all over the world and the fragmentation of what we might call the theatrical thrust into disparate movements like theatre of cruelty, tactile theatre, nude theatre, theatre of despair, etc., etc., or would you say, Mr. Friel, that the influence of Heidegger is only beginning to be felt in the drama and that Beckett and Pinter are John the Baptists of the great new movement?
Well, in answer to that, I'd say that—I'd say that I'm a middle-aged man and that I tire easily and that I'd like to go out for a walk now; so please go away and leave me alone.

The facts. What is a fact in the context of autobiography? A fact is something that happened to me or something I experienced. It can also be something I thought happened to me, something I thought I experienced. Or, indeed, an autobiographical fact can be pure fiction and no less true or reliable for that. Let me give you an example.

When I was a boy we always spent a portion of our summer holidays in my mother's old home near the village of Glenties in Co. Donegal. I have memories of those holidays that are as pellucid, as intense, as if they happened last week. I remember in detail the shape of cups hanging in the scullery, the pattern of flags on the kitchen floor, every knot of wood on the wooden stairway, every door handle, every smell, the shape and texture of every tree around the place. My father and I used to go fishing on the lakes near the village. Now there were about eight of them that we used to go to. And, although I haven't seen them for, I'm sure, twenty-five years, I know them with a knowledge that is special and sacred and so private that it's almost apprehensive. But what I want to talk about now is a particular memory of a particular day. There's no doubt in my mind about this. It's here and now before my eyes as I speak. The boy I see is about nine years old. And my father would have been in his, say, in his early forties. We're walking home from a lake with our fishing rods across our shoulders. It's been raining all day long. It's now late evening, and we're both soaked to the skin. And for some reason—perhaps the fishing was good, I don't remember—my father is in great spirits and is singing a song, and I'm singing with him.

And there we are, the two of us, soaking wet, splashing along a muddy road that comes in at right angles to Glenties' main street, singing about "how my boat can safely float through the teeth of wind and weather". And that's the memory. That's what happened. A trivial episode without importance to anyone but me—just a moment of happiness caught in an album.

But wait. There's something wrong here. I'm conscious of a dissonance, an unease. And what is it? Yes, I know what it is. There is no lake along that muddy road. And, since there is no lake, my father and I never walked back from it in the rain with our rods across our shoulders. The fact is a fiction. Have I imagined the scene then? Or is it a composite of two or three different episodes? The point is: I don't think it matters. What matters is that for some reason—and we're back now to our opening ideas of our expiation and exorcism—for some reason this vivid memory is there in the storehouse of the mind. For some reason the mind has shuffled the pieces of verifiable truth and composed a truth of its own. For to me it is a truth. And, because *I* acknowledge its peculiar veracity, it becomes a layer in my subsoil. It becomes part of me; ultimately, it becomes me.

Before I leave my childhood and youth, I want to look back briefly at that bizarre process called my education. For about fifteen years I was taught by a succession of men who force-fed me with information, who cajoled me, beat me, threatened me, coaxed me to swallow their puny little pies of knowledge and attitudes. And the whole thing—I know it now of course—was an almost complete waste of time. I'm not resentful about this. I don't feel scarred or damaged by it. And I'm certainly not blaming those grim men who prodded me through examinations. They were victims as much as I. But surely this isn't education:

> Beginning of Tudor reign 1485; Dias discovers the Cape 1486; Columbus discovered America 1492; Vasco da Gama discovers the Cape route to India 1496.

Or

Hence, loathèd Melancholy,
  Of Cerberus and blackest midnight born,
In Stygian cave forlorn
  'Mongst horrid shapes, and shrieks, and sights unholy,
Find out some uncouth cell,
  Where brooding Darkness spreads his jealous wings,
And the night-raven sings;
  There under ebon shades, and low-browed rocks,
As ragged as thy locks,
  In dark Cimmerian desert ever dwell.

That, incidentally, was John Milton. Or

A rhomboid is an oblique angled parallelogram with only the opposite sides equal.

Or

Arma verumque cano, Troiae qui primus ab oris
Italiam, fato profugus, Laviniaque venit
litora . . .

And so on and so on.

Yes, on second thoughts I am slightly resentful. And the little, little grudge I bear is directed at those men who taught me the literature of Rome and Greece and England and Ireland as if they were pieces of intricate machinery created for no reason and designed for no purpose. They were culled out of the air, these contrivances, and planked in front of us, and for years we tinkered with them—pulling them apart or putting them together again or translating or scanning or conjugating— never once suspecting that these texts were the testimony of sad or happy or assured or confused people just like ourselves. And there we were, so engaged in irregular verbs and peculiar declensions that we never once smelt blood or felt gristle. Yes, I resent that slightly. Indeed, I was fairly long in the tooth before I made the modest discovery for myself that literature wasn't some kind of political dynasty where Elizabethans were ousted by Puritans, who gave way to Restoration dramatists, who in turn were routed by the Augustans, who were supplanted by the Romantics, who were followed by the eminent Victorians, etc., etc., etc.—a kind of literary monopoly invented by critics and academics for the torment of students.

I'm now going to make a detour past those ten years when I taught school myself, because I regret them. And there's nothing more boring or indeed more boastful than a public confession of venial sins. I don't regret the teaching. In fact, I liked teaching. At least I liked doing what I thought then was teaching. Because what I was doing was putting boys in for maths exams and getting them through. In fact, I fancied myself as a teacher because I worked hard at teaching the tricks, and the poodle dogs became excellent performers. And I regret, too, that I used a strap. Indeed, I regret this most of all. It's a ghost I have called up many a time since. But he still won't be atoned to. I suppose he's right.

And before I leave those ten years I might as well mention that this was when I first began to fumble with short stories and with plays. This was the time when I got married. And this was the time when I first began to wonder what it was to be an Irish Catholic. In short this was when for the first time in my life I began to survey and analyse the mixed holding I had inherited—the personal, traditional and acquired knowledge that cocooned me: an Irish Catholic teacher with a nationalist background, living in a schizophrenic community, son of a teacher, grandson of peasants who could neither read nor write. The process was disquieting. It *is* disquieting because it's still going on. But what I hope is emerging is, in the words of Sean O'Faolain, "a faith, a feeling for life, a way of seeing life which is coherent, and persistent, and inclusive and forceful enough to give organic form to the totality of my work."

But back to the facts. In the year 1960 I left teaching and, as they used to say, embarked on a career of letters. By then I had had some pale success with short stories and radio plays. I'll come back to that chameleon word *success* in a moment or two. And, by doing some journalism as well, I was making just about enough money to keep going.

And it was about that time that I had to make a decision. Now, if you want to be a playwright, you must either arrange to be a child of theatrical parents and be born preferably in the greenroom in the interval between act 1 and 2 of *Separate Tables;* or you will have to have been dragged to theatrical matinees every Wednesday and Saturday by an eccentric maiden aunt; or played the Gravedigger in the school production of *Hamlet;* or at very least you will have to have been an usher for the local amateur dramatic association. Now I was privileged in none of these ways. And now I found myself at thirty years of age embarked on a theatrical career and almost totally ignorant of the mechanics of play-writing and play production, apart from a modest intuitive knowledge—

just like a painter who has never studied anatomy or like a composer with no training in harmony.

So I packed my bags, and with my wife and two children went to Minneapolis in Minnesota where a new theatre was being created by Tyrone Guthrie, and there I lived for six months. That period is a story in itself. Immediately after it ended I thought it was the most important, or, as they say now, traumatic, period I had ever experienced. And, of course, it was nothing of the kind. The really traumatic experiences are sly and dark and devious and generally slip into the consciousness through an unlocked window. But it *was* an important period in a practical way. I learned about the physical elements of plays, how they're designed, how they're built, how they're landscaped. I learned how actors thought, how they approached a text, their various ways of trying to realise it. I learned a great deal about the iron discipline of theatre, and I discovered a dedication and a nobility and a selflessness that one associates only with a theoretical priesthood. But, much more important than all these, those months in America gave me a sense of liberation. Remember this was my first parole from inbred, claustrophobic Ireland, and that sense of liberation conferred on me a valuable self-confidence and a necessary perspective so that the first play I wrote immediately after I came home—and that was *Philadelphia, Here I Come!*—was a lot more assured than anything I had attempted before.

And now to return to that strange word *success*. I've written nine plays, and of these two are classified as "successful", more vulgarly as "hits". If one is to pursue this jargon, the other seven plays are "flops". Now for a writer these terms have no meaning—the word *success* has no meaning. I'm not being at all obtuse or grandly aloof. People may like a play of mine or hate it—that's another question. It may be performed all over the world or just once in a basement theatre in Cork. It may be a well-constructed play or a badly constructed play. It may be simple or obscure. But these are other considerations entirely. But for the writer there is no success, just as there is no "success" in rain falling or the sun shining. In a strictly limited sense, yes, but only with reference to a hierarchy of values that have meaning only for the writer himself—*then* he can assess a play as successful. But what *he* means is something very different from public acclaim or from press awards or bestseller lists. What he means is this—that this particular work is in tune with the body of his previous work, that it is a step forward in the revelation of his relationship with his own world, and that, at the time of writing, the idea and form are coincidental and congruent and at one. *Then* he knows he has written a success, and *this* knowledge is the only abiding satisfaction he has. Everything else is trivial.

What did I do in Minneapolis? The honest answer to that is, very little. I lived in a languishing hotel called the Oak Grove, and I spent my days and evenings in the theatre, literally skulking about in the gloom of the back seats. The Guthrie Theater was a very courageous concept: an attempt to establish a classical theatre in what is traditionally considered the philistine Midwest and thousands of miles away from New York, which is the tawdry Mecca of American theatre. And, because this was a pioneering effort determined to succeed, everybody was extraordinarily keen and dedicated and enthusiastic and busy. It was no place at all for a drone. For a few weeks I managed to make myself almost invisible. I slipped into the building with the workmen in the morning and slipped out with the actors at night. But eventually an obese and evil-looking stage-door man—appropriately called Chuck—stopped me and demanded to know my business. And just as I was stammering a garbled explanation, one of the actors volunteered, "He's OK, Chuck; he's an observer." And that fortuitous christening instantly gave me not only an identity but a dignity: an observer—part of the great communal effort—pass, friend.

I moved from the gloom of the back row down to the orchestra. People began to nod to me. I got a pencil and paper and occasionally pretended to jot down profound observations. Some of the less secure actors even began to ask my advice about their performance, God help them. It was all very gratifying. But there were some disadvantages. Up to this I could crouch in the dark and scratch and grunt and make faces and mutter to myself. But now I had to sit in smart attention and gaze at the stage for hours on end. It was very, very tiring. When I got back to the Oak Grove at night, it was hours before the muscles of my face would surrender the intelligent, alert look I had assumed all day. Observers may contribute little to the life of the theatre but they work harder than anyone else I know.

The years that followed immediately after that visit to Minneapolis were busy. I wrote five plays. I watched over their launching in Dublin and traveled with them to London or to New York for their first production outside the country. It would be churlish to say that it was all work and worry, because it wasn't. There was a lot of fun, because theatre people are the best company in the world. I mean actors of course, not impresarios, who are mere hucksters in the merchandise of drama. But actors are a very special people. Their stock characteristics, their gaiety, their effusiveness, their temperaments, their easy charm, their volatile affections—all the things that most people dislike in them—I find fascinating. I don't think their lives are unreal. If there is such a thing as a real life—and presumably a real life would be some kind of lifestyle that would reflect the very essence and accidents of existence, then surely actors are much closer to that image than the nine-to-five businessman.

But there was worry too. And the reason for the worry is that the playwright is never fully his own man. The painter completes his picture, and the public looks at his work on the gallery wall. The poet or novelist produces his book and through it talks directly to his reader. But the playwright requires interpreters. Without actors and without a performance his manuscript is a lifeless literary exercise, a kite without wind, a boat waiting for a tide. And the day he completes a script, he has won a battle and takes on a war. First of all he has got to get a management to put on his play. He then has to get a director—and nowadays directors have pushed themselves into such power in the theatre that they expect writers not only to approach them with awe, but to surrender the entire interpretation of a play into their artistic hands. Right. He gets a management; he gets a director; he gets his actors; and rehearsals begin.

From here on, the pain or the pleasure the writer experiences depends on his attitude to his director and to his actors. And my attitude is this: I look on my manuscript as an orchestral score, composed with infinite care and annotated where necessary with precise directions. This is in no way a judgment in quality but a statement of character. I look to this director and to the actors to interpret that score exactly as it is written. It is not their function to amend; it is not their function to rewrite or to cut or to extend. It is their function, and it's their only function—and an enormously difficult one—to interpret what's given to them. And I use the analogy of the orchestral score with deliberation because I have never known a conductor who would even dream of tampering with the shape of a symphony nor an instrumentalist who would think of rewriting a score before performing it. But I have yet to meet the director or the actor who wouldn't casually paraphrase lines of dialogue or, indeed, transpose whole scenes. Hence the war, or at least the twitching truce.

Of course, there are playwrights who will disagree with me, who are happy to rewrite on request during rehearsal, even after the play has opened. And their thesis is that theatre is a communal enterprise to which the writer and the actor and the director contribute on a sort of ad hoc principle. And one of their most dubious maxims is "If it works, it's right." Well, of course, I think they're completely wrong. These people belong in show biz. But there are so many of them, and they have such strong support from directors and actors that those of us who believe in the responsibility of the script are considered cranks and difficult to work with. So be it.

But to get back to the main thoroughfare. When I spoke earlier of a faith, a feeling for life, a way of seeing life, I wasn't of course talking of a schematised set of religious beliefs. I meant the patient assembly of a superstructure which imposes a discipline and within which work can be performed in the light of an insight, or a group of ideas, or a carefully cultivated attitude. Or, as Seamus Heaney puts it with much less contortion, "There are only certain stretches of ground over which the writer's divining rod will come to life." And when I refer to Ireland as being inbred and claustrophobic and talked of the tortuous task of surveying the mixed holding I had inherited, I had in mind how difficult it is for an Irish writer to find his faith. He is born into a certainty that is cast-iron and is absolute.

The generation of Irish writers immediately before mine never allowed this burden to weigh them down. They learned to speak Irish, took their genetic purity for granted, and soldiered on. But for us today the situation is more complex. We are more concerned with defining our Irishness than with pursuing it. We want to know what the word *native* means, what the word *foreign* means. We want to know have the words any meaning at all. And persistent considerations like these erode old certainties and help clear the building site.

People often urge me to write a play "about the trouble in the North". You have the dramatic situation, they tell me; you have the conflict; you know the scene. As if this is what writing is about—take the do-it-yourself kit up to your study and assemble the pieces according to the enclosed leaflet. But, of course, they're not really offering me the stuff of a play any more than the people who say to me: "I'll tell you somethin' that happened to me. Now if I had your talent I could make a damned good story out of it. What happened was this." And they know they're offering me nothing, these people. All they're doing is strut in front of me. What they're saying is "my life is full of excitement, not like yours, and if I *only* had the knack, if I *only* had the education, if I *only* had the time, I'm the buck would churn out the books." There was a time when I thought these were well-meaning people. Perhaps they are. But now I think they're just sad.

Exhibitionism. Exorcism. Expiation. In spite of my opening comment, it seems to have been all ostentation, all parade, the swagger of the first-person singular. But when you ask me have I anything to declare, and I say, only this and this, I assume that you'll look beyond the innocent, out-spread hands.

Brian Friel's Other Island

Aodhan Madden / 1971

In 1963, when Friel said his ambition was to write the "great Irish play," he explained his goal in terms that were at once parochial and universal: "Such a play is one where the author can talk so truthfully and accurately about people in his own neighbourhood and make it so that these folk could be living in Omagh, Omaha or Omansk." Asked again in 1970 how he would like to see his work developing, Friel told Fergus Linehan: "I would like to write a play that would capture the peculiar spiritual, and indeed material, flux that this country is in at the moment. This has got to be done, for me anyway, and I think it has got to be done at a local, parochial level, and hopefully this will have meaning for other people in other countries." Friel's next play, *The Gentle Island,* seemed to aim specifically at representing Irish life at a local, parochial level in such a way that it would resonate metaphorically as a microcosm of the entire country. Friel spoke to Aodhan Madden of the *Sunday Press* during the week before the play's Dublin opening.

Brian Friel, living the part of "gentle islander" himself in the tweeds of his adopted Donegal, leans on a shillelagh backstage at the Olympia and says that if a new Sean O'Casey rises directly from the ashes of the Northern holocaust, it won't be he.

Ireland's premier playwright lives in the shadow of Derry's war-scarred walls, in the tiny border village of Muff. But he does not consider himself the writer to pull down the Joxerian blinds on the Northern

From the *Sunday Press,* 28 November 1971, p. 31.

drama. Oh yes, he says, what's happening in our island provokes tensions in all of us, tensions which the writer will channel indirectly into art.

His new play, *The Gentle Island,* which opens at the Olympia on Tuesday, may have echoes of Belfast and Derry, but Friel's vision is not confined to the imaginative span from the Shankill to the Falls. Ostensibly, *The Gentle Island* is about the life and times of one family who live on a tiny island off the Donegal coast. The island is Inniskeen. The island is a microcosm of Ireland, the life of the islanders, their relationships, their behaviour, the interaction of the island people, the visitors who come among them, the problems that beset them, all reflect in a way, Friel's view of Ireland. "We see most facets of Irish life, love, hate, loneliness, tensions in the life of the gentle island" says Friel.

"The title *The Gentle Island* is satirical" Friel says, "and it's a direct translation of the word Inniskeen", but the play itself is not satirical. It is a serious slice of island life, a metaphor for Ireland.

Friel is like an Irish islander himself, quiet, solid, the tweeds reflecting a tranquil life-style far removed from traffic and trauma. He's clearly ill at ease in the stuffy, gloom-filled dressing room at the Olympia with its heavy dusty furniture, the opulent old costumes, the brooding Victoriana and its echoes of Dan Lowry. For him, I'm sure, it's the wilds and the wastes of Donegal where the grass grows audibly and the murmur of nature is the heart of the real Ireland.

He was born in Omagh in 1929, lived 26 years in Derry and then retreated to Muff. How near is he, emotionally, to Derry's agony? He shrugs his shoulders. "I think you people in Dublin are nearer to it than I am." A clown's mask peers down from a heap of comedy costumes. "The violence in Irish life may be suggested in my play but it is not specifically reflected in the story."

The conversation switches to *The Mundy Scheme,* the satire in which Friel converts the Emerald Isle into a vast graveyard for rich American Hibernophiles. "That one died of a coronary after just a few nights in New York. It's impossible to predict what American reaction is going to be like."

Failure does not deter him. "Successes are merely a bonus" he says adding a Wildean quip, "The play's a success, let's hope the audience is." His most successful play is probably *Lovers.* Universal International want to film it now. His other box office boost, *Philadelphia, Here I Come!* has already been filmed and will be released soon. Is he wary of film people mucking around with his plays? Friel gives a gentle shrug. "If one is going to sweat over something like that, then one might as well commit suicide." It's a chance that playwrights just have to take. He wrote the screen script for *Philadelphia* himself, but admits that he didn't do a good job of it because he has no experience of that technique.

Yes, he would like working on films. No, he absolutely detests television.

He is certainly our best known, probably our best living playwright. His plays have been staged all over the English-speaking world, many of them have been translated into a dozen languages. Two of his plays have been the toast of Broadway. But he's a man of quiet modesty, success sitting gently on a bushy Northern brow. He has been savaged by righteous critics. Labels like 'anti-cleric' have been hurled venomously at him . . . but Friel's answer is the greatest weapon of all . . . silence.

And yes, he is writing another play . . .

Brian Friel: Derry's Playwright

Eavan Boland / 1973

In the summer of 1970 the poet Eavan Boland had interviewed
Brian Friel along with four other writers from Northern Ireland—of both Catholic and Protestant backgrounds—for a
three-part *Irish Times* series on "The Northern Writers' Crisis of
Conscience." The three articles—labelled "Community," "Crisis" and "Creativity"—sought to take the writers back to their
unwitting acceptance in childhood of the received beliefs of
their respective communities, to identify the moment that
impelled each writer to recognize the state of crisis in the
North, and to explore each writer's reflections on the possibility of articulating some response to the Northern situation in
his work. All five of the writers expressed wariness of "too
immediate, too personal a response" to the political situation.
Although Friel suggested that it might be better for the writer
to remain on the sideline rather than following the footsteps of
writers elsewhere who "are becoming more and more committed socially," he acknowledged that the crisis was "inevitably . . .
bound to affect my work." By the time Boland interviewed Friel
in 1973 the Northern crisis had made itself felt in his next play,
The Freedom of the City. Friel's play about three unarmed civilians
being gunned down by forty British soldiers after a civil rights
march was widely seen as a response to Bloody Sunday, 30 January 1972, when British troops opened fire in the Bogside area
of Derry, killing thirteen civilians, seven of whom were less than
nineteen years old. The play opened in Dublin on 20 February

From *Hibernia* (Dublin), 16 February 1973, p. 18.

1973, and a production directed by Albert Finney opened at the Royal Court Theatre in London just one week later. British journalists flatly referred to the play as "a re-creation and elaboration on the events of Bloody Sunday." Friel told an interviewer for BBC Radio Four he had been working for eighteen months on a play called "John Butt's Bothy" that eventually became *The Freedom of the City*. But the original play, with a focus on poverty, "never could find its foundations" until events in the city of Derry "gave the play the definition it required." "From my point of view," Friel said, "it was a happy coincidence of imaginative creation and historical actuality." In his *Hibernia* interview with Boland, Friel goes into greater depth in talking about the ways in which Bloody Sunday is and is not relevant to *The Freedom of the City*. But he also offers one of his most thoughtful explorations of the questions in his mind when he faced an interviewer in London the same week. "Should a writer be involved in the crises through which he lives?" Friel asked himself, "Should he use his art to write propaganda? I just don't know."

I interviewed Brian Friel in 1970 at his home six miles south of the Derry-Donegal border, looking across the expanse of the Foyle. He spoke then of the difficulty of finding a theme; as I was leaving he handed me a new novel to read by an American poet, James Dickey, called *Deliverance*. I knew of Dickey as a respected, ironic artist, very far from a household name. Two years later and some months *Deliverance* has become a film, grossing almost as much as *The Godfather,* and Brian Friel has found a theme.

When *The Freedom of the City* goes on the Abbey stage, and very shortly afterwards appears at the Royal Court in England, he is prepared for a certain amount of misinterpretation by his audience. Already it has been suggested that the play is about Bloody Sunday, but, as he explains, it is not:

"It's not about Bloody Sunday. In fact, the play began long before Bloody Sunday happened. I was working on this theme for about ten months before Bloody Sunday. And then Bloody Sunday happened, and the play I was writing, and wasn't succeeding with, suddenly found a focus. I was stuck until this point, and this was a kind of clarification. The play, in fact, is the story of three people who are on a Civil Rights march in Derry city in 1970. The march finishes in the Guildhall Square. There's a public meeting. Then the British Army moves in, breaks up the meeting and these three people take refuge in the Guildhall and find themselves in the Mayor's parlour."

At first glance, *The Freedom of the City* provides the scenario of a political play, even from Friel's brief outline of it. Yet it would be surprising if it was. There has never been anything of the polemicist or the propagandist in his work, with the possible exception of *The Mundy Scheme*, which he now dismisses as 'bad just because it wasn't half good enough.'

In fact, far from being concerned with the impersonal decisions which affect life, Friel is obsessed with the personal, interior world of self-deception which only comes to light in crisis, if ever. For example, the insight which Cass McGuire has into her life comes only when she is confronted at the end of it with the ruin of her illusions: similarly in the 'Foundry House,' one of the finest short stories Friel has written, the nun in America who maintains an illusory sense of her family's fortunes long after they have declined, is far more indicative of the concerns of Friel's work than any political stance could be. He is an artist preoccupied with the individual and his cryptic humiliations, rather than with the public gesture, as, for example, John Arden is.

An indication of how independent his work is of the moment, the political watershed, can be assessed by the fact that *The Freedom of the City* began as a play set in the 18th century and constructed around evictions. At that time it was titled "John Butt's Bothy." Though that plot and place have disappeared, Friel still regards his new play, like its embryo, as being a study of poverty.

One of the things which makes him wary of reaction to *The Freedom of the City* is the aesthetic worry about how near an artist can afford to be to his subject.

"This play raises the old problem of writing about events which are still happening. It's the old problem of the distinction between the mind that suffers and the man who creates. The trouble about this particular play in many ways is that people are going to find something immediate in it, some kind of reportage. And I don't think that's in it at all. Very often an accident in history will bring about a meeting-point, a kind of fusion for you. And this is what happened. This is a play which is about poverty. But because we're all involved in the present situation people are going to say 'this is a very unfair play,' and of necessity it has got to be unfair in this public kind of way. I hope that people will come to see this with an open mind. But, of course, they may come and see in it only a confirmation of some kind of prejudice in the play anyhow."

Friel's emphasis on the chasm between the mind that suffers and the man who creates proves two things: one of them is simply that he has read Eliot's influential essay, which draws that distinction; secondly, that he is a prey to the confusion which an essentially private, scrupulously honest artist must feel living next door to a public uproariously violent situation. Because he is a private artist, the abundance of themes which the violence seems to offer means little to him as a writer, however much it may affect him as a man. Therefore, the focus of *The Freedom of the City* is simply applicable to that play, and represents no new, rich seam which he can work: "I don't think it's a breakthrough. I would love to think it was. But life's not as easy as that."

In this way he describes his dilemma as a playwright. As a person, naturally enough, he is as bewildered as anyone by the continuing horror of the situation in the city where he was born, and in which he grew up. But he evidently does not look to that situation to provide him with achievements and insights in art. When I asked him what his deep objectives were as a writer, he was, understandably, in his own words, 'circuitous.' "I suppose I want some kind of definitive statement that would give myself some kind of clarification. Yet what that statement would be about I don't know. If I did that would be the whole answer."

Friel is far happier talking about the machinery of theatre than about the meaning of his contribution to it. He sees a crisis in theatre which is not peculiar to Ireland: "All over the English-speaking world theatre is in a state of chaos. And in this country, where we don't have a theatrical tradition, we don't know whether we should attend theatre, or go and be entertained by it, or go as a kind of package tour to it. This may be the fault of directors or the writers. In any case, it exists."

From everything which Friel has said, those who go to *The Freedom of the City* expecting to find a resolution to the violence of the North, or an insight into the spirit of Derry, are likely to be disappointed. Naturally, this is so, since they would be searching through a play for what is more properly the province of a White Paper or a Ministerial directive. If, however, they go looking for a subtle increase and expansion of a playwright's skills and concerns they will think the experience worthwhile. The plot of the play should whet the appetite but if it satisfied it then one would feel Friel had fallen for the bait of reportage rather than art. He is unlikely to do that, for he has served one of the most exacting apprenticeships in Irish writing, having known the rejections of his work—as, for instance, of *Philadelphia, Here I Come!* by the Abbey, and *The Mundy Scheme* by the New York critics—as well as a great deal of success.

Currently he is working on a new play. But it is at so early a stage in its development that he is unwilling to talk about it. In a few months he is going to America to see *Crystal and Fox* being performed there. Finally, he has this to say about writing about Northern events; it could serve as a caveat to other writers who draw too freely on the present situation: "The trouble with Derry at the moment is that there is an articulation there, but it's a kind of clichéd articulation, because everybody is so obsessed with the media and what has happened yesterday that we have all got answers for everything."

However Friel, the Derry citizen, may respond, Friel the artist is likely to continue feeling he has an answer to few things, and that those answers he has are suspect. In this time of ready remedies it is a welcome stance.

Can the Critics Kill a Play?

Fachtna O'Kelly / 1975

Following its concurrent runs in Dublin and London, *The Free-dom of the City* was produced on Broadway in February 1974, where it closed after nine performances. Despite being termed "a genuine masterpiece" by Richard Watts of the *New York Post*, Friel's play seemed too Irish for Clive Barnes, a Londoner by birth, who wielded immense power as the drama critic for *The New York Times*. Calling the play "luridly fictionalized," "far-fetched," and "impossible," Barnes rhetorically asked, "Can we really be expected to believe that the British Army would mobilize against these three people 22 tanks, two dozen armored cars, four water cannon and 'a modicum of air cover'?" In the controversy surrounding the play's closure, Watts termed the play's sudden collapse "outrageous"; Joseph Papp of the New York Shakespeare Festival dismissed Barnes as "Lilliputian in his viewpoint" and said, "one man's prejudiced opinion should not determine the fate of a play"; and Paul O'Dwyer, the president of the City Council, wrote a letter to the editor charging the critic with defending "the Empire" instead of reviewing the play. Friel's next play, *Volunteers,* once again ran afoul of Gus Smith of the *Sunday Independent* in Dublin. After asking "Why Friel Doesn't Write about Civil Rights," Smith had panned Friel's play dealing with civil rights, saying *The Freedom of the City* was ineptly structured with "no tension, no drama, no climax." Smith's unsympathetic review of *Volunteers,* under the headline "Friel Must Dig Deeper," prompted a response by Seamus Heaney in the pages of *The Times Literary Supplement* in an arti-

From the *Irish Press,* 28 March 1975, p. 9.

cle titled "Digging Deeper." The following week Fachtna
O'Kelly of the *Irish Press* gave Friel the opportunity to respond
to the critics himself.

When playwright Brian Friel's new magnum opus, *Volunteers,* opened in
the Abbey Theatre, Dublin, earlier this month it was received with almost
universal put-downs by the critics of the national newspapers.

One notice said that "as a realistic play it is mildly amusing," another
said it was a humbling experience for such a fine writer as Friel and, for
the Abbey, another misjudgment, while a third critic concluded his
review by asking "Your point, Mr. Friel—your point?"

Hardly a very flattering series of notices. And it would seem that
they have had some effect on the Abbey's box office for seat occupancy,
as the term goes, is hovering around the 50 percent mark, about 25 percent down on the yearly average.

Once again, the reviews raised the whole question of the role of the
theatre critic: the effect of notices on attendances and the contribution
that they can make to the existence of "live" theatre in Ireland.

As far as Mr. Friel is concerned, the critic can be one of two things.
"He or she may be a kind of litmus paper, so perfectly attuned to popular taste that they can actually reflect it.

"Or the critic can, over a period of time or through the quality of
stuff written, build up a certain amount of respect and a worthwhile and
deserved reputation. I believe that we have an abundance of the first
kind in Ireland but, I think, a lack of the latter."

In the case of *Volunteers,* he points out that the critics did not write
anything different to what they had said in the past. "They were possibly
a bit more obtuse than usual," is as much as he'll say.

The effect of bad notices can be twofold, he believes. They may
firstly put an audience completely off going to a play or, secondly, they
could mean that people would attend a play but in a conditioned rather
than an open frame of mind.

"But more important than its effect on attendances is the fact that a
barrage of bad notices can very often submerge a play for three or four
years. It often takes that long for a real opinion to emerge and it also
means that foreign theatres will be slow to put on a work which has been
poorly received by the critics in Ireland," he adds.

Obviously, he is of the opinion that theatrical criticism in Ireland is
not all that it should be. He believes, however, that the fault lies not with
the individuals involved but the newspaper managements.

"For instance, I don't see any point in sending a man to review a play when he has been working for the rest of week on news stories. It is inevitable that his attitude will be affected by a kind of news story consciousness," says Mr. Friel.

Newspapers would have to search around for the best possible man and one whose opinions were not being trivialised by the rest of his work. The assessment of a theatrical experience was, of course, a particular craft and one which needed a mind free of other attitudes.

"In the end, the responsibility lies with the newspaper managements. They must ensure that the critics they appoint are not also expected to report on things like weddings or other news events. Either that, or the reviews must be done by a complete outsider."

Critics, indeed, can help the playwright considerably and he instances the case of Nathan, who had been of very considerable assistance to Sean O'Casey in the formation of his plays.

As for himself, Mr. Friel adds, he does not pay that much attention to notices written by the theatre critics. "I read them certainly and I observe what they are saying. But they certainly don't affect me personally."

Is the Play Still the Thing?

Elgy Gillespie / 1978

Brian Friel's play *Living Quarters* was produced in Dublin in 1977 but the playwright gave no interviews. In 1979, when *Faith Healer* opened on Broadway and *Aristocrats* had its premiere in Dublin, Friel continued to decline all interviews, prompting journalists to write about Friel's aversion to "the vulgar glare of publicity." In 1978, however, Elgy Gillespie published a series of articles in *The Irish Times* under the headline "Is the Play Still the Thing?" On 28 July the last article of the series appeared with the subhead: "In her final article, Elgy Gillespie talks to Brian Friel and Fergus Linehan." Despite the verb used in the subhead, the interview may have been conducted by correspondence. Friel took the occasion to reflect on the state of theater in Ireland and on the ways—and on the reasons—that Irish playwrights differ from the politically committed playwrights of their generation in England.

Northerner Brian Friel has written some vastly different plays since *Philadelphia, Here I Come!* and that must in part be due to the way times have vastly changed. Many people feel that his is still the strongest and most original voice of Irish theatre, and that his plays need to be re-appraised at intervals to be seen in shifting contexts. His last play was *Living Quarters* at the Abbey. He is working on his newest play at home in Donegal and the thought of renouncing stage-writing, he says, never enters his head.

"I detect no signs of either a theatre revival or a theatre decline in the North. In Belfast the Lyric continues as usual and the Arts Theatre

From *The Irish Times*, 28 July 1978, p. 8.

has been reopened. Coleraine has got the new Riverside and Derry hopes to have a new theatre with a permanent company in a few years. Maybe this all adds up to a revival. I don't know. The proliferation of theatre buildings is no yardstick. It is what takes place in them that is important.

"For example, over the past 15 years in the U.S., civic-minded people right across the country have been possessed by a frenzy to build theatres and arts centres. These elegant and expensive buildings now exist. But a theatre revival? I see no sign of one.

"Nor can I explain why young writers are not attracted to the theatre here. Artists in this country always seem to have found the novel and poetry and the short story more satisfying forms. (And even though playwrights are frequently reminded that we aspire to poetry, Eliot believed that 'the majority, perhaps, certainly a large number, of poets hanker for the stage.')

"Perhaps the complicated organisation and trappings of the theatre frighten the young writer off. Perhaps the acquisition of the necessary craft. Perhaps the fact that the work can be realised only through actors ('the intervention of performers' is Eliot's revealing phrase, suggesting that he believed drama closer to literature than to the theatre). Perhaps the whiff of the market-place. Perhaps—particularly in this country—the total lack of an informed critical response. Perhaps—again something peculiar to this country—the blurring of the distinction between professional and amateur theatre, a confusion that tends to diminish both the seriousness of professional theatre and the parish values of the amateur theatre.

"You go on to talk about the new group of young English writers—Brenton, Bond, Hare—and ask 'Why can't people of that sort write here?'

"We are on firmer ground here. All the young men you mention are committed to the Left, some of them professed revolutionaries, who look to the theatre as a pulpit because they believe that it is the legitimate, and perhaps only, function of theatre to change the political face of the world.

"Ireland does not seem to infuse her writers with that kind of political zeal. Or to put it another way: Irishmen and women with that kind of vision and commitment find modes other than the arts to express themselves. Of course, we have had and will have plays and novels and poetry and short stories that can be called 'political'. But where we differ from the English playwrights you mention is, I suggest, that we don't think of ourselves as politicians, nor do we consider politics our commitment.

"There was a time when I would have agreed that, given certain conditions, great playwrights could be nurtured. And I would have pointed to the Moscow Art Theatre—Chekhov, and to the Provincetown Players—O'Neill, and to the Abbey—Synge. But the older I get, the more sceptical I am of this thesis.

"I still believe that you can have the happy concurrence of the man and the moment, when a great dramatist's capabilities are a product of, and in return generate, a period of distinctive intellectual ferment. But the moment alone does not make the man, nor the man the moment.

"My present view is more stern. Financial assistance is helpful. Competent actors in a well-equipped theatre are helpful. The existence of a well-informed critical atmosphere is helpful. But in the end not one of these things alone will make a dramatist. He appears. The very most we can do is make his birth and growth less uncomfortable.

"Ever since the Greeks, there have been long periods when theatre went into decline, became submerged, surfaced again. I see no sign of such a decline now. But if it were to happen, let it happen."

Broadway? Who Cares!

Ronan Farren / 1980

The first-night audience for *Faith Healer* on Broadway in April 1979 was attentive and absorbed, but reviews were mixed. Douglas Watt of the *Daily News* found the strangely enthralling play to be rich in language and imagery. But Richard Eder of the powerful *New York Times* termed Friel's monologues "stagnant and tedious." Clive Barnes had changed papers but not his position on Friel; his *New York Post* review dismissed the play saying, "Pretentiousness carves its own tombstone." By the time glowing reviews appeared in *Newsweek, Time* and *The New Yorker,* the play was already dead—though not necessarily by its own hand. *Faith Healer* was not produced in Dublin until sixteen months later when it opened at the Abbey just before *Translations* appeared as the inaugural production of Field Day in Derry. Talking to Ronan Farren in Dublin before *Faith Healer* opened there, Friel readily acknowledges the risks he took but offers a compelling account of what he was hoping to achieve with the experimental form of that play. While contrasting the New York and Dublin productions of *Faith Healer,* he laughs off any possibility that *Translations,* with its emphasis on the Irish language, might ever go to Broadway.

Brian Friel has been spending the past few weeks between Dublin and Derry, watching over rehearsals of two of his plays. *Faith Healer* opens tonight in the Abbey, and *Translations* sets off next month, via Derry and Belfast, on a tour that will reach Dublin in the second week of the Theatre Festival, and will then go on to 11 other towns.

From the *Evening Herald,* 28 August 1980, p. 8.

It might be tempting to describe this double event as a high point in Friel's career, if one didn't have him sitting there in the Abbey's Green Room dismissing the coincidence: "That's just ineptitude, you know."

In fact he finished *Faith Healer* over two years ago and it appeared in April last year on Broadway, where its reception was warm but not sufficiently laced with ballyhoo to bring in the jaded New Yorkers.

Translations, about to be premiered in Derry, is a historical play set in a Donegal Gaeltacht at the time the first ordnance survey was being conducted: a time of upheaval with long-lasting effects.

Brian Friel is a modest, almost a shy man, who vigilantly avoids anything resembling pretentiousness about his own work. His respect for some of the academic commentators is tempered by the realisation that they sometimes see things that he, the author, did not intend.

He has been described as a moralist and a social commentator. Some people would claim to see a thread of pessimistic exegesis on the subject of society in today's Ireland, running through the plays. He's reluctant to concede much of this.

"When you begin writing perhaps you stance yourself in some kind of a public place or on a public issue, and perhaps you're pompous enough to believe you may have something of significance to say about it. But I think as you get older—I'm 51 now—these issues don't exercise you nearly as much.

"You're still sensitive to issues like the North and the condition of this island, and even—which is a kind of public issue—an Irishman writing in the English language . . ."

There were, of course, political elements in *Volunteers* and even more so in *The Freedom of the City*.

"And the play we're working on in Derry at the moment has relevance to the language issue and also to the political issue."

We turn to *Faith Healer*. Near the beginning of the play, Frank Hardy (Donal McCann in the Abbey production) muses:

"Faith healer — faith healing. A craft without an apprenticeship, a ministry without responsibility, a vocation without a ministry."

Much has already been made of the analogy element: for faith healing read the artistic gift, the mysterious thing known as talent. Sometimes it brings fruit, sometimes it is barren.

Again Brian Friel is wary:

"I think as a play and as theatre it has got to succeed at its own level first. And if there are extensions into that kind of analogous situation . . . fine."

There are three characters in *Faith Healer,* which consists of four

monologues. Did he not run a risk that the usual dramatic tensions running between characters would be lost in this shape, with each character
appearing alone on the stage?

"You do lose what are commonly accepted to be the normal dramatic tensions or the normal dramatic interest, but I think there's a possibility you can succeed on different levels . . . On the level of storytelling, for example. The play, in fact, must find its main thrust at that
level: people simply telling stories about their lives, the way, for example,
Eamon Kelly does his one-man shows.

"I think it's a very austere form and it makes demands on the audience."

Does the chatty character in a Friel play, talking of his past life,
invariably add in a dash of fiction?

"I think it's a different kind of reality. Telling the truth in another
way. That truth is more important to him and more valid than any other
one."

He does not consciously set out to create this kind of "truth".

"No. I was talking to some young man yesterday, an American who's
doing a thesis (on Friel's plays) and he mentioned this. He quoted other
plays where I had apparently done the same thing. You forget . . ."

So much for the insights of the thesis-makers.

A playwright is in the business of communication, but it might sometimes be suggested that audiences don't grasp the full implications of
what he's saying.

"I think they will extract their own meaning from a play which may
not necessarily coincide with the precise one that I had. But in some way
I think that's another form of communication. That brings us back to,
What is the truth? again."

Faith Healer closed on Broadway after a few performances, an event
that seems to have left Friel unmoved.

"I like what happened in New York. James Mason played the faith
healer and I thought it was magnificent. It was superb acting, and I
enjoyed working with him. He's so hard-working . . . He's 73 or so now,
but he takes great care of himself, diets, does an hour and a half of exercise every morning. The acting instrument is in marvellous condition."

So what of the notorious New York critics?

"Broadway is a theatrical warehouse where theatrical merchandise is
bought and sold and if you have a well-packaged and slick piece of merchandise it will have some kind of a run. New York has as much to do
with what's happening here as 'Dallas' has."

He wasn't in the slightest disappointed by the Broadway closure.

"I've had so many plays that flopped on Broadway that it doesn't worry me in the least. In fact I like working in the regions of America, but it's part of the American cycle that it is almost impossible to stay out of Broadway. In the regional theatres that's in your contract that the play can go into Broadway."

As well as the flops, Friel has had several highly acclaimed and long-running Broadway productions, particularly *Philadelphia, Here I Come!* and *Lovers.*

Donal McCann is obviously going to be a very different kind of character in the lead, as he's in his thirties, whereas Mason is over 70.

"Mason did a kind of retrospective on his life. He told his story in retrospect, and McCann in some way is telling his story as if it's in the present . . . It's a nice distinction."

Friel is tireless in sitting in on rehearsals—something many playwrights avoid and some directors resent. The Abbey's Artistic Director, Joe Dowling, is directing *Faith Healer.*

"Joe has done two or three plays of mine and we work well together. We have acquired a kind of discreet language. I like working with him very much."

The others in the *Faith Healer* cast are Kate Flynn and John Kavanagh.

Translations is Friel's fifteenth play. It is set in 1833, in a hedge school.

"What is supposed to be happening on stage—it's a kind of theatrical conceit—is happening in the Irish language. The audience subscribes to the pretence that they are listening to the Irish language."

Translations is being put on by the new company set up by Friel and actor Stephen Rea, under the name Field Day Productions. It is partly funded by the Northern Ireland Arts Council.

It opens in the Gate Theatre on October 6, directed by Art O Briain, with a cast that includes six Northern actors and two Englishmen. Among them are Ray McAnally, Stephen Rea, Nuala Hayes, Mick Lally and Liam Neeson.

He is quite definitely not looking towards Broadway with this one.

"Can you imagine an American producer asking you, what the play is about and you saying, 'Well, it's set in a Gaeltacht hedge school in Ireland in 1833 . . .'"

Brian Friel laughs, the laughter of experience, laughter without rancour.

Why Friel and Rea are Having a 'Field' Day

Lynne Riddel / 1980

The New York premiere of *Faith Healer* in April 1979 was followed by a "sensational" Dublin production in late August 1980. A month later Friel's *Translations,* the first production of the new Field Day Theatre Company, would open in Derry. Field Day was the brainchild of Brian Friel and Stephen Rea, the Belfast-born actor who had met Friel during rehearsals for the Royal Court production of Friel's *The Freedom of the City* in 1973. Working in London on that politically charged play, the lapsed Catholic from Derry and the lapsed Protestant from Belfast found they shared "an instant rapport." Then after six years of scarcely seeing one another, Rea gave Friel a call in 1979. When the two met, Rea says, "we both wanted the same things and we decided to work together to achieve them." Friel and Rea formed Field Day (choosing a name that echoed their surnames) to establish a theatrical voice free of the constraining influence of either London or Dublin and to offer that voice to Irish people, primarily in the North, who had lacked access to professional theater. Although Friel's previous plays had gone to Broadway or even opened on Broadway, the world premiere of *Translations* was to be in Derry, which lacked a civic theater. When approached by Friel, the City Council suggested that the play could be performed in the Guildhall, a bastion of Unionism that had ironically been the setting of *The Freedom of the City.* In order for Field Day to mount its first production and take it on tour, Friel not only had to request subsidies from the

From the *Belfast Telegraph,* 15 September 1980, p. 8.

Derry City Council, the Northern Ireland Arts Council and the
Arts Council in Dublin, he also had to appeal for a commercial
sponsor and publicize the financial needs of the company.
After years of declining all interviews, Friel found himself in the
position of actively seeking publicity in order for the new venture to succeed. Although he describes his motivation to Lynne
Riddel of the *Belfast Telegraph* as "an act of piety," Friel had told
Fionnuala O Connor of *The Irish Times* that the personal reasons motivating Rea and himself were hard to express in English. Although "no exact word existed," O Connor said, "dúcas
or *Pietas* would do, a sense of loyalty or dutifulness towards
one's home." Talking to Riddel a week before the Derry opening, Friel explains something of the genesis of *Translations* and
the genesis of Field Day.

The electric combination of Derry playwright, Brian Friel, and Belfast
actor, Stephen Rea, is an unusual yet productive one.

Rea, who started in BBC radio in Belfast at the age of 17 and gained
acclaim as *Playboy* at the Old Vic in 1975, and Friel, who has written more
successes than can be quickly mentioned, have combined forces to establish the Field Day Theatre Company in Londonderry.

The name itself has slight connections with the present production
but Rea said it was just "a convenient hook" on which to hang the company.

Rehearsals are currently under way for the first production of Friel's
new play *Translations* which will receive its premiere in the Guildhall next
Tuesday night, September 22.

The following week, the play will be the first dramatic production at
the newly renovated Grand Opera House in Belfast—an event both men
are particularly looking forward to. After a two-week stint at Dublin's
Gate Theatre, the company will tour eleven towns in the North and the
South.

But the inspiration behind the establishment of an independent
company in Derry and the choice of Derry's Guildhall for a world premiere have raised a few eyebrows in the arts world where critics are more
used to reviewing a Friel premiere in Belfast, London, or Broadway.

When quizzed about their decision, both Friel and 35-year-old Rea
seem puzzled by the question.

To them, the decision is as natural as sunlight—a progression which
is only to be expected.

Friel points out that his new play is set only 20 miles outside Derry and the city seemed to be a natural center both functionally and spiritually.

The play is set in a Hedge School in 1833 when the new English language National Schools are about to open and the British Army is carrying out the first Ordnance Survey of the area. This involves finding English translations or phonetic equivalents for local place names and the main characters, both English and Irish, stand at a moment of cultural transition.

The idea for the play came from a book entitled *Memoirs of Londonderry*, written by Colonel Colby, the man in charge of the Ordnance Survey.

"I played around with the idea for a couple of years, and then decided to write a play about it," says Friel. "My home in Muff just over the border is opposite Magilligan which the Army used as their base camp during the exercise, so I was reminded of the idea nearly every day."

Rea's involvement in the company came through a working relationship with Friel. He has appeared in two of his plays in London and Dublin but as an accomplished West End actor, Rea's move, at the height of his career, is a mystery.

"London is a convenient piece of machinery in which to perform plays," he says. "But sometimes that very machinery can lack life and I feel the London machinery has totally ground to a halt, for me anyway."

His reasons for joining the Field Day partnership are varied. He explains that the enterprise is involving him in certain areas of dramatic production that are completely new, although he also has an acting role to play as well.

"I normally just walk into rehearsals, read the script and act and that's as far as my part goes," he says. "With Field Day, I'm involved in everything."

But there are deeper reasons why Rea's involvement has been so intense.

"As an actor, I am always trying to improve and at this point of time, I feel that Ireland is the best place to do it. I think I can gain something by being part of theatre here," he says. "There is no reason why people here should have to go to London to see good productions. Many actors feel they could play forever in front of London's totally absorbing audience but I believe there is more to be gained elsewhere."

And in this statement, Rea touches the edges of the vague explanation behind both men's involvement in the project.

In Friel's words: "It's an act of piety. By saying that I mean that I have no overriding obligation but it just seemed the right thing to do."

Their dutiful act involves an eight-week tour on both sides of the border with the first half of the itinerary spent in Derry, Belfast, and then Dublin.

After that, *Translations* will be performed in seven provincial Ulster centres including Newry, Dungannon, Armagh, and Enniskillen, followed by a short tour of the south. This series of one-night stands has created obvious financial burdens and there have been appeals from the company for an extra £10,000 to add to grants already favoured from both the Dublin and Belfast Arts Councils.

"This is in no way a commercial enterprise," says 51-year-old Friel. "We accept that we are going to be out of pocket at the end of the venture."

The cast of ten includes Ray McAnally, Liam Neeson, Nuala Hayes and Anne Hasson and the production is being directed by Art O'Briain. But there is no expected additional cost problem for accommodating the team in Derry.

Both men say that being in Derry some of the expected problems have actually been removed. They say that while accommodation expenses are only to be expected in any production, cooperation from staff at the Guildhall has helped tremendously.

Londonderry City Council have spent more than £13,000, taken from the supplementary estimates, on providing new lighting and technical equipment and a new temporary stage has been specially designed and built around the old stage in the Guildhall's splendid assembly hall.

Both men are full of praise for the Guildhall staff and councillors.

"Nobody realised how difficult things were going to be but we received nothing but co-operation from staff," says Friel. "They have helped us not only in major financial ways but also with advertising, typing and general work."

"I feel they have set an example for other councils to follow and while many hide behind excuses of financial restrictions, Derry has managed to cope with all the problems that a major production entails," he added.

Certainly councillors and council staff have shown their enthusiasm for the project by being present at every publicity function and although they have kept very much out of the limelight, both Rea and Friel say their help has been invaluable. And while rehearsals continue amidst, in the words of Rea, "the usual complacency and panic," questions are being asked about the future of the company and the possible implications the set-up might have for building a civic theatre in the Maiden City—a scheme which has been close to the hearts of many for almost ten years.

But if there are plans to continue the company after November, neither Friel nor Rea are willing to say.

"We are not going to sit down and plan something around the company, but we hope to do something similar as soon as possible," says the playwright.

But Friel, who has been a leading campaigner in the fight to bring a permanent theatre to Derry, says hopes could hinge on audience reaction to the premiere.

"Certainly, the money doesn't seem to be around any longer, but I hope this venture and the publicity it creates in Derry, will help plans along the way," he says.

As the curtain comes down on the company's last performance in the Cork Opera House on November 15, it seems impossible to believe that the ideals and hopes riding on the project will fade.

For Rea, the project will provide invaluable experience in an already distinguished career and it will also have fulfilled a few personal dreams about creating a "people's theatre."

For Brian Friel, a world premiere will never seem quite the same again after this home-town production and performance.

New Play to Set Fire to the Foyle?

Liam Robinson / 1980

Preparations for the Derry opening of *Translations* attracted extensive coverage in Dublin. On 20 September the *Irish Press* emphasized Friel's policy of including "as many Derry people or people from the North" as possible in the cast. Besides documenting the Derry background of four women in the play, the reporter noted that this would be the second appearance in Derry's Guildhall for "Ballymena actor Liam Neeson," who twelve years earlier had appeared "on a couple of boxing bills in the Guildhall for his local Ballymena Club." Talking to an *Evening Press* reporter, Friel stresses the local roots of the play in Donegal and the connection of the play's themes with his own familial history.

Getting Brian Friel to set the Foyle on fire as a curtain-raiser to a renaissance of the great healing power of theatre is the steadfast aim of Derry Council. Or so it seems to any observer who pauses in this proud city, which has not surrendered to bomb law, to catch a glimpse of preparations for the mounting of the world premiere of *Translations* in the Guildhall next Tuesday.

City Councillors declare that they are delighted that Friel, Stephen Rea, and the newly formed Field Day Theatre Company have chosen this city in preference to other established theatre venues throughout Ireland and the British Isles for their premiere. And this is not idle cant in the cause of culture.

The Guildhall, which was once a symbol of how two cultures could

From the *Evening Press*, 19 September 1980, p. 6.

meet in peace and throw away their cares in front of the footlights, carries still its ironsides of scaffolding, sinister reminders of the logic of the bomber.

But inside, to create a suitable setting for the premiere, alterations and improvements to the Assembly Hall are being made. A new stage suitable for professional and amateur shows has been built and a whole new lighting system has been installed.

Paddy Woodworth of Field Day management says: "The Council has been terrific to us. They have given us office space with excellent facilities, the use of the phones, and a rehearsing room. And they are even helping us to get the posters out."

Field Day is an independent theatre touring company based in Derry which gratefully acknowledges generous sponsorship from the Arts Councils on either side of the border and the patronage of Derry City Council and the local Arts Association.

Brian Friel came together with Stephen Rea, who was born in Belfast, started his career in the Abbey and made a big name for himself in the English National Theatre Company, when the Arts Council asked the playwright if he were interested in getting a professional venture on the road. And so it was done.

To demonstrate that the new company is planting its roots firmly in Derry it is making overtures to the children of the city. This is how Roy Hanlon, a Scotsman with Irish ancestors who has created an enviable career for himself on the London stage, finds himself cast in a strange role, a school lecturer.

He says: "I like visiting the schools, reading excerpts of the play to the children, telling them how a theatre functions, and trying to lift their enthusiasm." He has three children himself—one of them called Siobhan—but he would not like to introduce them to some Derry street scenes. He says: "It is hard to become accustomed to the sight of armed troops endlessly patrolling the place."

Friel's new play, *Translations,* is set far from the noise of Saracens.

"There is no question of the new company or the play," he says, "being part of a crusade for anything. The action takes place in the Ireland of the 1830's when the students of the hedge schools were living through a very significant phase in history. It is an Irish-speaking place in Donegal at the time when the Education Act of 1831 was coming into operation and the national schools were bringing about the decay of the hedge schools."

"These hedge schools masters were very erudite; that is why there are Greek and Latin lines in the play. These unfortunate masters were often very drunk, too, from loneliness. They lived hard lives far from home.

"At this time, too, the first National Ordnance Survey was being carried out by the British Army and they were thrown among an unfamiliar culture. The abrasiveness of the play is formed by the conflict of these two cultures.

"I suppose I became interested in this theme because my great-grandfather was a hedge school master, and my grandparents were Irish speaking—mainly I often thought to exclude us children from their conversation. And there is a famous book by a Colonel Colby who conducted the survey. This book I have been looking at for years and I suppose it was the seed for *Translations*."

After a week in the Guildhall, the play will move to the refurbished Grand Opera House in Belfast and then on to the Dublin Theatre Festival for a fortnight. Then it will recross the border for a tour of seven northern towns.

The cast in Derry says it could indeed set fire to the Foyle.

Mapping Cultural Imperialism

Stephen Dixon / 1980

Given his newfound volubility to promote the work of Field Day, Brian Friel was even willing to talk to London journalists in anticipation of the production of *Translations*. But Friel emphasizes that *Translations* was intended to be an Irish play for an Irish audience, describing that impetus as "talking to ourselves." Friel explores the thematic implications of *Translations* as not only about the absorption of one culture into another but also about the disquiet between two aesthetics. He also talks about the form of *Faith Healer*, noting that the play's monologues should be seen in the context of traditional Irish storytelling.

Derry in the drifting, drenching September mist. Green-uniformed RUC men cluster in doorways. From time to time an Army Land/Rover squelches past, with the inevitable man riding machinegun at the rear. The outside of Derry Guildhall, where Brian Friel is adding the final polish at rehearsals of his new play, *Translations,* is forbidding: a high wire fence all around and a gauntlet to run of locked gates and security men.

A County Tyrone ex-schoolteacher, Brian Friel writes plays that are very dark indeed. *Volunteers* dealt with the plight of a group of Irish political prisoners who opt for working on an archaeological dig, supervised by warders, only to find that a kangaroo court back at the gaol has sentenced them to death for collaboration. *Freedom of the City* directed at the Royal Court by Albert Finney, was about an unauthorised civil rights march dispersed with CS gas.

His present success at Dublin's Abbey Theatre, *The Faith Healer—*

From *The Guardian*, 27 September 1980, p. 11.

which played on Broadway last year with James Mason and Donal Donnelly in the cast—is about an alcoholic showman / faith healer who tours
Scotland and Wales and meets his destiny in an exceedingly unpleasant
manner in Donegal. Given the surroundings, and the reputation, one
could be forgiven for feeling a little nervous about meeting Brian Friel.
What a pleasure to report that one's mild paranoia was totally
unfounded.

Now in his early fifties, and a full-time writer since 1960, Friel is a
Puckish, dapper man of immense good humour. He has the looks and
manner of a particularly amiable and philosophical publican. *Translations,* after its Derry opening ("I think it is important that it starts its life
here in Derry," he says) will move to the newly renovated Belfast Opera
House and then feature in the Dublin Theatre Festival, which begins
tomorrow, before touring Cork, Galway and other cities.

Friel's stance in *Translations* seems perversely uncompromising even
for him. It is about an Irish hedge school in the 1830s—but as he points
out: "In Ireland we are still talking to ourselves in theatrical terms, and
for very good reasons. If we are overheard—as we often are—then that's
fine."

Perhaps the popular image of hedge schools needs to be explained
before Brian Friel proceeds to demolish long-cherished myths: they
were, it is widely believed, extremely clandestine affairs, with priests
tutoring children under pain of appalling retribution from the British
authorities if discovered.

"The phenomenon of the hedge schools," says Friel, "is not quite as
furtive as the received idea of it. On the one hand there is the folk memory, and on the other there is *our* particular hedge school, which is very
prosaic. The play is about the absorption of one culture into another;
but I hope it goes a bit deeper than that—about the disquiet between
two aesthetics.

"Under the Education Act of 1831 the national schools were imple-
mented, and pupils were leaving the hedge schools and starting at the
national schools, as there was a formal shift from Irish-speaking to English-speaking. That is the first thread of the thread of the play.

"The second thread concerns the first ever ordnance survey of this
country, done by Sappers of the Royal Engineers. They accurately
mapped the whole country, and new place names were put on those
maps. The towns and villages were given Anglicised names—a whole
country was rechristened. And, obviously, this involved quite a culture
shock."

The play marks a new departure for Friel, whose work has attracted its share of hostile or puzzled notices, both in America and Ireland, since the huge success of *Philadelphia, Here I Come!* in 1964.

He returns to a favourite theme: modern Irish dramatists talking to themselves, in national terms.

"The four monologues in *The Faith Healer*, for example, have to be seen as stories because the Irish consciousness is more receptive to this; it is a tradition that goes back to the seanchai—the travelling storyteller."

For Friel, the Dublin Theatre Festival is just one of the venues for *Translations*, but the city's theatregoers are already looking forward to it in a year when the Festival seems more inward-looking and "Irish" than in previous years. Last year's had an international flavour, Princess Grace of Monaco, Michael Redgrave and the National Theatre, Cyril Cusack in *A Life*. This year Ireland concentrates on her own storytellers.

Finding Voice in a Language Not Our Own

Ciaran Carty / 1980

The Derry reception of *Translations* was "euphoric," "electric," "triumphant." Applause punctuated the speeches; the audience leapt to its feet at the final curtain in a standing ovation that united Unionists and nationalists; calls for the author voiced a palpable excitement. In his curtain speech, Friel offered what one observer termed a miracle of emotional brevity by telling the audience that the play had fulfilled one of St. Columcille's prophecies. Friel said that, while living in Iona, the saint had prophesied: "The town of the Oaks will in the second half of the twentieth century open its arms to the Field Day Theatre Company." "And so it did," Friel said. Then in three languages, reflecting those spoken in the play, he said "thank you" to the audience in Latin, Irish and English. Critics hailed the play as "a watershed in Irish theatrical history." Noting that passages in the play surpassed O'Casey and Synge, the *Irish Press* declared that "Friel has become the heir apparent to the throne of those literary giants." Some of the euphoria in Derry, however, reflected concerns that went beyond the literary merits of the text. London critic James Fenton noted in the *Sunday Times* that "a great deal of the pleasure of the occasion derived from the sheer achievement of assembling a new company of Irish talent and staging a world première in such surroundings." Yet the response to the play in Derry went beyond civic pride in a cultural triumph. Ciaran Carty would observe that Friel and Rea had chosen Derry for the opening precisely

From the *Sunday Independent* (Dublin), 5 October 1980, p. 16.

"because it embodies the meeting of two cultures" and, as a result, "the place became an extension of the play." After its sold-out performances in Derry including an additional matinee to accommodate some of the crowds turned away, the Field Day production of *Translations* moved to Belfast and then to the Dublin Theatre Festival. Although Ciaran Carty's interview appeared in the *Sunday Independent* just before the play opened in Dublin, Carty had talked to Friel during the final week of rehearsals in Derry. In their extended conversations, Friel locates the genesis of *Translations* in the replacement of the country's place names but stresses that situation's metaphoric implications for Irish writers who must use "a language not our own." Friel discusses the English presence in Ireland and contrasts the impetus for propagandist theater in England with the situation confronting the Irish playwright.

He plops a tea bag into a cup of boiling water. "I'm used to drinking tea in green rooms and it's always filthy," he apologises.

Not that we're in a conventional green room: the huge first-floor room of the Guildhall, with its high ceiling and panelled walls, has been made available to Field Day for rehearsals by Derry City Council.

That Field Day should be in the Guildhall at all—to say nothing of Unionist mayor Marlene Jefferson leading the applause on opening night—is in itself remarkable.

To the minority in the North this intimidating neo-Gothic building overlooking the Foyle has always been a symbol of domination.

"This is theirs, boy, and your very presence here is a sacrilege," jeered Skinner in Friel's 1973 play *The Freedom of the City*. With two other demonstrators he had taken refuge from C.S. gas in the mayor's parlour when troops broke up a Civil Rights march. Mistaken for an IRA assault force, they came under fire from the British and were shot as they surrendered: a savagely ironic analogy to Bloody Sunday.

But all that is changing. The Guildhall has fallen to words rather than bullets. Even with the recession biting deep—over 10,000 jobs have been lost in the area—a power-sharing Council offers Derry the beginnings of hope.

Friel's play is in keeping with this new tolerance. He hasn't written a polemic. Theatre for him has never been a soap-box. His plays explore the ambiguities and confusions that pervade life; the truths of his characters are never more than approximations.

"The play found expression in the issue of actual place names," he tells me, "but I think in some way my concern is more with the whole problem that the writers in this country experience: having to handle a language that is not native to him.

"There's a line where the hedge school teacher says that they'll have to learn these names and they'll have to make them their new home. And in some way that's what the play is about: having to use a language that isn't our own.

"But I'm not talking about the revival of the Irish language. I'm just talking about the language we have now and what use we make of it and about the problems that having it gives us.

"The assumption, for instance, is that we speak the same language as England. And we don't. The sad irony, of course, is that the whole play is written in English. It ought to be written in Irish."

Much of its theatrical impact comes from Friel's inspired device of having all the characters speak the same language but with a translator all the time interpreting what the English and the Irish are saying to each other: a recurring reminder of the fundamental differences that can be embodied in the same language.

"Somebody asked me if it had a political message," says Friel ruefully. "Well, if it has, I don't know what it is.

"Of course, it's also concerned with the English presence here. No matter how benign they may think it has been, finally the presence of any foreigner in your land is malign. Even if the people who were instrumental in bringing it in have the best motives—as some of them had.

"We forget that it was the minority here—to step into that jargon— it was the Catholics who sent for the British troops in the height of the problem. And now the 'Brits Out' calls are coming from the same people."

But politics are merely incidental to Friel's preoccupation with words. "It's not literal history that shapes us," points out the teacher in *Translations,* "but images of the past embodied in language."

As a playwright he has been conditioned by this experience as much as anyone else: perhaps more so. "It's a problem dramatists here never really faced up to: the problem of writing in the language of another country.

"We're a very recent breed. Poets and novelists, I think, belong to a less fractured tradition than we do. We've only existed since Synge and Yeats. There was no such thing as an indigenous Irish drama until 1904."

Dramatists from Ireland before that always had to write for the English stage: to pitch their voice in an English way. "They had to do that if they were to practice their craft. The whole Irish drama tradition from

Farquhar to Behan is pitted with writers doing that. Ultimately they were maimed.

"But there's a big change now. What many are doing is writing for ourselves. Not in any insular or parochial sense but they want to be heard by their own people. And if they're overheard by anyone else, that's a bonus."

But having said that, he is at pains not to be thought to be making a cult of Irishness. "John McGahern once told you in an interview that he did not want to be thought of as an Irish writer. And I can see the danger in that. But I think it's an appellation that other people put on you. So what the hell. You go and do your job."

Which is how Field Day came about: to give life to the idea of writing for an Irish audience rather than primarily for Broadway or the West End. The logical follow-through comes after Dublin with a series of one-night stands in Magherafelt, Dungannon, Newry, Carrickmore, Armagh and Enniskillen.

"But we're the most reluctant producers," he laughs. He formed Field Day with Stephen Rea ("The name is derived from both our names") because it was the only way to get money from the Northern Ireland Arts Council to perform *Translations*. "They only fund existing establishments so we had to become an establishment."

Now they find themselves into something much larger than they had anticipated, having to worry about everything from getting out contracts to putting up "no smoking" signs. "It's not like going into the Abbey where everything is provided and all you do is sit in on rehearsals and that's it!"

Even with £40,000 from Belfast, £10,000 from the Dublin Arts Council and £13,000 for a new stage and lighting system in the Guildhall from Derry Council ("their help and enthusiasm has been incredible"), Field Day is unlikely to break even.

"The issue is how small the deficit can be kept to. But the response has been so good that I'm much less worried than I was.

"We haven't given any thought to what's going to happen next. Perhaps the play will go to Hampstead. I'd love to see it performed in Belgium or Montreal or parts of Russia where there's the same problem of two cultures and languages coming together. But that's all romanticising."

Friel has lived all his life around Derry. "We moved here from Omagh when I was ten. My father was a teacher and I became a teacher too, but gave it up to write stories for *New Yorker*. They paid such enormous money I found I could live off three stories a year."

Tyrone Guthrie invited him out to Minneapolis to the first of the regional theatres he had started. "I don't know what I learned there but I suppose it was some smell of what theatre was about."

Out of the experience came *Philadelphia, Here I Come!* in 1964, which became the longest-running Irish play on Broadway, a record not surpassed until last year's triumph of Hugh Leonard's *Da*.

Since then he has had play after play on Broadway *The Loves of Cass McGuire, Lovers, The Mundy Scheme, Freedom of the City, The Faith Healer*—yet international success has failed to lure him away from the North.

He continues to live with his wife Anne and four children a couple of miles over the border in Muff, Co. Donegal.

Which is not really surprising. All his plays are set in Ireland and rooted in the Irish experience: that is where his material is.

His plays give universal form to the particularities of his experiences: the way he finds to express an idea invariably becomes an extension of that idea. "The crux with a new play arises with its form," he says. Thus *Philadelphia* has two actors to personify, Gar's inner and outer selves. *The Faith Healer* consists entirely of monologues, emphasising the separateness of the characters. *Translations* is rooted in the varying nuances inherent in the same language on different tongues.

He boils another kettle, to all appearances like a tweed-jacketed teacher in some school common room. Derry is full of his former pupils, to whom he's known by the nickname Scobie.

"A play offers you a shape and a form to accommodate your anxieties and disturbance for this period of life you happen to be passing through," he explains. "But you outgrow that and you change and grope for a new shape and a new articulation of it, don't you?"

He is a meticulous craftsman, attending every rehearsal, never letting go of a play until it is a reality on the stage. "The dramatist ought to be able to exercise complete control over the realisation of his characters.

"The director can bring an objective view to the script that a writer can't have. But I'm very doubtful about the whole idea of a director interpreting a play in any kind of way that's distinctive to him.

"A good director hones in on the core of what a play is about and realises that and becomes self-effacing in the process.

"A director is like the conductor of an orchestra and the actors are the musicians. They are all there to play the score as it is written."

If that makes Friel a conventional playwright, he's not bothered. He prefers to work within the possibilities of theatre rather than trying to make it something else. He has shunned the fashions of English theatre, avoiding both the Pinteresque concern with dramatising mood and the Howard Brenton vision of theatre as a vehicle for politics. The English he argues can indulge in the rhetoric of propagandist drama because it's safe there: they're secure in continuing culture which has hardly changed in hundreds of years.

"But here we're continually thrust into a situation of confrontation. Politics are so obtrusive here."

He gestures out the window. The British army barracks dominates Derry from the opposite bank of the Foyle. Below the entrance to the Guildhall is protected by a perimeter of barbed wire.

"For people like ourselves, living close to such a fluid situation, definitions of identity have to be developed and analysed much more frequently.

"We've got to keep questioning until we find some kind of portmanteau term or until we find some kind of generosity that can embrace the whole island.

"That certainly is the ultimate aim, isn't it?"

Talking to Ourselves

Paddy Agnew / 1980

Following its triumph in Derry, the Field Day production of
Translations moved to Dublin, where it was "the huge, overwhelming, tears-and-fisticuffs-if-you-can't-get-in hit of the Festival," according to a London reviewer. In Ireland the play was
widely regarded as the "most important theatrical event of the
year," and David Nowlan of *The Irish Times* concluded that Friel
"has now overtaken John Millington Synge as the prime writer
of dramatic literature in Ireland this century." Although the
play was taken in some quarters as straightforward history, Friel
emphasized the contemporary significances of the play. Friel
told an interviewer for Radio Telefís Éireann that the play raises
two issues that had "never been properly resolved in this country": the English presence and "the problem of expressing ourselves through an acquired language." Although the latter issue
is "more concerned with ourselves," Friel acknowledged that in
some way it "is also inhibiting the relationships between this
island and England": "You know, you and I could list a whole
series of words, for example, that have totally different conno-
tations for English people than they have for us—words like *loyalty, treason, patriotism, republicanism, homeland.* So that in fact
there are words which we think we share and which we think we
can communicate with, which in fact are barriers to communication." When *Translations* opened in London, Friel again
acknowledged that to some extent the play has to do with "the
relationships between Ireland and England, and to that extent
I suppose it's a play about how two countries can understand

From *Magill,* 4 no. 3 (December 1980), pp. 59–61.

one another." But, Friel insisted, "I'm really more concerned with the effect that this historical event had on the people within the island of Ireland." In his most extensive commentary on *Translations* in an interview with Paddy Agnew for the Dublin magazine *Magill*, Friel emphasizes the issues the play raises for Irish speakers of English. Voicing concerns remarkably similar to Hugh's final stance in *Translations*, Friel says that people in Ireland must both recognize the foreignness of the English tradition and find ways to "make English identifiably our own language." He also explains how the process of translating Chekhov's *Three Sisters* led him to George Steiner's *After Babel*, which in turn resulted in a reworking of the text of *Translations*.

In the programme notes for Translations *you cite a quotation from Martin Heidegger about the nature of language. This same quotation appears as the foreword to George Steiner's* After Babel, *a scholarly work about aspects of translation and language. How and why did you come to read Steiner?*

I came to *After Babel* because I was doing a translation of *Three Sisters*. Although I do not speak a word of Russian, I had been working on this play with the help of five standard English translations. It was a kind of act of love, but after a while I began to wonder exactly what I was doing. I think *Three Sisters* is a very important play, but I feel that the translations which we have received and inherited in some way have not much to do with the language which we speak in Ireland.

I think that the versions of *Three Sisters* which we see and read in this country always seem to be redolent of either Edwardian England or the Bloomsbury set. Somehow the rhythms of these versions do not match with the rhythms of our own speech patterns, and I think that they ought to, in some way. Even the most recent English translation again carries, of necessity, very strong English cadences and rhythms. This is something about which I feel strongly—in some way we are constantly overshadowed by the sound of English language, as well as by the printed word. Maybe this does not inhibit us, but it forms us and shapes us in a way that is neither healthy nor valuable for us . . . The work I did on *Three Sisters* somehow overlapped into the working of the text of *Translations*.

The fact that you opened the play in Derry would imply that you felt the play had a relevance to the North, in general, and to Derry, in particular, which it does not have to the rest of Ireland, or to anywhere else for that matter?

Not really, no. The reason that we wanted to rehearse in Derry was because the town of Derry is close to the fictional location of the play.

When the director, Art O Briain, came here he felt this was the obvious place to rehearse this play. So we looked around Derry and to our surprise the Guildhall were enthusiastic about the venture.

Do you feel then that the play has a relevance to places like Belgium or Quebec, where there is a problem of two cultures?

Yes, I think so. Those are two places where I would love to go with this play. I am sure there are areas of Russia, perhaps Estonia or southern Russia, where their languages have faded, as has Irish . . . Of course a fundamental irony of this play is that it should have been written in Irish.

The old schoolmaster, Hugh, at one point says that "certain cultures expend on their vocabularies and syntax, acquisitive energies entirely lacking in their material lives." Do you feel that, in a sense the loss of our Celtic background means that we have lost a vital energy?

What Hugh is saying there is that societies which do not have material wealth or material stability are inclined to compensate for this by the invention and use of a language which is more ostentatious and opulent than the language of an economically secure society . . . What I am talking about however is the relationship of this island to the neighbouring island. We have all been educated in an English system, we are brought up in school reading Wordsworth, Shelley and Keats. These are formative influences on our lives and there is no possibility of escaping from this.

We must accept this. But we must make this primary recognition and it is a recognition which we must never lose sight of: that there is a foreignness in this literature; it is the literature of a different race. If we assume that we have instant and complete access to that literature, we are unfair to it and to ourselves. And we constantly make that assumption because of the common language error.

If I can quote from the play, "we must make them our own." We must make them (English language words) distinctive and unique to us. My first concern is with theatre and we certainly have not done this with theatre in Ireland. The only person who did so in this country was Synge. Nobody since him has pursued this course with any persistence or distinction and indeed this is one of the problems of the theatre in this country. It is a new and young discipline for us and apart from Synge, all our dramatists have pitched their voice for English acceptance and recognition. This applied particularly to someone like Behan. However I think that for the first time this is stopping, that there is some kind of confidence, some kind of coming together of Irish dramatists who are not concerned with this, who have no interest in the English stage. We are talking to ourselves as we must and if we are overheard in America, or England, so much the better.

Does the same principle apply to other areas of Irish life, namely that we have not found our own voice?

I suppose so, but probably the voice can only be found in letters, in the arts. Perhaps this is an artist's arrogance, but I feel that once the voice is found in literature, then it can move out and become part of the common currency.

Is the English which we speak still "full of mythologies of fantasy, hope and self-deception"?

I think so, certainly in our political lives.

Is it wrong then to suggest that this is a political, polemical play?

I really do not know. I am the last person to ask, really. Apparently *An Phoblacht* did a piece on it which says that the character of Doalty is the central figure, that a man who does not know the seven times table, can still have a deep instinct which is true and accurate.

Because he says "I have damn little to defend . . . but what I have got, they'll not get without a fight"?

Something like that, I suppose. But someone else suggested to me that the key figure is Owen, who was described to me as a typical SDLP man, but people are entitled to take their own interpretation out of the play. Perhaps there is some kind of validity in that, that the figure of Owen is an SDLP man and that if he is, then the task upon which he embarked was done with some kind of honour.

In the end, in terms of the narrative, the colonial presence is malign. This would suggest that simply there will be no solution to the Irish problem until the British presence removes itself or is removed?

We are not just talking about the present time and I am no expert in matters political, but in the long run of course I think that that is going to be true. There will be no solution until the British leave this island, but even when they have gone, the residue of their presence will still be with us. This is an area that we still have to resolve, and that brings us back to the question of language for this is one of the big inheritances which we have received from the British. In fact twenty miles from where we are sitting, you can hear very strong elements of Elizabethan English being spoken every day. The departure of the British Army will have absolutely no bearing on the tongue that is spoken in that area. We must continually look at ourselves, recognize and identify ourselves. We must make English identifiably our own language.

When Yolland describes his initial impressions of the Baile Beag community as being somewhere "at its ease and with its own conviction and assurance," does that not imply some sort of nostalgia for Celtic Ireland?

I have no nostalgia for that time. I think one should look back on the process of history with some kind of coolness. The only merit in looking back is to understand how you are and where you are at this moment. Several people commented that the opening scenes of the play were a portrait of some sort of idyllic, Forest of Arden life. But this is a complete illusion, since you have on stage the representatives of a certain community—one is dumb, one is lame and one is alcoholic, a physical maiming which is a public representation of their spiritual deprivation.

You talk of looking back on history with some sort of coolness. Is that what is implied by suggesting that "it is not the literal past, the facts of history, that shape us, but images of the past embodied in language"?

In some ways the inherited images of 1916, or 1690, control and rule our lives much more profoundly than the historical truth of what happened on those two occasions. The complication of that problem is how do we come to terms with it using an English language. For example, is our understanding of the Siege of Derry going to be determined by Macaulay's history of it, or is our understanding of Parnell going to be determined by Lyons's portrait of Parnell? This is a matter which will require a type of eternal linguistic vigilance.

"Confusion is not an ignoble condition," says Hugh, but in the Irish context can we afford to be confused?

I think most of us live in confusion; I live in confusion. Hugh's words are perhaps a fairly accurate description of how we all live, specifically at the present time. Other countries perhaps have access to more certainties than we have at the moment. I was talking specifically about Ireland.

Friel and a Tale of Three Sisters

Donal O'Donnell / 1981

Friel may have imagined that *Translations,* a play set in a nine-teenth-century Gaeltacht, would primarily be of parochial interest, providing an occasion for Irish people of the North and South to be "talking to ourselves." But then the rest of the English-speaking world got the chance to eavesdrop on the conversation. *Translations* opened in New York in April 1981 and at the Hampstead Theatre in London in May, just after *Faith Healer* had finished its run at the Royal Court. Although he attended rehearsals for a week, Friel did not bother to go to the London opening of *Faith Healer,* noting that his plays had never been received with anything more than "tepid warmth" in England. All that was to change, ironically, with Friel's Gaeltacht play. *Translations* garnered London accolades as "a national classic," the most eloquent Irish play "since *The Plough and the Stars,*" a play with "a grace and conviction rarely encoun-tered" that is "so well written that the final effect is bracing rather than dispiriting." The play transferred to the National Theatre touching off another round of raves. Meanwhile, the second world premiere by Field Day in Derry's Guildhall was not going to be a new Irish play but Brian Friel's Irish version of Chekhov's *Three Sisters.* The audience in provincial Derry, well away from the metropolis of either London or Dublin, would be listening to three sisters talking to themselves about life in provincial Russia, well away from the metropolis of Moscow. Discussing issues involved in his translation of *Three Sisters,* Friel explores Irish affinities with Chekhov. Three weeks before the

From the *Sunday Press,* 30 August 1981, p. 19.

opening of *Three Sisters,* Friel and Rea had asked poets Seamus
Heaney and Tom Paulin, scholar Seamus Deane, and broadcaster David Hammond to serve as directors of Field Day.
Despite that move to expand the company, Friel told Donal
O'Donnell that Field Day did not want to "acquire a roof" or
become an institution. Instead, Friel explains something of his
vision for a transient, independent venture that might function
to "de-colonise" the imagination.

A week tomorrow Northern playwright and author Brian Friel will see
the fruits of almost a year's "labour of love" when his Field Day Theatre
Company performs the world premiere of his "translation" of Anton
Chekhov's *Three Sisters.*

The production is only the second to come from this unique company, founded by Mr. Friel and Belfast-born actor-director Stephen Rea
last year for the performance of Mr. Friel's own highly successful play
Translations.

All concerned with the production are full of praise for Mr. Friel's
adaptation of the world classic. While aiming essentially at Irish audiences, he believes that it will have a wider appeal and a continental tour
is being considered.

The decision to tackle the daunting task springs from Mr. Friel's
admiration of Chekhov. "The cliché is that we in Ireland have some special kind of affinity with Chekhov. I am not sure whether this is true or
not, but I think it is potentially true," he told me during final rehearsals
in Derry's magnificent Guildhall where *The Three Sisters* opens on September 8.

"I think that the problems of performing Chekhov in this country is
that the translations that have been available have been British, which
results in Chekhov being placed at a remove from us. In a way, I think
one of the functions of Field Day enterprises is in some way to 'de-
colonise' the imagination.

"I don't know a word of Russian, of course, and so I feel a wee bit
diffident about using the word *translation.* What I did was simply to put
six texts in front of me and tackle each line at a time, to see first of all
what was the meaning of it, then what was the tone and then eventually
what was the sound. It took nine months in all," he said. The result is that
Mr. Friel has sought to resolve the problem that has faced Irish theatre
playing Chekhov.

"What has always happened up to this is that Irish actors have to assume English accents so you end up with being an Irishman pretending you're an Englishman, pretending you're a Russian! In some way the whole thing gets further and further away from us, I think."

Although he sees his adaptation as "re-freshing" Chekhov, Mr. Friel has left unaltered the setting of the original. The story is of the three Prozorov sisters, Olga (Sorcha Cusack), Masha (Eileen Pollock) and Irina (Olwen Fouere) and their brother, Andre (John Quinn) who live in a large provincial garrison town some distance from Moscow at the beginning of this century.

"It is a story of their hopes and ambitions for their lives, how these ambitions are being thwarted and stultified."

Mr. Friel took the opportunity to explain the uniqueness of the Field Day Theatre Company, and its future plans. "Ideally, of course, we would like to do a brand new play, preferably an Irish one, preferably a new Northern play. But, then, on the other hand, we feel very strongly that if there isn't something we want to do and believe in fully, we will just do nothing.

"We haven't an institution that we have to serve and we don't want to acquire a roof. We want to be transient in the aesthetic sense as well as in the practical sense, which gives us independence."

The play has a cast of 14 and true to the concept of Field Day it has a strong Northern element, as both Mr. Friel and Stephen Rea believe it is important that the North should be articulated in this way.

Thirty-six-year-old Stephen Rea, who hails from the Antrim Road area of Belfast, will not be on stage this time. Instead he faces the "huge challenge" of directing the production.

"I have only directed a couple of short plays, in London eight years ago, but this task is enormous by comparison. It is a brilliant play with massive technical difficulties but we have a great text, a great design team and Mícheál Ó Súilleabháin's music is lovely," he said.

Participation the Field Day productions is "by invitation only" and casts are handpicked so that each actor is just right for their role. Without exception the members of the cast whom I met, expressed genuine delight at being "honoured".

In the case of Sorcha Cusack, it was she who first suggested to Brian Friel and Stephen Rea, whom she met while playing in London: "I wish you would remember me for one of your plays sometime."

For North-Belfast–born Eileen Pollock, paradoxically, her role as one of the sisters is her first opportunity to perform with an Irish company in Ireland, North or South.

Her only previous experience in Chekhov was when she was in the cast of *The Seagull* at Queen's University, where she admits they didn't approach it very seriously.

"Brian's translation is much better than others at extracting the humanity of the situation, tragedy and all, with a ripple of humour. It is very hard work and while it is not an Irish play, it brings it into the understanding of the Irish actor," said Eileen.

The third "sister", Olwen Fouere, first learned of her invitation through her agent. She read the script, liked it and accepted, although she had other acting commitments from which she had to be released.

The big challenge to her in the play is adapting to the Northern-Irish idiom in the Friel "translation". The play has been brilliantly structured between Friel and Chekhov, she said. Like the others in the cast she is very enthusiastic about the whole idea behind Field Day and for her there is the added excitement that *Three Sisters* is providing her first contact with a Northern playwright and actors.

The Saturday Interview: Brian Friel

Elgy Gillespie / 1981

A car bomb would abort the dress rehearsal for *Three Sisters,* and two bomb scares the day the play opened resulted in some of the opening night dialogue being drowned out by a circling helicopter, spotlighting some of the difficulties of staging a world premiere in Derry. But when Elgy Gillespie of *The Irish Times* got through the security fence during rehearsals, she found Friel willing to discuss the reasons for his reluctance to give interviews, his response to the reception of *Translations,* and his reasons for doing a translation of Chekhov.

Behind the iron fence the Guildhall looks immaculate and hollow, like a film-set facade. The laughing security staff (why are Northerners always so good-humoured, even at a time like this?) unlock gate and door, urging you down a stately hall and up sweeping marble steps. Stained glass windows depicting captains and kings, in a manner tactlessly overt, proclaim debts to bodies across the water.

The new play being rehearsed and performed there is Brian Friel's own translation of Chekhov's *Three Sisters,* and it is to make music to Irish ears, as the second Irish production of the Field Day Theatre Company, which has scored so ubiquitously with *Translations.* That starred Stephen Rea as Owen, but this time Friel's co-director in Field Day is himself directing. So both Field Day directors have, to an extent, submerged original selfhood and personal development for the good of the company production, which opens here next Tuesday and comes to Dublin for the Theatre Festival.

From *The Irish Times,* 5 September 1981, p. 14 ("Weekend" section, p. 6).

Brian Friel slipped out to the corridor and boiled the kettle for tea. In his fifties now, his high-cheeked face seems to acquire more Thady Quill puckishness as time goes on. He has an exceedingly gentle manner, and a beautiful voice with very musical modulations. When he split his evening pants at the Harvey Awards last Spring, he described himself as "backing out of the limelight," and does not give any credence to success. ("For the writer there is no such thing as success just as there is no 'success' in the rain falling or the sun shining.")

Until Field Day, he loathed press interviews and never gave them if he could help it. It's easy to see why; he is so mild and equivocal in manner that it is easy, even inevitable, for journalists to put their own bias or construction upon his words, by quite unconsciously giving them certain inflections. He is the opposite of cityish witty, urbane, forceful.

But he is not doctrinairely political in a republican sense, as you might have decided upon the reported evidence, and in any case he has himself admitted that he always comes to regret the causes he involves himself in.

His passionate involvement in Field Day, we can safely hazard, is not about nationalism in a narrow way. It's about questioning everything, just the way he questions everything as he talks. The journalists would easily put them down as statements, if they were taping them and relaying word for word. This, he explains, is why he's no good at them. "Things seem so much more definite in the way I'm quoted in interviews."

So why, to ask the obvious question, had they chosen *Three Sisters*, and what was so wrong with other translations? "We wanted a classic, we felt a classic would be what Field Day needed at this point. We're still defining ourselves by exploration and we both still feel this development is an integral part of our career." But so much energy, to be expended in the drag of touring, the recounting of box office receipts (at which neither Rea nor Friel excel) when they could be acting, writing?

Friel makes a little movement of his head, approximating to a shrug, the better to downplay commitment. "Oh, it's very draining. But I suppose we must be getting something back from it . . ." If he were forced to be more definite about Field Day's artistic and political aims? He wasn't sure what those two things mean, or how they move in relation to each other, he quietly replied. Oh, so he just didn't want to be preachy about it?

"I'd love to be preachy but I'm not sure what the sermon is. We can only define afterwards what the sermon is." After the tour will come *Angel* for Stephen Rea, a film with a script by Neil Jordan, in which he plays a saxophonist besotted with Charlie 'Bird' Parker. But for Friel? "Afterwards I'll have to get my own life back into shape, I suppose."

Field Day emerged quite naturally, when the Arts Council suggested Stephen Rea as the man to come over and play in *Translations*. The Guildhall turned out to be the ideal place to rehearse, generous as it is with facilities and goodwill towards them. Rea didn't want to just come, and go back to London again. "Both of us felt there was some tiny little space we might fill that we could focus the whole North thing on . . . but we knew we must have impermanence built in. This could be our last play, or we could go on for another twenty years." In fact, Tom Mullarkey's plans for a new Derry theatre are still knocking about the Guildhall somewhere, awaiting the finance to help found a home for a second Northern rep company—but that wouldn't be relevant to Field Day.

"We don't think it's necessarily of value to have a building to offer up piety towards; no matter how modest, you'd have to continually ask yourself what to do with it, you couldn't just do something or do nothing. It's part of the fluxiness to not know if we'll be doing something or not, and we feel fluxiness is the most important thing for us now." So there might easily not be a Field Day by next year?

"If a great new play emerged tomorrow, specially if it was a Northern play, we'd jump at it. Or else we might put out a magazine or do something completely different."

Nevertheless, Friel and Rea were exhausted and depleted at the end of their last tour, and also had very serious money problems. They have now acquired a business manager, Noel McKenna, to take care of that end, and they rejoice in grants from both Northern and Southern Arts Councils as well as help from Derry's city fathers. They find nothing sullying about the promotional end. They have also expanded Field Day's board to include poets Seamus Heaney, Seamus Deane and Tom Paulin and the BBC producer Davy Hammond. Friel says he is quite unmoved, both by the spectacular acclaim for *Translations* at the National Theatre, and by the euphoria that greeted its first night last year in Derry.

"I'm too old for euphoria, and the spectacle of first nights in particular. They belong to Broadway. Euphoria on first nights makes me wonder what's wrong with the play."

Of course *Translations* was an easy, accessible, lovable sort of play. "It's deliberately very traditional with three acts and a rural setting. I think that as Stephen and I put it before, we are talking to ourselves really, and if America and England overhear us, that's us delighted."

Translations swung instantly into warmth and heat, as Friel puts it, talking to himself—"but not in a narrow Sinn Fein way"—he was surprised at the breadth of its reception. Whereas the more austere, less playlike *Faith Healer* had a more hazardous, tumultuous career and a bad reception. You feel, Friel says, as you do about a sickly child, for a panned play.

"But as Guthrie said, a playwright only survives as a body of work. Now the thing is this one. Your children grow up and leave home after their run; the newborn babe-in-arms is the one you concentrate all your love upon."

I asked about his lifelong love with Chekhov, so evident in the echoes of *Aristocrats. Why* must he be rewritten for us?

"It's a work of love. The first purpose in doing *Three Sisters* like this is because for a group of Irish actors, only American or English texts are available. If it's an English text of a Russian scenario, there's a double assumption there. I felt we should be able to short-circuit this double suspension so that they can assume a language that can simply flow out of them.

"Of course Fen is perfect for England, but if you do use that one you must get your actors to assume English accents because it's English music. As English as Elgar. The officers say 'Jolly good. Wasn't it splendid.'"

Wasn't that explanation going to sound, perhaps, exaggerated and caused simply by nationalistic sentiment?

Friel said he would have to be careful of that. It was a risk. "But there's the other thing, that the received method of playing Chekhov is just to take up a stance on the downstage right or left, stare into the middle distance and talk desultorily about philosophical questions. Whereas there should be a great reality, about the acting as well as about the words. Again there's a calculated risk about tackling it a new way.

"It's all a question of music. The audience will hear a different music to anything they've heard in Chekhov before."

Had Friel resorted to a literal translation of the actual Russian text? No, he simply sat down at his desk with six English versions in front of him. But on one occasion, in particular, he did when he wasn't sure what to do about the soldier bringing in a samovar as a gift to the sisters, when samovars are normally given only to long-married matrons. So why should everyone be shocked if you don't happen to know samovars aren't given to girls? Friel wanted to be both "absolutely faithful", and true to naturalism.

"In the end I just funked it. I put: 'Oh my God, look what he's done.

Samovars are only given to old maids', which made it different again. The ideal condition would be to have a playwright who was fluent in Russian. But if you have to forego the one, I think it's better for the translator to be a dramatist. There are bigger truths beyond that of the literal translation."

Friel Takes Derry by Storm

Ulick O'Connor / 1981

Despite its headline, Ulick O'Connor's article appeared before *Three Sisters* had opened. Talking during rehearsals, Friel explains why he wanted to do Chekhov in an Irish idiom. Elsewhere Friel said he had heard of "a director who told Irish actors to pretend that they were English in order to get the accents right when they started working on a Chekhov play." Such practices emphasized the need for what Friel termed the "decolonisation process of the imagination." Talking to O'Connor, Friel goes into greater detail than elsewhere about the uniqueness of Derry's past and speculates about Derry playing a vital role in the redefinition of the entire island.

For more than half a century the Guildhall in Derry has been a symbol of imperialism. As you go up the carved wood staircase there are busts of Queen Victoria, Edward VII and George V lining the walls. Massive stained-glass windows proclaim the victories of King William III, or the association of Derry Burghers with Worshipful London Guilds.

The names of the original councillors engraved on the wall tell their own story, Babinton, Turner, Pollock, Hasting, Cooke. You almost expect to hear Elgar's "Pomp & Circumstance" intoned in the background.

What you do actually hear is "My Lagan Love" being picked out on a piano by actor Jimmy Lynch of "Z Cars" fame. He is one of the cast, along with Eamon Kelly, Olwen Fouere, Eileen Pollock, Sorcha Cusack, taking part in Brian Friel's new translation of Chekhov's *Three Sisters* presented by Field Day which opens next Tuesday.

This group, founded by Brian Friel and Stephen Rea, have tem-

From the *Sunday Tribune* (Dublin), 6 September 1981, p. 2.

porarily taken over what was once Derry's Loyalist emporium. In the vast Assembly Hall, which once resounded to the shouts of Orange rhetoric, you can hear now hammering and the sound of saws as a set is being constructed. The other rooms are occupied by costume-makers, stage-managers, designers.

In one of them I met Brian Friel. He is 51, lean like a whippet and has alert chestnut-coloured eyes that dart about as if they were determined to miss nothing.

"For a long time the people were on the outside looking in, now we're on the inside looking out," is how he puts it.

For six months he and Stephen Rea have cast and organised this enormous venture with help from the Northern Ireland Arts Council. Their actors are from all parts of Ireland, North and South, with different backgrounds, and represent the blend which Brian thinks should be part of the new Ireland.

"I wrote this play in an Irish idiom because with English translations Irish actors become more and more remote. They have to pretend, first of all, that they're English and then that they're Russians. I'd like our audience to see Captains and Lieutenants who look as if they came from Finner or Tullamore. The decolonisation process of the imagination is very important if a new Irish personality is to emerge."

Brian hasn't written anything for a year because of his preoccupation with Field Day. I asked him was it worth it.

"Well, I believe in a spiritual energy deriving from Derry which could be a reviving breath throughout the North. I think there is more creative energy here than anywhere else. Derry doesn't look to either Belfast or Dublin, but to itself, that's why I want to work here—piety perhaps."

Why should Derry be different from other parts of the North?

"For one thing they were a dispossessed people living in a state they never subscribed to, with Donegal lying just across the bay. Janus-like they had one head looking to the North and one looking to the South. Now, however, the dispossessed are coming into their own and if this island is to be redefined the essence of redefinition could come from here."

Not only is Brian Friel Ireland's greatest living playwright but he is one of the few writers who has come out firmly in favour of a united Ireland. He didn't relish growing up under partition.

Freedom of the City, which is about the occupation of the Guildhall where Brian is now conducting rehearsals, has overtones of Bloody Sunday when the British Army shot 13 civilians. It is the only major creative work to come out of the Northern Ireland troubles; it failed predictably in London, sold out in Chicago and would have been a sell-out in New York if the critics of the leading paper, the *New York Times* had not slain the play in a few sentences. *Translations* which was the first production of Field Day at the Guildhall has taken London by storm and is now in the repertory of the English National Theatre.

"I am amazed by this," Brian says. "I never thought that a play set in a Gaeltacht in 1833 could have evoked the response it has in London." He wrote the play, he says, "to tell us more about ourselves, to assist in the process of self-discovery in our people."

An Irishman's Diary: Play's Logic

Niall Kiely / 1981

Friel had already gone on record as saying that one of the
ironies of *Translations* was that the play should have been written in Irish. Such a play would, of course, have been inaccessible to English-speaking theater audiences. But what about an
audience that did not need translations for either the Irish or
the English of *Translations?* A proposal for a bilingual production for a bilingual audience prompted the translator of *Three
Sisters*—then playing in Belfast before embarking on a series of
one-night stands around the North—to respond with an unam-
biguous "Nyet."

Colm O Torna, of Comhalachas Naisiunta Dramaiochta, could not really
explain why playwright Brian Friel didn't want Aisteoiri na Tire to use a
bilingual translation of *Translations,* which makes its debut in the First
National Language next Saturday at the Taibhdhearc in Galway. (Thereafter *Aistriúcháin,* the translation by Maynooth's Professor Brendan
Devlin, a Co. Tyrone man with a feel for the play itself, will play weekends
at venues around the country.)

Readers who haven't seen or read quite a bit about *Translations* may
skip the next esoteric bit, but the problem will fascinate anyone interested in the theatre. Friel, you may remember, employed an astonish-
ingly effective theatrical convention in that all the actors spoke English
but the natives were understood by the audience to be speaking in Irish,
with the English characters using their own language, resulting in much
mystification, misunderstanding and some splendid comic effects.

"It works quite well in Irish, too," O Torna allowed. "But I would

From *The Irish Times,* 17 September 1981, p. 9.

have thought the jokes would have been even more obvious using both languages especially as Aisteoiri will be performing to audiences who understand both. Art O Briain was in favour of both. Tomas Mac Anna suggested we try it both ways, experiment, but the author may think it is an intrinsic part of his play."

Friel himself, back in his Co. Donegal home after a Derry hospital visit to Davy Hammond (in Altnagelvin for tests but since in the pink of health) told the Diary that he felt only an all-English or all-Irish form would suffice. "Translating it into any language, you'd have the same problem. I think you'd have to invent a different theatrical conceit if you did away with it. Otherwise, it doesn't make sense in a way; the conceit is part of the strange logic of the play."

Rehearsing Friel's New Farce

Ray Comiskey / 1982

Since Friel had insisted from the outset that he wanted Field
Day to remain transient aesthetically as well as literally, to be
independent, it was perhaps to be expected that he would want
to do the unexpected. *The Communication Cord,* the next play
Friel wrote after *Translations,* was a farcical send-up of some of
the issues treated much more seriously in *Translations.* Julie
Barber of Field Day said Friel wrote *The Communication Cord*
mainly because the critics took *Translations* too seriously:
"While Brian was pleased with the success of *Translations* he felt
the critics treated it with far too much reverence." His penchant for the unexpected extended even to his response to
applause on opening night. Although his curtain speech at the
conclusion of *Translations* two years earlier was acclaimed as "a
miracle of emotional brevity," Friel trumped his own performance at the curtain call for *The Communication Cord.* With both
cast and audience joining in prolonged cries of "Author,
author" as they awaited his entrance through a door downstage
left, Friel "entered from a door upstage centre, bowed in the
confusion, and uttered not a word." One of the last lines of his
farce about confusion in communication had been "maybe
silence is the perfect discourse." According to David Nowlan of
The Irish Times, "Friel had, in just ten seconds, re-enacted his
whole drama." Talking to Ray Comiskey in Derry during the
final week of rehearsals, Friel discusses the serious implications
of farce and the thematic implications of *The Communication
Cord.* He points to similarities between that farce and *Transla-*

From *The Irish Times,* 14 September 1982, p. 8.

tions and indicates the way the goals of Field Day were continuing to evolve.

The visitor to Derry's Guildhall has to pass under the disapproving gaze of Queen Victoria, whose statue stands in the main hall, facing the grand staircase. She rests, plain and voluminous, a reminder of one tradition, while in the magnificent chamber upstairs the architectural expression of that tradition unites the strands which once bound it together. The high-ceilinged, wood-panelled space is all curlicues and soaring stained glass, presided over by the great organ whose pipes stand at one end like a row of reproving major-domos. A mixture of power, commerce and the ecclesiastical, the atmosphere is charged with dour burgomaster solidity, no doubt reassuring to those who come from the tradition it so splendidly represents.

Next week it will be host to a new play by a man from a rather different cultural lineage. Brian Friel's latest work, a farce called *The Communication Cord* which deals with the problem of language and communication, will receive its world premiere there. But if Friel's background is quite different from what the Guildhall stands for, his play is part of his own efforts and those of the theatre company he founded with Stephen Rea, Field Day, to focus attention on aspects of the various tradition here today and likely to be changed, but not gone, tomorrow.

In its underlying linguistic concerns the new work has some common ground with the playwright's earlier *Translations,* and it fits in with the emerging interests of Field Day. So how did the company come about? "It hadn't any formal beginnings," said Brian Friel, "in that Stephen and I sat down and said 'now what we must do for the next three or five years is this, and we must attempt it in this kind of way.' It began more casually, where a group of people with a kind of intuitive understanding of various things found themselves coming together on the enterprise."

He explained: "We think of ourselves as Derry-based, northern-focussed, but absolutely in terms of the whole island. The Derry base is important because in some way Derry is an important psychic town on this island. The northern focus is very important because—and what I'm doing now is articulating things that we didn't begin with but which emerged with the practice—both Stephen and I feel, maybe in some kind of silly way, that the North is going to be one of the determining features of the future of this island." In practical terms, he said, it means rehearsing and opening in Derry, having round the enterprise a predominance of northern people, and touring "from Coleraine to Kerry", but always with the one constant, which is the theatre.

Would the North's likely influence on the future be due to the old moulds being questioned more there than in the South? "Yes, I think they are. Field Day is not about changing the North—I hate using grandiose terms like this—but in some way the very fact that it's located in the North and has its reservations about it, and that it works in the South and has its reservations about it, it's like, as somebody said, an artistic fifth province.

"We're not," he added, "talking in precise political terms at all. We're talking about some kind of awareness, some kind of sense of the country, what is this island about, north and south, and what are our attitudes to it. Leaving aside the Chekov, the first play we did, *Translations*, was about how this country found a certain shape. This farce is another look at the shape this country is in now. There's a strong element of satire in it, so we're talking about, not political realities, but perhaps, insofar as any theatre can affect anything, some kind of minute little adjusting attitudes."

About cultural realities as they affect a personal sense of identity? "Yes."

In his mild-mannered way he acknowledged the difficulty of avoiding pretentious language when dealing with a subject like this. "You find yourself saying extreme things that you need to qualify immediately." Somebody said he was sick of the term, national identity, and what the hell does it mean? "It means something very important, because it's your national ID in some way, isn't it?"

How does this farce, his first venture into the form for which, he said, he had no models, fit into this picture? "Well, a farce is a very serious enterprise. It's supposed to entertain and be very funny, and if it isn't it has failed as a farce." He paused and laughed. "You say that and get it out of the way. But then, I think that it's a perfectly valid way of looking at people in Ireland today, that our situation has become so absurd and so"—he searched for the right word—"crass that it seems to me it might be a valid way to talk and write about it."

What are the attractions of satire in this? "There's always a strong satirical element in farce. It's not subtle like you get in comedy. It's very broad and in farce it's simply the satire that says man is an unthinking animal, he has no intelligence and he acts intuitively and instinctively, and he doesn't know why he does it; so if something happens he just responds to it in the same way."

With this it goes back to the question of communication in *The Communication Cord?*

"It does. It's an extension of that. In other words, what function does language have then. In the case of *Translations* we were talking about the function of a fractured language, an acquired language and a lost language. In this case it's saying—I don't want to go back to the grandiose language—but it's saying, again, that perhaps communication isn't possible at all."

Communication in the sense in which it's spoken about in this play?

"Right. One of the lines in the play is 'perhaps silence is the perfect discourse'." He shrugged and said: "Maybe."

The very act of creating the play is, in itself, a denial of that line. Behind the hall in which it will be performed, in a big, echoing room overlooking the Foyle, the cast of eight were rehearsing under the eye of the director, Joe Dowling. It's an often tedious business, doing things over and over, getting lines, interpretation, positions, actions and—particularly in farce—the timing right to make it work. During a break the director spoke about handling farce, and its nature.

"There's an awful lot of nonsense talked about farce," he said. "People assume there's some special technique, which is not true at all. Because a farce really is just heightened comedy, by pace or whatever. But it's got to be real, absolutely disbelieving. A lot of what in recent years has come to be known as farce, like the Brian Rix farces, starts from such an utterly unreal basis that they lose impact quickly. It becomes a burlesque. But a Feydeau farce, or this farce, or Leonard's use of farce, each of these has been based on reality, and you work from that."

Is it a question of types and of making them believable?

"I think it is, but there's more than that in them, though, in some of the characters. It's a question of the actors finding that little bit more. You've got the academic, the senator, the peasant in this, but it's a question of mining it away so you've got more and more character and less and less type."

"One could say they're types because they fit into particular categories, but Friel's skill as a writer is that he never leaves it at that. He always has some twist to the character."

This is the final week of rehearsals, known as the technical. The cast will have moved into the great hall to work on the actual stage, getting accustomed to the set and props, the doors and stairs of the restored traditional cottage in which the action takes place; and at the week's end the lighting has to be worked in.

"That'll be just hell," said Joe Dowling. "The last week of rehearsal always is."

Then comes the premiere next Tuesday, after which it moves to Belfast's Opera House on September 27th, followed by a tour of the north and south, finally reaching Dublin at the Gaiety on November 1st and winding up with a week at the Everyman in Cork. But the fact that it will not be a part of the Dublin Theatre Festival has led to all sorts of rumours down here, so the question was put to Brian Friel to answer himself.

"There's absolutely nothing sinister about it," he said. "We were invited to the Festival and we considered at one stage that we might go. We would have liked to go because we got a very generous offer from the Dublin Theatre Festival which would have solved all the financial problems for us this year, but it was simpler for us to stick to the tour we had outlined. That's really all there was to it. We will go to Dublin when the time comes."

Finance, in fact, remains a perennial problem for Field Day. About two-thirds comes from the Arts Council in Belfast, with the bulk of the remainder coming from its counterpart in Dublin, not to mention some "modest amounts" from the Northern Ireland Tourist Board, Irish Shell and subscriptions from programme advertisers. It hangs over plans now being explored to tour America with the new farce and *Translations*, and it means a "hand-to-mouth" existence for the company.

"Arts councils of their nature never give you all the money you need," said Brian Friel, "and that's fair enough. There's always a gap between what they give and what you require. Of course, I worry endlessly about it, but in the long term I don't really worry all that much, because I think we'll survive as long as we need to survive."

As long as the will is there?

"Right. If we were getting a million dollars tonight it would be great for this year. But we're not looking to an endless future. That's what I'm really saying."

The Man from God Knows Where

Fintan O'Toole / 1982

The six directors of Field Day were all natives of Northern Ireland. But at the time Field Day was formed, only one of the six still lived there. Friel's suggestion that Field Day arose from a sense of rootlessness or impermanence—that the very place where one is at home is also a place where exile or disinheritance is imposed—has ironic echoes in the lives of all the directors. Fintan O'Toole talked to Friel at his home in Muff, across the border from Derry where Friel had grown up. A 1981 interview with Friel had appeared in the *Belfast Telegraph* under the headline: "The Man from Muff." But even as he talked with O'Toole, Friel was preparing to move once again—this time to an older, smaller house twenty miles further into Co. Donegal. Besides talking about his sense of exile, Friel expresses the hope that Field Day might help reclaim a sense of inheritance. He also discusses issues involving language, saying *The Communication Cord* seeks to disrupt categorization of his work, and talks about *Faith Healer* as presenting a metaphor for the craft of writing. O'Toole's interview appeared just before the Field Day production of *The Communication Cord* opened at the Gaiety Theatre in Dublin for a one-week run.

The first thing I wanted to ask you was about the sense of place in your work and the fact that so many of your characters seem to lack a sense of place, to be dislocated. Does that have any parallel in your own life?

That's a real academic's question, isn't it? I'll try to answer it. Are we talking now, we are? Seamus Deane has written a number of essays on

---

From *In Dublin*, no. 165 (28 October 1982), pp. 20–23.

me, and that's one of his persistent points, that I'm some sort of displaced person, you know? If there are parallels in my own life I don't know. There is certainly a sense of rootlessness and impermanence. It may well be the inheritance of being a member of the Northern minority. That could be one of the reasons, where you are certainly at home but in some sense exile is imposed on you. That may be a reason, I mean I'm groping at answers to this. In some kind of a way I think Field Day has grown out of that sense of impermanence, of people who feel themselves native to a province or certainly to an island but in some way feel that a disinheritance is offered to them.

Is Field Day then an attempt to re-claim that inheritance?

Yeah, but the difficulty is what to re-claim. You can't deposit fealty to a situation like the Northern situation that you don't believe in. Then you look south of the border and that enterprise is in so many ways distasteful. And yet both places are your home, so you are an exile in your home in some kind of sense. It may be an inheritance from a political situation, I think it may very well be and I think the people that are gathered around Field Day—there are six of them—I don't want to speak for the other five, but I think this could be a common sense to all of them. Someone has suggested, maybe it was Paulin suggested, that it's a kind of an attempt to create a fifth province to which artistic and cultural loyalty can be offered.

There's also a close sense of family in your plays and of the kind of bonds that the family imposes on the individual.

Maybe it's part of the same thing again, that there's some kind of instinctive sense of home being central to the life and yet at the same time home being a place of great stress and great alienation. I'm not really very good at this kind of question, Fintan, because the question's a kind of abstract based on a body of work, isn't it, and I sort of look from enterprise to enterprise, from job to job, you know what I mean? So it's really a kind of an academic's question, isn't it?

So do you never look back on your work and attempt to pick things out?

No, not at all. Only when you find, for example, that categories are being imposed on you, for example after three plays in particular—after *Faith Healer,* which was kind of an austere enterprise, *Translations,* which was offered pieties that I didn't intend for it, and then *Three Sisters* and in some way I felt I'm being corralled into something here. By other people. And this was one of the reasons I wanted to attempt a farce.

Were you consciously attempting an antidote to Translations *when you were writing* The Communication Cord*?*

Oh, yes. Well, consciously at two levels. Firstly for Field Day, because

I felt it would be appropriate for Field Day to have something like that at this point but also from my own point of view, because I was being categorised in some sort of a way that I didn't feel easy about, and it seemed to me that a farce would disrupt that kind of categorising. There's risks involved in doing that sort of thing. I think it's a risky enterprise doing a farce. But I think it's worth it.

When you started off with The Communication Cord, *were you aware of trying to use the mechanisms of classical farce?*

Yes, it's something like a meccano set—you get on with various pieces of it and you put them all together. Maybe it's different from the usual farce in that the play itself was to some extent an attempt to illustrate a linguistic thesis. But apart from that it's just a regular farce, isn't it?

Yes, but it does also carry on a concern with language that has been evident in your work for the past five or six years. So it's a farce that is also, in one sense, to be taken very seriously.

It's a form to which very little respect is offered and it was important to do it for that reason, not to make it respectable, but to release me into what I bloody well wanted, to attempt it, to have a go at it.

Were you aware of almost being canonised after Translations?

Ach, not at all, ah no, that's very strong. But it was treated much too respectfully. You know, when you get notices especially from outside the island, saying 'If you want to know what happened in Cuba, if you want to know what happened in Chile, if you want to know what happened in Vietnam, read *Translations,*' that's nonsense. And I just can't accept that sort of pious rubbish.

I was wondering whether your concern with language, indeed with your profession as a playwright, stemmed from a re-examination of that profession. You said in 1972 that you were thinking of going back to writing short stories instead of plays.

Ah, I don't know. The whole language one is a very tricky one. The whole issue of language is a very problematic one for us all on this island. I had grandparents who were native Irish speakers and also two of the four grandparents were illiterate. It's very close, you know. I actually remember two of them. And to be so close to illiteracy and to a different language is a curious experience. And in some way I don't think we've resolved it. We haven't resolved it on this island for ourselves. We flirt with the English language, but we haven't absorbed it and we haven't regurgitated it in some kind of way. It's accepted outside the island, you see, as 'our great facility with the English language'—Tynan said we used it like drunken sailors, you know that kind of image—that's all oul rubbish. A language is much more profound than that. It's not something we produce for the entertainment of outsiders. And that's how Irish theatre is viewed indeed, isn't it?

It is very often. And isn't it the dilemma of the modern Irish playwright that to actually make a decent living out of writing plays you have to find an audience in Britain and the States, while the enterprise that you're involved in is more about trying to write primarily for an Irish audience?

Are you confusing an economic dilemma with an artistic dilemma? Is that what you're saying?

Well, doesn't the fact of having to make a living force certain conditions on you?

It doesn't, no. Not in the slightest. Because in the case of *Translations* I was really sure that this was the first enterprise that Field Day was going to do and I was sure we were in deep trouble with that play. We thought Field Day will never even get a lift-off because of this play, because here is a play set in 1833, set in a hedge school—you have to explain the terminology to people outside the island, indeed to people inside the island too, so I thought we were on a real financial loss here. But that is part of the enterprise, and this is one of the reasons why I attempted the translation of Chekhov. It's back to the political problem—it's our proximity to England, it's how we have been pigmented in our theatre with the English experience, with the English language, the use of the English language, the understanding of words, the whole cultural burden that every word in the English language carries is slightly different to our burden. Joyce talks in the *Portrait* of his resentment of the Jesuit priest because he 'possessed these words long before I possessed them'.

Did theatre come before short stories?

No, I wrote stories first. I know now why I stopped writing short stories. It was at the point when I recognised how difficult they were. It would have meant a whole re-appraisal. I mean, I was very much under the influence, as everyone at the time was, of O Faolain and O'Connor, particularly. O'Connor dominated our lives. I suppose they really were some kind of imitation of O'Connor's work. I'm just guessing at it, but I think at some point round about that period, the recognition of the difficulty of the thing, you know, that maybe there was the need for the discovery of a voice and that I was just echoing somebody else.

What was the effect for you of suddenly, with your fourth play, having a great success and productions in America and becoming at least for a time a famous playwright?

We'd need to be very careful about language. It [*Philadelphia, Here I*

Come!] was a very successful play, and it's a play that in some kind of way haunts you too—people say 'Oh yes, you're the man that wrote the play called *Philadelphia Story*, aren't you?'—so, famous and successful, I don't know.

Did you see it again when it was revived in the Abbey recently?

I did, yeah.

What was it like seeing it again?

I've really no interest in it at all. None whatsoever. I would go to a thing like that out of duty to the actors and to the theatre, but I've really no interest in the enterprise itself. I would feel minor irritations at the way things are written or expressed but no interest at all. Even things like *The Communication Cord*, which are still running, I have no interest in it really. It's finished and it is as it is, and I'm drawn on to the next enterprise.

You wrote in the sixties I suppose four plays which concentrated on different aspects of love—Philadelphia, The Loves of Cass McGuire, Lovers *and* Crystal and Fox. *You then stopped writing about love. Was it just that you had said all you wanted to say?*

I just don't know the answer to that. I don't think there's a point when you say 'I've nothing more to say about that' because I don't think you start from that premise and say I've got this to say about anything. You don't have anything to say about anything. You delve into a particular corner of yourself that's dark and uneasy, and you articulate the confusions and the unease of that particular period. When you do that, that's finished and you acquire other corners of unease and discontent. There are continuing obsessions, like the political thing is a continuing obsession, and I've written two or three demonstrably political plays. And I keep saying to myself I'm never going to write another political play because it's too transient and because I'm confused about it myself, but I know damn well and I'm sure I'll have another shot at it again sometime.

With The Freedom of the City, *which was obviously a very complex play, are you afraid that in certain circumstances an audience might take a very crude and a very blunt political message from it?*

That wouldn't worry me anyway. 'Have I sent out certain young men?'—that sort of thing wouldn't worry me at all. I think one of the problems with that play was that the experience of Bloody Sunday wasn't adequately distilled in me. I wrote it out of some kind of heat and some kind of immediate passion that I would want to have quieted a bit before I did it. It was really—do you remember that time?—it was a very emotive time. It was really a shattering experience that the British Army, this disciplined instrument, would go in as they did that time and shoot thirteen people. To be there on that occasion and—I didn't actually see people get shot—but I mean, to have to throw yourself on the ground because people are firing at you is a very terrifying experience. Then the whole cover-up afterwards was shattering too. We still have some kind of belief that the law is above reproach. We still believe that the academy is above reproach in some way, don't we?

Your active involvement in politics was in the sixties in the Nationalist Party.

Yeah, I was a member of the Nationalist Party for several years. I don't remember how long. Those were very dreary days because the Nationalist Party . . . it's hard to describe what it was. I suppose it held on to some kind of little faith, you know. It wasn't even sure what the faith was, and it was a very despised enterprise by everybody. We used to meet once a month wherever it was in a grotty wee room and there'd be four or five old men who'd sit there and mull over things. It was really hopeless.

Did you ever regret the fact that you moved to Donegal from Derry shortly before the troubles began?

I regretted it in many ways, yes. I think it was in '68, and the trouble began in '69 and we might have been better to be in there. Just to be part of the experience. Instead of driving into a civil rights march, coming out your front door and joining it might have been more real. It would have been less deliberate and less conscious than doing it from here.

Coming back to what I was asking you earlier about your recent plays, which seem largely concerned with your own craft, Faith Healer *was first staged in 1976 in New York. Was that a reflection of a concern with the power of the writer, with what you yourself do?*

I suppose it has to be. It was some kind of a metaphor for the art, the craft of writing, or whatever it is. And the great confusion we all have about it, those of us who are involved in it. How honourable and how dishonourable it can be. And it's also a pursuit that, of necessity, has to be very introspective, and as a consequence it leads to great selfishness. So that you're constantly, as I'm doing at this moment, saying something and listening to yourself saying it, and the third eye is constantly watching you. And it's a very dangerous thing because in some way it perverts whatever natural freedom you might have, and that natural freedom must find its expression in the written word. So there's an exploration of that—I mean the element of the charlatan that there is in all creative work.

And even more so in the theatre because even at a distance you're acting as a showman?

Yes. It's a very vulgar medium, in the Latin sense, and it's also vulgar I think too in the accepted sense. But I think it also has satisfactions that you wouldn't find as a novelist or as a poet. It's a very attractive enterprise to be involved in. You would find that even as a critic, because they're very attractive people. It's a very essential kind of life because it's giving everything to this one enterprise and once it's over then we go on to something else. It's essentially human in some way.

Of the six members of the Field Day Board only yourself and Stephen Rea are actively involved in theatre.

That's right. I think the important defining thing about them all is that they're all Northern people.

What is it about the South of Ireland that makes it impossible for you to give your loyalty to it?

Well of course I have loyalty to it, because in some way it's the old parent who is now beginning to ramble. In some way it could be adjusted and I think it could be made very exciting, I think. But I think it requires the Northern thing to complete it. I'm talking about the whole Northern thing.

You're saying then that there are certain qualities that are peculiar to Northerners and not found in the South?

Yes. I think the qualities are—I don't believe for one minute in Northern hardheadedness or any of that nonsense—but I think that if you have a sense of exile, that brings with it some kind of alertness and some kind of eagerness and some kind of hunger. And if you are in possession you can become maybe placid about some things. And I think those are the kind of qualities that maybe Field Day can express. Does this make any sense to you?

Yes it does. Do you think that that sense of exile gives you access as an artist to a more fundamental and widespread sense of alienation?

Yeah, but the contradiction in that is that we are trying to make a home. So that we aspire to a home condition in some way. We don't think that exile is practical. We think that exile is miserable in fact. And what's constantly being offered to us, particularly in the North, and this is one of the problems for us is that we are constantly being offered the English home, we have been educated by the English home and we have been pigmented by an English home. To a much greater extent than you have been. And the rejection of all that, and the rejection into what, is the big problem.

What is home for you? Is it a sense of a group of people with a common purpose? Is that in itself going to give you some sense of belonging?

I think now at this point it would, but once I would achieve it and once it would be acquired then I'd be off again.

There is in a way a contradiction for you, isn't there, because it seems necessary for you as a writer to have a sense of being on the outside, and yet you're striving with Field Day to transcend that?

I think there is some kind of, there is the possibility of a cultural whole available to us—w-h-o-l-e, we're living in the other one. How to achieve that and how to contribute to that is one of the big problems, and the problem is confused and compounded by the division of the island. It's also confused by our proximity to England. You can't possibly—and don't even want to—jettison the whole English experience, but how to pick and choose what is valuable for us and what is health-giving for us, how to keep us from being a GAA republic, it's a very delicate tiptoeing enterprise. I think the possibilities for your generation are better in some kind of way.

Doesn't the whole Field Day project then depend on political nationalism and on the achievement of a united Ireland?

I don't think it should be read in those terms. I think it should lead to a cultural state, not a political state. And I think out of that cultural state, a possibility of a political state follows. That is always the sequence. It's very grandiose this, and I want to make notice of abdication quickly, but I think they are serious issues and big issues, and they are issues that exercise us all, the six of us, very much. But you've also got to be very careful to retain some strong element of cynicism about the whole thing.

That presumably is very much part of The Communication Cord.

Oh that's part of it. I want it to be seen in tandem with *Translations*.

Doesn't the whole enterprise of Field Day though beg the question of the power of art to affect society? I mean theatre is by and large peripheral; it's just treated as another social event.

But it's got to succeed on that level. It's got to succeed on that level first. You can't suddenly say 'To hell with all those middle-class fur coat people'—fuck them out we want the great unwashed. You've got to take the material you have. There are other theatre groups who are into something else. If you're into agitprop or if you're into political theatre or if you're into street theatre—that's their enterprise. We're not into that kind of enterprise. I think what we're saying is: we'll go to the people who are there but we'll talk to them in a certain kind of way. You know, we're living with what we have. We're trying to talk to them in a different voice and we're trying to adjust them to our way of thinking.

Doesn't the health of the whole thing, though, need an audience which is capable of change? Do you believe that the current theatre audience which tends to be middle-class and to have certain expectations is capable of being adjusted in this way?

That's truer in Dublin than it is elsewhere, because there is a theatrical experience and a theatrical tradition in Dublin. There is no theatrical tradition in Belfast. There's very little anywhere else around the country. And this is in some kind of a way why it's nice and cosy to say you know we get such great response when we're doing the one-night stands, that's nice and easy. But in some way it's true on a different kind of level—that these people watch you very carefully. They watch you almost as if we were cattle being paraded around on a fair day. They watch us with that kind of cool assessment. And they're listening. I think they hear things in theatre because they haven't been indoctrinated in the way a metropolitan audience is. They hear different sounds in a play. They are great audiences in a different kind of way to a Dublin theatre audience. Going back to your question—you say you're speaking to the same people. We're not in fact speaking to the same people apart from Dublin. This is one of the reasons why—we're happy to go to Dublin and play for a week and the only reason we would go and play for four weeks would be to make money which would fund us then next time round. It's not a question at all of turning your back on the capital city but we're into something else I think.

The Communication Cord is probably the most formally conservative play you've done for a long time. How important is a sense of form to you? There are people who would say that for a writer to be focussing so strongly, as you are, on the tools of his own trade, on language, is in some way incestuous considering the urgency of so many things that need to be said.

Do you think it's a valid criticism?

I don't think so personally because I think the problem of language is a profoundly political one in itself.

Particularly politics on this island, where you listen to a cabinet minister from Dublin and he's speaking such a debased language that you wonder how in God's name can this man have anything to do with your life at all. I think that is how the political problem of this island is going to be solved. It's going to be solved by language in some kind of way. Not only the language of negotiations across the table. It's going to be solved by the recognition of what language means for us on this island. Whether we're speaking the kind of English that I would use, or whether we're using the kind of English that Enoch Powell would use. Because we are in fact talking about accommodation or marrying of two cultures here, which are ostensibly speaking the same language but which in fact aren't.

Your own work as a writer is very much bound up with that clash of cultures, and there's the old cliché about times of trouble leading to a flowering of literature. Do you ever feel that you're feeding off the suffering here?

We're looting the shop when it's burning, you mean? I mean this is often said, and it's said of all the Northern poets particularly. I don't know. The experience is there; it's available. We didn't create it, and it has coloured all our lives and adjusted all our stances in some way. What the hell can we do but look at it?

Brian Friel and Field Day

Radio Telefís Éireann / 1983

As with its two previous productions, Field Day had four weeks of rehearsal in Derry prior to the September 1982 opening of *The Communication Cord*, Friel's farcical take on some of the same issues involved in *Translations*. Unlike the two previous years, the cameras of Radio Telefís Éireann were on hand to film interviews as part of a documentary to be transmitted six months later. The RTÉ cameras stayed with the Field Day company after it went on tour throughout the North, including Friel's birthplace of Omagh. A year earlier, while *Three Sisters* was in rehearsal, Brian Friel and Stephen Rea had asked four others to join them as directors of Field Day. Although the RTÉ documentary included interviews with all six Field Day directors—Friel, Rea, poet Seamus Heaney, poet and scholar Seamus Deane, poet Tom Paulin, and broadcaster David Hammond—the focus was clearly on Friel, who was interviewed multiple times in a variety of settings. The extended conversations not only explored Friel's assessment of *Translations* and *The Communication Cord* but also afforded him opportunities to look back on his career and ahead to the future of Field Day. Indeed, the documentary allowed all six directors to reflect on their own visions for Field Day. It also showed, however, that Friel was already sensing a conflict between the need to protect himself as a writer and the encroaching demands on his time of the enterprise he had founded.

Transmitted on Radio Telefís Éireann, 14 February 1983. The documentary report, with a script by Seamus Deane narrated by T. P. McKenna, was produced by Seán Ó Mórdha, and included interviews with the six directors of Field Day: Brian Friel, Seamus Heaney, Seamus Deane, David Hammond, Stephen Rea, and Tom Paulin.

NARRATOR: Brian Friel watches a rehearsal of a scene from his new play, *The Communication Cord.*

[Extract from rehearsal.]

NARRATOR: He doesn't revise the script during rehearsal. That remains fixed. The cast learns to discover the finality of its shape and cadences.

[Extract from Friel commenting during rehearsal.]

STEPHEN REA: If you look at Brian's plays, there's an extraordinary freshness of subject matter, for a start. And just everything about the play—each new play—is different and unexpected. I mean you could never predict what he's going to write *next* time. Having seen *Translations,* you *couldn't* have predicted *Communication Cord,* you know, a farce and all that kind of territory that he's dealing in.

[Extract from Friel commenting during rehearsal.]

NARRATOR: All this is taking place in the Guildhall in the city of Derry, an ornate pile of red Victorian Gothic backing onto the river, facing the city walls. The Guildhall was for sixty years the home of a gerrymandered Corporation. Its stained-glass windows commemorate historic moments in Unionism, in this instance the coronation of King George V. But now the Guildhall houses another kind of theatre.

BRIAN FRIEL: It's a problem because—the poet, it's a single imagination talking to another single imagination—in the case of the dramatist he has got to take five hundred people or a thousand people and forge them into one single, receiving imagination. And even then he's not even speaking directly to those people. He's speaking through the medium of actors and directors and designers. So that's always the big problem—it's an interpretative art. And in many respects it's a very vulgar art form. So that's the first big fear—that the piece isn't going to be interpreted as you heard it in your head originally.

INTERVIEWER: What do you expect or demand of a first production?

FRIEL: I don't think you bring those kind of imperatives to it. I think in some kind of way immediately before rehearsals begin you have got some kind of ideal sound in your head of what the play is like. Then as rehearsals go on it acquires the authenticity that those particular actors *bring* to it. And then the problem always is that after a first production, those become the definitive sounds of the play. So even though there are subsequent productions and maybe better productions, in some way the defining sounds have been fashioned and forged by the first production.

INTERVIEWER: You, I think, have surprised Field Day, and I think you're going to surprise your public. You're following *Translations* with a farce, a full-length farce.

FRIEL: Yes, I think that, of course, on the kind of easy level that's a kind of a strange and maybe slightly dangerous thing to do. But a farce is a very serious business, I think; a farce is a very stern look at how man behaves because it says that perhaps if we've looked at man as a rational and thinking and sensitive animal, this time we say man is also a different kind of animal. He's an unthinking, amoral mixture of innocence and roguery, and that's a perfectly valid way of looking at people, I think.

[External scene of Friel in a car; followed by shots of posters.]

NARRATOR: Brian Friel passes through a checkpoint at the border. He sees the banners and placards go up to announce the new production. Everything here—geography, architecture, roads—smacks of politics, of difference and division. But on this occasion there is a widely shared anticipation. The publicity enhances a communal sense. Yet this play and most of the others by Brian Friel are studies in broken communities—failures in sharing, and shared failures.

FRIEL: I think there's certainly that theme, apparently. I'm not really very conscious of this, but when it's pointed out to me I've got to accept that it *is* there, that this whole business of failures in communication and even in the term *the communication cord,* I think, suggests some kind of alarm and disaster. I think those elements are there in the other plays. I think there's another element that people don't look at, and I think it's a projection of some kind of dual personality in a lot of the plays. In other words, in a lot of the plays—I discover this now in looking back over the bulk of the work—that there are very often two characters: one who is a very extrovert, quick-talking, glib character and another who's a kind of morose and taciturn and . . . less immodest, let's say. And in some way I think perhaps those reflect some aspect of myself and perhaps some aspect of a member of the minority living in the North.

[Scene of Friel, Heaney and audience members entering the Guildhall.]

NARRATOR: On the opening night, however, everybody comes. It's not an occasion exclusively for the minority or for any group. These people all live in or come from or are coming to a city renowned both for its bitterness and for its warmth. It's small enough and tightly bound enough for the most intimate of enmities and friendship. All sides have their codes—of dress and address, of accent, of gesture. A great deal of this is subdued in the ecumenical limelight of this opening moment. But the conversation is nevertheless self-conscious, both off stage and on.

[Extract from *The Communication Cord:*

> JACK: But your thesis is nearly finished, isn't it?
> TIM: I don't know. Maybe.
> JACK: What's it on again?
> TIM: Talk.
> JACK: What about?
> TIM: That's what the thesis is about—talk, conversation, chat.
> JACK: Ah.
> TIM: Discourse Analysis with Particular Reference to Response Cries.
> JACK: You're writing your thesis on what we're doing now?
> TIM: It's fascinating, you know. Are you aware of what we're doing now?
> JACK: We're chatting, aren't we?
> TIM: Exactly. But look at the process involved. You wish to know what my thesis is about and I wish to tell you. Information has to be imparted. A message has to be sent from me to you and you have to receive that message. How do we achieve that communication?
> JACK: You just tell me.
> TIM: Exactly. Words. Language. An agreed code. I encode my message; I transmit it to you; you receive the message and decode it. If the message sent is clear and distinct, if the code is fully shared and subscribed to, if the message is comprehensively received, then there is a reasonable chance—one, that you will understand what I'm trying to tell you—and two, that we will have established the beginnings of a dialogue. All social behaviour, the entire social order, depends on our communicational structures, upon words mutually agreed on and mutually understood. Without that agreement, without that shared code, you have chaos.]

[Shot of various newspaper reviews.]

NARRATOR: The first night is over. The reception given the play is warm, even enthusiastic. Friel has a success on his hands.

FRIEL: Graham Greene defined success as the postponement of failure. And I think that's very accurate. I think especially in, as I call it, this vulgar medium and this immediate medium that I'm involved in, that all you hope is that everything doesn't collapse on you. I don't think there's such a thing as success in theatre, and not with a particular play really.

INTERVIEWER: The audiences might disagree.

FRIEL: Fine, that's a kind of bonus. If audiences are there and are warm and responsive and generous and if there's a lot of them—that's a bonus. You get a quick satisfaction from it but it's not a sustaining satisfaction.

NARRATOR: Skepticism like this has deep roots. Born in 1929 in Omagh, brought up in Derry since he was ten, Brian Friel has the Border mentality. Its most conscious element is the experience of life in the North. Its hinterland, almost its subconscious, is Donegal, or the memory of it. His first play, appropriately called *This Doubtful Paradise*, appeared in 1959 after he had spent a decade teaching in Derry. There was nothing doubtful about the childhood paradise of a quiet town like Glenties, where he used to spend his summer holidays at his grandmother's home. The Ballybeg of his plays has at least some of its roots here. Glenties and the lonely landscapes of Lettermacaward or Dooey— these are the lost kingdoms of Friel's youth and of his imagination. A dream landscape, it concentrates the duality of Friel's existence—North and South; a silent present, an eloquent past; exile and ancestry. His close friend, the singer and broadcaster David Hammond, speaks of the original home.

DAVID HAMMOND: This is the townland of Dooey. It's about ten or twelve miles north of Glenties. This is the area, indeed the very spot, that Brian Friel's family left three generations ago to go and settle in Glenties town. Many of the images are still abundant in this countryside of those times. We have the whitewashed house, the thatch, the small fields, the stone walls, the donkey. There are all these images, romantic images, and Brian Friel has never used them in his plays.

NARRATOR: But in one short story, we do catch a glimpse of the Donegal of Friel's boyhood. And in it we sense the nourishment it provided for his mature imagination.

[Extract from a 1974 RTÉ dramatisation of "Mr. Sing My Heart's Delight" that shows a boy getting off of a bus and walking along a Donegal lane overlooking the ocean while a voice-over narration conflates and edits two paragraphs from Friel's story:

On the first day of every new year I made the forty-five-mile journey by train and bus and foot across County Donegal to my granny's house which sat at the top of a cliff above the raging Atlantic at the very end of the parish of Mullaghduff. Even on the best day in summer, Mullaghduff is a desolate place. The land is rocky, barren, uneven, covered by a brown heather that never blooms and hacked into a crazy jigsaw by hundreds of tiny rivulets no more than a foot wide which seemed to flow in as many different directions and yet cunningly avoid crossing one another. Granny's house lay at the most accessible end of this vast waste, three miles from the nearest road. This annual visit of mine, lasting from January until the nights began to shorten sometime in March, was made primarily for Granny's benefit: during those months Grandfather went across to Scotland to earn enough money to tide them over the rest of the year. But it suited me admirably too: I missed school for three months, I got away from strict parents and bothersome brothers and sisters, all younger than I, and in Granny's house I was cock-of-the-walk and everything I did was right.]

HAMMOND: Friel's family, his mother's family, have a reputation for being musical. It's still very strong, that reputation, in this countryside. And I can imagine in this house many a ballad and song was sung.

NARRATOR: And many's a dream was dreamed. Some of them were dreams of escape, like Gar O'Donnell's.

[Extract from *Philadelphia, Here I Come!*]

NARRATOR: With *Philadelphia, Here I Come!* in 1964, Friel had arrived. The divided mind of Gar epitomised not only his own but a whole community's plight, an antic disposition worn in a climate of tragedy.

FRIEL: Yes, I don't like taking one play out of the context of the general work and saying this was a more important play or a less important play to me. I don't think the work can be measured in that kind of way. I mean I prefer to look on it all as some kind of continuum. Of course, I was very fortunate with that play. And that had to do with, I suppose, some point of development in myself and the moment in which that play appeared; and there was a kind of happy confluence of those two things. But I don't feel that the play has any major significance for me.

NARRATOR: And of course it is true that *Philadelphia* is only one play in a rich context. The continuity and consistency of Friel's achievement are remarkable. With an unwavering focus and a sharpening technique, he has steadily incorporated into his plays an ever subtler examination of the public forces that mold the private life, the private forces that remold the public life. He writes with the energy and scruple of a man who seeks a correspondence between fact and value, and with the irony of one who regards the search as at once a necessary and a naive one.

SEAMUS HEANEY: I think since what we think of as the great days of the Abbey Theatre, since the days of Synge earlier and then O'Casey later, no Irish dramatist has achieved the authority that Friel has. Now I would make a distinction between authority and reputation or fame. Reputation, fame, are, you know, bandied about; they come and go, as fashion comes or goes and as reviewers dictate. But authority is to do with having both an inward command of your own themes and imagination, having of course a professional command of your medium; but that professionalism or that artistry and that inner certitude being related to the outer world that the artist is in. Now it seems to me Friel has both revealed the nature of Irish society to itself and has by his artistic experiments revealed his own growth to himself in the course of a large body of work. So I would place him at the centre.

[External view of Derry.]

NARRATOR: The centre is Derry, the border town in a beautiful setting of river and hill, the half-ruined site of a terrible and intractable conflict. Nothing betokens insecurity more than the security forces, especially in this city. They patrol within the walled centre, around The Diamond's War Memorial. But Derry because of its position as a border town has always had a certain extramural dimension, a sense of place not walled in by stone or boundaries.

TOM PAULIN: I've never thought of it in terms of a fifth province, though I always feel coming to Derry that it's a city that's right on the dangerous edge of things in Ireland, that it is different from any other city in Ireland, that it's neither in one state nor in the other. So perhaps in that sense we are outside.

[Archive footage from Sunday, 30 January 1972, of troops firing on civilians.]

NARRATOR: In one infamous afternoon the Northern crisis came to a head in Derry. The first victims fell at Free Derry corner. The state struck to put an end to a trouble that it had begun. An official slaughter followed by an official whitewash changed everything. Derry after January 1972 underwent a psychic recession from both North and South. It learned, like Belfast and the other towns and villages, to be schooled in violence.

SEAMUS DEANE: I think especially since about '72, which was the bloodiest year and which was the year that made it emphatically clear to everybody that whether we like it or no—no matter what other kinds of sermons are delivered—that the fact of violence, and the relationship between violence and political breakdown, and the relationship between those two things and the creation of anything is one that we have to endure and live with and learn in some ways to be creative with.

[Excerpt from rehearsal of *The Communication Cord*.]

NARRATOR: Inevitably the violence challenged the artist with his rage for order. Friel's work registered the impact. Yet the violence brought in its wake another more pervasive threat—indifference, apathy. The result was an even deeper disillusion, a more deathly exhaustion.

HEANEY: I'd put it this way: I think that there is something exhausted in the country at the minute. I think there's also a sense of a change—the relationship with the British thing. While politically there are still maintenances going on, there is in some deep place in the Unionist psyche, in the Northern Catholic Nationalist psyche, and in the psyche in the Republic—some deep place that knows—a sense of an ending.

NARRATOR: Out of convictions and circumstances like these, Field Day emerged. It was the brainchild of Brian Friel and of Stephen Rea. It had a specific aim. It wanted to turn blinded and stifled energies towards light and release. It wanted to reassemble, re-collect, and recollect all the shaken imageries of the country's imagination. It was a faintly immodest ambition, but that hardly mattered.

REA: You know on its most basic kind of level it's talking about doing plays about the Irish people as absolutely well as you can do them and showing them to the Irish people; that's really at its fundamental level. On a broader basis than that, of course, you can say: giving some kind of a voice to some energy that's in this country, which is unexpressed because politics are moribund at the moment, and because Irish people have no particular focus, I don't think, that's creative. I think that we can provide that focus. I mean that's very grandiose in a way. I think Yeats provided it at a particular time of political stagnation in the country. I think he provided that focus. And I think—I'm afraid I think we could provide it too, you know.

NARRATOR: A broadcaster, an actor, a playwright, and three poets. Three from a Protestant, three from a Catholic background. Seamus

Deane, Stephen Rea, David Hammond, Seamus Heaney, Tom Paulin, Brian Friel—these are the directors of Field Day. They begin imagining for themselves and for others a world elsewhere, a fifth province.

FRIEL: It's a nice idea, a fifth column or a fifth province. There probably is an element, yes, there is an element of that in it. There is something slightly underground about it and there certainly is something grapevinish about it, because we aren't sure what we're attempting and what we're doing but we're absolutely certain about the intuitions that have brought us together.

DEANE: I think all six feel that the discourse has been determined for them by the social and political circumstances, not only those by which we were formed but those which in very recent years have in some ways transformed us. I refer, of course, to the so-called Northern Troubles. But the sense that these Troubles have created, oddly enough, a deeper apathy than that from which they initially arose and *that* sense—there's a mystery there. There's also some kind of terrible loss involved there. And it's out of that sense of loss—to investigate in what that loss consists—that the discourse has arisen.

[External view of traffic signs.]

NARRATOR: At Ballygalley roundabout all the signs point North. But other signs point towards the end of a long road, towards a void. John Montague, a native of this area, once wrote, "A civilization died here" and now, once again . . .

PAULIN: Well, I think it's the idea that most people in England certainly are fed up with what's happening in the North of Ireland and now want to pull the Army out. And most people, I would have thought, in the North of Ireland realise that the British government wants to get out of the North of Ireland. I think some of us feel that we have to make some kind of affirmation, some sort of cultural statement now to fill the void that is going to come very soon.

NARRATOR: The chief icon of the North is the war memorial—garrison and siege, bitter defiance, noble sacrifice. Long memories are made of this. Violence dominates the past as well as the present. Energy is petrified into the heroic or the grieving gesture. This is a land of slogans embodied in statues: "What we have we hold"; "No surrender"; "Not an inch". Everything bespeaks the garrisoned, the military mentality.

DEANE: I think one—in a way sad but in another way telling—fact about the North is that of all the movements it has had, it has never yet had a cultural or a literary movement. All of the writers or artists we have had have tended to migrate south or to England or to the Continent. I think in a way that—though this is merely hazarding a guess—if Field Day is to pick up any audience it's going to pick up that audience that at one time gave its fidelities to political commitment ten years, fifteen years ago, and now feels that politics is going to change nothing, in fact politics is only going to make everything worse, as it has done.

NARRATOR: In such unrewarding climate, poetry seems a peripheral activity. So how do the poets in Field Day—Heaney, Deane, and Paulin— contribute?

FRIEL: I think the poets are essential to it. We have three of them in the directorate. They're essential because in some way the poetic voice is the purest artistic voice. It's not diluted by audiences or by theatre tickets or by sale of paperbacks or that sort of nonsense. So that in some way they ought to keep us pure.

HEANEY: Brian is, of course, the only begetter in a way of the thing— Brian and, it should be said, Stephen Rea. And this is an important, I think, aspect of it: that the actor and the writer are together; now *they* together moved the thing to produce *Translations*. But there is a moment in *Translations* which, I think, relates to the poet thing. There's a character in that play, *Translations,* who cannot speak and she is being rehearsed by the son of the schoolteacher, Manus. And the play begins with Manus having coached her to the point where she can say "My name is Sarah". Through events that happen in the play, including the arrival of the British soldiery, the girl is *stunned* in a way and at the end she can't speak her name. Now I think one of the functions of the poetic imagination within any given reality or group or country is in some way to speak the name—the name of things as they are at the moment—to speak that reality. And I think Brian's welcome for the poet is really a solidarity with that idea, that that is the function of the poet and, secondly, that the function of Field Day is a poetic function.

NARRATOR: With *Translations,* the first Field Day production, the group found a focus and a voice. It was a clear focus but an ambiguous voice. Chance had designed the perfect image for the group.

REA: The significance of *Translations,* of course, is huge. Who knows why Brian picked that subject to write about at a moment when we picked to do this enterprise? When the play became the enterprise and the enterprise was the play, I mean that was just, we were kind of jamming in a way that way, I think. I've said that to Brian and he said, well, that's the bit of luck that you deserve because of the craziness of doing the thing in the first place.

NARRATOR: So there it was, a play tensed across a linguistic and cultural divide, set in the past, remembering the future, two languages and two cultures at odds but intimate.

[Excerpt from *Translations* of the love scene between George and Maire, who do not understand each other's language.]

HEANEY: There is no doubt about it that the moment when Field Day initiated itself and spread its wings a little, that is after *Translations,* the actual sense of occasion—the sense of a current of energy running, the sense of people *dis*covering something that was covered in them, again—was almost palpable.

[External scene of pedestrians.]

NARRATOR: It is painful to contemplate the North's dilapidation. On top of the political crisis, there has come an economic blight so severe that it has reached far beyond the minority ghettoes and towns which have never known anything else. Posters and slogans, warnings and notices, bomb zones, no-parking areas—the still moments of a dolorous afternoon in a dark season. There is an infinite weariness in the atmosphere of this provincial town. Is this any different, really, from its counterparts in the South? Commerce is much the same anywhere. But the North has always insisted on its difference, even in that.

PAULIN: There is certainly, I mean I suppose there's always been this gap between North and South; there's a traditional hostility that goes back at least 200 years. You can even see it in remarks of the United Irishmen towards people in Dublin, even though they were then fighting for a united Ireland. And, of course, now—though I think many people from the North are skeptical about certain things in the Republic—*still* it is finally a better state than what exists in Northern Ireland. It has elections; it is democratic. There are all sorts of things that need change there, but we feel it'll only be changed when the imaginative force of Northern culture is reattached to Southern culture.

NARRATOR: The bombing campaign, now extended over a dozen years, has reduced some areas to ruin and turned the towns into armed camps. Alerts, checks, and endless surveillance have become regular features of daily life and promise to remain so. The old people move in the half-blitzed militarised streetscapes, which once must have been friendly and familiar places.

FRIEL: I think that, to be certain, you're a maimed people in this country. One can only read that in one's own life. We're a maimed people to the extent that there was a language in use in this country—that language is gone; that we haven't yet acquired our new language because the language we use is a language that is an inherited or an imposed language—without being dramatic about these things. So that if there's a sense of decline, it's in that sense that we are still trying to establish who we . . . we're trying still to *identify* ourselves. And I think when we say we're trying to identify ourselves, I'm not quite saying that we're trying to define a national identity—that's a different kind of thing. When you talk about a national identity, I'm not quite sure *what* that means. But when we try to identify ourselves, it means you've got to produce documents, you've got to produce sounds, you've got to produce images that are going to make you distinctive in some way. If there's a sense of decline about how the country is, it's because we can't readily produce these identification marks.

INTERVIEWER: And do you think that Field Day might produce a new vocabulary?

FRIEL: Field Day, I think, may offer us the possibility of choosing what those identification marks might be. And if those choices, if those identification marks, are available to people, they can then choose them, and they can identify themselves by them. They may not *choose* to use them.

[External scene in Omagh.]

NARRATOR: Field Day goes on the road. Theatre goes out to the people in the hope that the people might come in to the theatre. In Omagh they do. Here Friel is in his native place. Although on the road, there is little sense of dislocation. The audience is large, the community small. So the audience is known to and by the author. It is a close but not quite closed society. A wave of public support lifts the company. It is carried towards a recognition of what it is there to do.

REA: Yes, I think we *have* stepped in. I think that Brian and myself and the rest saying "let's do this now" means that we *have* stepped in, in a way. I mean people may choose to ignore that but I think that we have taken on some kind of cultural responsibility and one can't be ashamed of that. I think that's true. Instead of operating just as individuals pursuing our own skills and our own careers and meeting with whatever success is there, I think we've at this point said let's pool the resources and take up that responsibility.

NARRATOR: To take it up, to lift out of these streets and out of these memories that world elsewhere, that other province, but not by turning away from this one.

FRIEL: I don't think there's any question of turning our back on the

North or being disappointed with the South. There's certainly no question of turning our back on Britain; in this enterprise we don't even see Britain; it doesn't exist as far as we're concerned. I think yes, of course, there's an element of dissatisfaction with the North and there's certainly an element of dissatisfaction with the South. We are not going to supply any comprehensive answer to the whole thing. But in some way, if we were to create, as somebody else has suggested, a fifth province; if there was a possibility of establishing *some* kind of centre ground—and I don't mean that in political terms or bridge building—but in some kind of artistic centre ground that would draw on the massive and turbulent energy of the North and the more established and, perhaps, slightly spent energy of the South, we then might have something that would be of intense artistic value for the country.

NARRATOR: Thus, Field Day *has* to enter the public arena. It issues statements and theatre programmes. It exercises its language in the world of propaganda and appeal. Cast in a different mold, it begins to learn that it must endure the same heat. It is a world of competing theatres and theatre groups. The arena is the stage, the page, the street.

DEANE: Sure, politics is a danger to us but then we're maybe a danger to politics as well, in a sense. We're not afraid of the public arena, as obviously the politician isn't. But at the same time, I don't think that any politics or any politician can come along with any conviction now and try and persuade either us or anybody else that there is a new dawn, that there is another horizon, in the passing over of which we will find Utopia. The politicians have, in a sense, been burnt out. Some of them, let it be said, some very fine people have been destroyed by the heat of a situation which they in many cases didn't help to generate. In a situation like that I don't feel so much threatened by politics or the politician. I think the subtler threat is the threat that the artist might feel: I'm an artist, therefore I should have a decontamination; I should stay free of politics. There's no freedom from politics. We are politicians in a sense by being artists.

NARRATOR: Yet there is an obvious danger. Tensions within the individual and the group, between the group and others, are inevitable. The choice, once made, has to be made over and over again.

FRIEL: One of the big problems, particularly if you're involved in theatre, and particularly now because of Field Day, is there is a conflict between creating the work, which means, indeed, the suppression of the personality, and this is one of the essential things for any artist. So that I'm caught in a situation where I'm trying to protect myself and protect my work on one level and at the same time trying to keep this enterprise of Field Day vibrant. I don't know whether I'll be able to do these two things; maybe one will have to go. Because there certainly is a conflict between appearing in public as I'm doing at this moment and suppressing the personality, which is necessary for the work.

NARRATOR: In Derry, where the new Troubles began and where the new group had its beginnings, the river divides Bogside from Waterside, Donegal side from the Derry side. It is a monotonous, an exhausted separation. Something else is demanded, and the desire for that other world, for another beginning out of this ending, is making itself felt.

HEANEY: More fundamentally I would go back to what I would sense is a general malaise, although that is too coarse a word, a general feeling that is abroad underneath the consumerism and underneath the hectoring and underneath all the codified positions and feelings, even the codified patriotisms, codified everything. Underneath the codes, there is a sense of need and it's that sense of need that we're trusting.

[Excerpt from *The Communication Cord* of Stephen Rea as Tim:

> Words. Language. An agreed code. I encode my message; I transmit it to you; you receive the message and decode it. If the message sent is clear and distinct, if the code if fully shared and subscribed to, if the message is comprehensively received, then there is a reasonable chance—one, that you will understand what I'm trying to tell you—and two, that we will have established the beginnings of a dialogue. All social behaviour, the entire social order, depends on our communicational structures, upon words mutually agreed on and mutually understood. Without that agreement, without that shared code, you have chaos.]

Field Day's New Double Bill

Patrick Quilligan / 1984

Throughout the years of his involvement with Field Day, Friel
had an evolving vision of what the organization might accomplish. In 1984, when Field Day was preparing a version of
Antigone by Tom Paulin and a version of Molière's *The School for
Husbands* as adapted by Derek Mahon, Friel saw Field Day as
having the potential to help bring into being a new notion of
Irishness.

Overlooking the River Foyle in Derry stands the Guildhall, to the East
the Waterside area of the city with the Bogside adjacent. The Hall, built
in 1890 and featuring the fine stained glass which depicts the city's history, provides a home once a year to Field Day Theatre Company.

It is owned by Derry City Council and since the inception of the theatre company four years ago the Council has generously given it over to
them for the extensive rehearsal period as well as providing free office
space for the planning of the comprehensive national tour, North and
South, which begins tomorrow.

Thus a creative link was forged between the two, unusual in that in
theatrical terms one became synonymous with the other. It is difficult to
think of another company with such a firm sense of place and also incon-
ceivable that a Field Day production would open anywhere but in Derry.

Derry was chosen for a number of reasons, not least the fact that it
had played second fiddle to Belfast for too long in the North's cultural
and artistic life. As important for the Field Day enterprise is its strategic
location straddling the two states, with a bird's-eye view of both. Not only
does it view both states, but its divided community looks to both for solu-

Excerpt from *The Irish Times*, 18 September 1984, p. 10.

tions. The severance from its natural hinterland hampered the city's economic and social development and the company felt it was an ideal place
to shed the burden of two conflicting heritages.

Brian Friel's *Translations* was Field Day's first production and it
brought together the playwright, now resident in Co Donegal, with actor
Stephen Rea and coincided, according to Friel, "with the vague and
amorphous hopes and thoughts we had about the whole enterprise".
The two founder directors gathered four others from both sides of the
community, Seamus Deane, Seamus Heaney, David Hammond and Tom
Paulin, who were committed to a re-examination of previously held
beliefs and not constrained by history in their present or future thinking.

"We're a Northern accented group," says Friel, "with a strong political element (small p) and that would concern itself with some sense of
disaffection most of us would feel at the state of two nations, which is
strongly reflected in the work we are doing this year. I would say that all
six of us are not at home in Northern Ireland and indeed all six would
probably not be at home in the 26 counties.

"We appropriated (from Richard Kearney) the phrase 'Fifth
Province', which may well be a province of the mind, through which we
hope to devise another way of looking at Ireland, or another possible Ireland, and this really is the pursuit of the company."

Friel believes that if this "new province" or new possibility is to mean
anything then it must first be "articulated, spoken, written, painted,
sung" and then perhaps the definition can be forged by legislators and
politicians.

"Already in crude political terms the island is at the point of some
kind of cataclysm, the Northern State certainly is and so also is the Southern State, where new definitions currently silenced or confused, are both
necessary and possible. Field Day is a forum where a more generous and
noble notion of Irishness than the narrow inherited one can be discussed."

The company is involved in other areas, but theatre remains the
activity with the highest public profile. This year they will tour 17 centres
throughout the country (the Gate Theatre, in Dublin, is second on the
itinerary, for a week from next Monday) with a bill of one-act plays by
Northern poets Tom Paulin and Derek Mahon. They are *The Riot Act*
based on *Antigone* by Sophocles and *High Time*, a "comedy after *The School
for Husbands* by Molière". Both will be staged in modern style and represent the first venture into stage writing for the authors.

A group of Irish actors normally resident and working in London
have been brought to Derry for this production, in line with company

policy of using indigenous talent of whatever hue or profession to provide an "Irish filter" not always available to Irish audiences. Friel's translation of Chekhov's *Three Sisters* in 1981 was a case in point.

Much has been made of the political element in Field Day and the
reputation, "unfounded" says Stephen Rea, of being solely the voice of
the minority community.

"Politics is an important ingredient but not the only one. We tour
the whole country in an attempt to reach a fresh identity that will contain
everyone and in that we are political. But we are deeply interested in theatre as an art form, in setting new and different theatrical standards,
which I'm not saying we always attain. But we strive towards that and for
this production we have gathered together a group of totally committed
actors with nothing to distract them."

But theatre's relevance to the harsh reality of people's lives is never
far from Rea's mind. He cites dismissal of the legitimacy of the miners'
case in Britain by right wing opinion and the confrontational international stance by the US in Central America as examples of the plight of
those who stand up and protest. Similar to the plight of the character of
Antigone in the play which he directs—she is unwilling to remain silent
in the face of injustice. Rea is reluctant to spell out the parallels in recent
Irish history and prejudice the artistic merits of the play.

Suffice it to say that "there is a sense in *Antigone* that if you respond
to a fixed position by a Government, in this case Creon, your response is
in some way evil or subversive; she is unable to do anything else but to
react in this way because the gauntlet has been thrown down. This play
applies not only to Ireland but has a universal message. Apart from the
obvious political relevance for us, it's a great play translated by an Irish
poet and we want it to be primarily theatrical."

Friel's Sense of Conflict

Michael Sheridan / 1986

In a profile assessing "the contribution of our most eminent living playwright," Michael Sheridan explored the ways in which Friel as a Northern playwright responded to the conflict and social upheaval that surrounded him. After praising *Philadelphia, Here I Come!* Sheridan focused on the ways *The Freedom of the City* responds directly and *Translations* responds metaphorically "to the Northern Ireland 'situation.'" Sheridan then introduced a substantial statement from Friel himself on the difficulties implicit in such a situation for the artistic imagination and for the artist's use of language. The first paragraph here is by Sheridan, and the remainder of this excerpt consists of a quotation from Brian Friel.

While he fights against the constraints of working in an embattled society and while he has articulated that problem in his work, Brian Friel is the first to recognise the incredible difficulties inherent in finding the means of expression for a playwright born and bred in a land with past and present troubles:

"I am sure that our writers find it distasteful or perhaps too remote from their imaginative reach to write about the troubles and in a way I envy them that fastidiousness or incapacity or whatever but for those of us who grew up with the situation, whose daily life and experience is pigmented with it, the question is not can or should we write about it, but how can we write about it and once we make that submission, and it always feels like a caving in, we are faced with two difficulties.

"The first difficulty is to negotiate between fealty to the tribe and

From the *Irish Press*, 1 October 1986, p. 9.

responsibility to creative imagination, between a kind of loyalty to all those beliefs and loves and enthusiasms and tradition that have helped to form us and at the same time to be faithful to one's own personal mythos, to the secret, the private, the unspoken, the inchoate.

"That is the first difficulty, to make that negotiation, because if that negotiation is not successfully accomplished, you become either a propagandist, or a megaphone for the more raucous element of your tribe, or far worse, you betray your inner spirit structure that must always refuse a worldly or public subscription.

"The second difficulty is language, because the Northern situation is so spoken about, it is almost spoken out, so spoken out, that the very language you employ to feel your way into it, to rediscover it, to give it artistic coherence, is knackered, worked to death.

"Ideally a new language should be forged and that is less possible in the theatre than in poetry or prose fiction. So burdened with that knackered language, what we do is an attempt to reveal the Northern situation in different ways, by elaborate metaphor, by historical analogy, or in a way, as some Irish writers are now attempting, by writing about the troubles as a situation comedy for television, where exhausted language and exhausted form complement and parody one another.

"I don't know, as I say, most of us are saddled with the problem and we like to believe that somewhere there is a rarefied existence where life is not trivialised by difficulties like these—where some kind of imaginary pure art can be wrought.

"But we know there isn't such a life, so we carry on and try to learn to negotiate as artfully as we can."

Brian Friel's Ireland: Both Private and Political

Matt Wolf / 1989

When *Aristocrats* had its first production at the Abbey Theatre
in Dublin in March 1979 (with Stephen Rea leading a cast
directed by Joe Dowling), Friel declined to be interviewed.
When the play appeared in London in 1988, directed by Robin
LeFèvre and starring Sinead Cusack and Niall Buggy, Friel did
not see the production nor did he agree to any interviews in
November when the play won the *Evening Standard* Drama
Award for best play of the year. Five months later, when a pro-
duction of *Aristocrats,* again directed by LeFèvre and starring
Buggy, opened on Broadway, Friel at last agreed to talk about
the play with Matt Wolf, the London theatre critic of *Variety* and
a regular contributor to *The New York Times* and *The Times* of
London. For the first time Friel acknowledged that the play—
which reviewers both in Dublin and London had praised as
Chekhovian—did indeed owe a debt to the Russian playwright.
As such, the play represented a vision of drama that must have
seemed to Friel in 1989 to be somewhat at odds with an increasingly politicized view of a "Field Day play" as articulated by
some of the Field Day directors. Friel's expressed desire to be
private reflects not just his distaste for being interviewed but,
rather, a wider conception of drama. As opposed to writing
plays that consciously address issues of imperialism and colo-
nialism, Friel was espousing a Chekhovian view of drama that
made room for the private, the personal, the idiosyncratic.

From *The New York Times,* 30 April 1989, sec. 2, pp. 7, 8.

Within a year Friel would complete *Dancing at Lughnasa,* the most directly autobiographical play of his career.

It was a rainy afternoon in New York, the day's rehearsals had ended, and the Irish dramatist Brian Friel was back in the city where he began his international career with *Philadelphia, Here I Come!* more than two decades ago. He was in town for the belated American premiere of his 1979 play *Aristocrats,* which opened Tuesday, and that meant submitting to a journalistic rite—the interview—which he is known to dislike. "I'm never quite sure what they're for," he said amiably over drinks at a Chelsea restaurant, worlds away from the nature and the quiet of his Greencastle, County Donegal, home. Indeed, in 1972 he took preventive measures to forestall such occasions by interviewing himself in a BBC radio "self-portrait":

"What other writers influenced you most strongly?

"I've no idea.

"Which of your plays is your favorite?

"None of them.

"Would you say, Mr. Friel, that the influence of Heidegger is only beginning to be felt in the drama and that Beckett and Pinter are John the Baptists of a great new movement?

"Well, in answer to that I'd say that . . . I'd say that I'm a middle-aged man and that I tire easily and that I'd like to go out for a walk now; so please go away and leave me alone."

Other points of information: he is 60 years old; born in Omagh, Northern Ireland, he moved to Londonderry when he was 10; in 1954 he married Anne Morrison, with whom he has five children, four daughters and a son; his introduction to the United States came in 1963 when he was invited by his friend and colleague Tyrone Guthrie to spend six months in Minneapolis during the start of the Guthrie Theater.

On this visit to New York, his discourse seemed almost puckish ("That looks like a harvest wreath; we should all do a Morris dance underneath it," he said with a laugh, pointing to an adornment on the restaurant wall), even as he still avoided grand pronouncements. New York theatergoers, meanwhile, have an overdue opportunity to sample the work of the writer considered the patriarch of contemporary Irish drama. Regularly produced both in England and Ireland, Mr. Friel's work last received a major New York production in 1981 with *Translations* at the Manhattan Theater Club. Now, the same theater is tackling his earlier *Aristocrats,* which will run through June 2. When the play opened last week, Frank Rich in *The Times* called it funny and harrowing. "Mr. Friel makes the Irish condition synonymous with the human one," Mr. Rich said. (The production occupies temporary quarters at Theater Four on West 55th Street, to allow the extension of Joe Orton's *What the Butler Saw* at M.T.C.'s Stage 1.)

The cast is headed by John Pankow and Kaiulani Lee, newcomers to the playwright's work, and the Irish actor Niall Buggy, who appeared in *Aristocrats* last year in London. Making his New York debut, Mr. Buggy plays the childlike, Chopin-loving Casimir, the lone brother surrounded by three sisters (a fourth is heard but not seen) in a family of Irish Catholic gentry in decline and clinging to shards of faded glory while their father dies, noisily, upstairs. *Aristocrats* played a limited engagement last summer at northwest London's Hampstead Theater and was named the season's best play in November at the *Evening Standard* Drama Awards. Robin Lefèvre, the London director, is repeating his assignment in New York.

Mr. Friel never saw the London production and seemed bemused to be watching it take shape in New York. "Once you've done a play and been through rehearsals, that's it. You cherish the memories of it," he said. He regards the play less as a subject for current discussion than as the re-emergence of a particularly creative time in his career: that between March 1979 and September 1980 that saw the premieres of *Faith Healer, Aristocrats* and *Translations,* three plays about myth making, family and language, all topics he continues to explore.

Faith Healer, seen briefly on Broadway with James Mason in 1979, tells of an itinerant healer who publicly dispenses balm even as he nurses private calamity. Its structure, four lengthy monologues performed by three actors in succession, distills the playwright's gift for narrative and provides a link back to his initial work as a short-story writer. (Mr. Friel was a contract writer for *The New Yorker* at age 21.)

Translations, set in 1833, uses the renaming of Gaelic places into English to chart a society caught in the same delicate balance that holds true today. In each play, Ireland is as much an imaginative as a physical terrain; all three, indeed, take place in or allude to Ballybeg, Mr. Friel's fictional County Donegal village, which the author likens to William Faulkner's Yoknapatawpha County. Both are small rural communities that allow their authors to cast wide thematic nets.

In general, the playwright rejects interpretation, perhaps as a reaction against his background as the son of an academic and a onetime teacher himself; still, dramatic influences are apparent in his work. Having written *Aristocrats* as he was beginning a new translation of *Three Sisters,* he acknowledges the play's debt to Chekhov, starting with its familial makeup and its locale, which he describes as "an old crumbling house with upper-class pretensions." He has long been drawn to Russian writers, and adapted Turgenev's *Fathers and Sons* for London's National Theater in 1987 and New Haven's Long Wharf last year. "I was unemployed, and I wanted to keep the muscles slightly flexed," he explained with a twinkle, implying that perhaps the attraction was greater than that.

And yet, he treads cautiously: "It's up to wiser people to point out the similarities. They're implicit rather than explicit." And he seems more interested in the phase of his life that began after *Aristocrats*—his cofounding in 1980, with an actor, Stephen Rea, of Field Day, a Londonderry-based theater company that had its debut production with *Translations*. All his plays since, except *Fathers and Sons*, have had their premieres with the company, and Field Day has gone on to publish poetry and pamphlets, the latter by noted academics like Fredric Jameson and Edward Said. One board member, Seamus Deane, the poet and critic, has edited a two-volume anthology of Irish writing from the year 550 to 1987, which will be published next year in both Gaelic and English.

Financed equally by the arts councils in Belfast and Dublin, Field Day tours one play annually, bringing theater to communities that would otherwise go without. The aim, Mr. Friel says, is to forge a cultural identity for Ireland free of the influence of both London and the nationalist mythologies of the Republic. "I don't for a moment believe that people are hungry to hear the things we say; that's self-aggrandizement," he declared. "One of the things that's reiterated again and again is that we represent a group of seven (on the board of directors) talking to ourselves. If we're overheard, that's great. What's constantly surprising is how many people seem alert to what we do.

"Our work is fulfilled when we take it into the national consciousness," continues the playwright, who achieved just that aim with his most recent Field Day play, *Making History*. It concerns the English-educated Gaelic chieftain Hugh O'Neill, who led a thwarted Ulster resistance against Queen Elizabeth I in the 1590's before fleeing in exile to Italy. The incident marked an end in the province to determined Irish resistance to British rule, but not before sowing the seeds of today's discontent.

Mr. Friel has written explicitly about "the troubles" in the plays *Freedom of the City* and *Volunteers*, but *Making History*, like both *Aristocrats* and *Translations*, roots politics in the personal and in a sense of history. Today, he remains vexed, he said, about what the political component of his work should be:

"I feel I don't ever want to write about politics, but sometimes it happens. It's not a deliberate policy to get involved in political drama. In fact, I'm far from sure of the wisdom or the validity of it. Politics emerges like flesh-and-bones for Octavio Paz, Chinua Achebe; it's hard to imagine African writing that isn't political. I want to be more private and I want isolation, but there's a seduction of political drama, of political art. These last 20 years have been stressful and oppressive."

Looking ahead, Mr. Friel is hopeful about plans for a new Field Day production of *Faith Healer*, to star Donal McCann, who was seen on Broadway last summer in *Juno and the Paycock*. He is also busy advising on Field Day's latest commission, an original play about Oscar Wilde by an Oxford professor, Terry Eagleton. And he's comically perturbed about an ongoing series of radio plays of his to be heard through tomorrow on Britain's Radio 3 and 4. "I must be dead because they're doing a retrospective of me," he said, eyes sparkling, no doubt recalling Hugh O'Neill's wish, in *Making History*, not to be embalmed in pieties. "They tell me they only do that to playwrights who are dead."

From Ballybeg to Broadway

Mel Gussow / 1991

After Brian Friel founded Field Day in 1980, the world pre-mieres of all his new plays—*Translations* (1980), *The Communi-cation Cord* (1982), and *Making History* (1988)—as well as his version of *Three Sisters* (1981) were all Field Day productions. Only his version of Turgenev's *Fathers and Sons* (1987) had gone elsewhere—to London's National Theatre. But when he finished *Dancing at Lughnasa,* he sent the play to the Abbey Theatre in Dublin, where the play was directed in April 1990 by Patrick Mason. Six months after an "incandescent" Dublin opening and with only a few cast changes, Mason's production crossed the Irish Sea and repeated its triumph at the National Theatre. After a sold-out run in London, *Lughnasa* returned in January 1991 to Dublin, where Friel was feted by the Lord Mayor and became the second living theatrical VIP to have his portrait hung in the Abbey. Mason's production of *Lughnasa* was slated for Broadway. But when the Gulf War delayed that transfer, the production returned to a West End theater in Lon-don, where it was still running when Friel's play won the Olivier award as play of the year. After a second cast was recruited to continue in London, the original cast headed for Broadway in October 1991, where the production received eight Tony nom-inations—the most a new play had ever received in the history of the Tony Awards—and eventually won three Tony Awards including best play as well as the New York Drama Critics Circle award for best new play. Left out of the festivities was Field Day. Friel had insisted from the beginning that Field Day should be

From *The New York Times Magazine*, 29 September 1991, pp. 30, 55–61.

transient, impermanent. Within its first year with six directors, Friel was saying the effort to keep Field Day vibrant required of him "the suppression of the personality." Although Friel would not resign from Field Day until February 1994, a process of disengagement had begun. Like Thoreau leaving Walden, Friel seems to have disengaged from Field Day for much the same reason he embarked on the venture—the need for independence, for charting a course free of gravitational forces that would impose a fixed orbit. Talking to Mel Gussow prior to the Broadway opening of *Dancing at Lughnasa,* Friel discusses the play's genesis, the translation of foreign classics into a distinctively Irish English, his sense of exile in Ireland, and his deliberate move from director to director in order to retain his freedom.

Late on a summer's evening in London in 1987, Brian Friel walked along the Thames Embankment with Tom Kilroy. The two playwrights had just left Britain's National Theater, where they had seen Friel's dramatization of Turgenev's *Fathers and Sons.* As they passed homeless men and women curled up in doorways and trash-filled alleys, the writers speculated about the lives of these unfortunate people. Friel said he had two maiden aunts who ended up like that—destitute and abandoned in London. Just before World War II, they had suddenly left the family home in the tiny village of Glenties in Ireland, and never returned. Caught up by the story, Kilroy suggested Friel write a play about it.

Back in Ireland, Friel took his friend's advice. It was in fact an idea that had been lodged deep in his memory bank—his remembrances of childhood summers spent with his mother and her sisters at his grandparents' house. For several years he had been trying to overcome a severe case of writer's block, but as he began to write, the play flowed freely. As *Dancing at Lughnasa* (pronounced LOO-na-sa, as in lunacy) evolved, it became the story of five sisters, all of them unmarried and living together, each stranded with an unrealized dream. The play is dedicated "in memory of those five brave Glenties women," and "out of piety" for his mother and her sisters, each of the characters bears the first name of the real-life model on which she is based.

In the play, as in others of his works, Friel uses autobiography as a taking-off point for art with a far more universally relevant purpose. Probing his life for ideas, he becomes "the miner and the mined." *Dancing at Lughnasa* deals with characteristic Friel themes (dispossession, dreams of departure, lost illusions) and also—a new theme for the playwright—the Dionysiac side of even the most religious and outwardly repressed people, as exemplified by the desire of the sisters to dance at the annual harvest fair of Lughnasa, dedicated to the pagan god, Lugh.

In a surging *coup de théâtre*, the women create a spontaneous revel—not at Lughnasa but in their rustic home. Carried aloft by the beauty and the frenzy of the dance, theatergoers also share a moment of ecstasy. The play concludes with a linguistic refrain of the earlier choreographic image. The character who stands in for the playwright says, "There is one memory of that Lughnasa time that visits me most often." Music of the 30's "drifts in from somewhere far away—a mirage of sound—a dream music that is both heard and imagined. . . . When I remember it, I think of it as dancing. . . . Dancing as if language had surrendered to movement—as if this ritual, this wordless ceremony, was now the way to speak, to whisper private and sacred things."

Even before it opens at the Plymouth Theater on Oct. 24, *Dancing at Lughnasa* has become Friel's greatest success, the capstone to date of a career that has produced more than 20 plays. In its prior engagements at Dublin's Abbey Theater and in London, the play earned critical acclaim and an Olivier award as best play of the season. It is the first new Irish play to achieve such wide popularity in England.

With its rueful and deeply compassionate family portrait and its provocative commentary on crosscurrents of paganism and Christianity, the play adds luster to the playwright's ascendent reputation. With the death of Samuel Beckett, he is Ireland's finest living playwright (his most accomplished peers are Hugh Leonard and Thomas Murphy). The author of *Philadelphia, Here I Come! Aristocrats, Faith Healer, Translations* and *Dancing at Lughnasa,* Friel is at 62 very much in his prime, a writer on a level with Sean O'Casey and John Millington Synge.

Joe Dowling, who has directed plays by all three playwrights, says that in Friel's work, "lives unfold before you" offering "revelation within revelation." He continues: "I don't know of any other playwright in the English language who will go out on a limb as often as he does. He is the one who has most consistently over the last 25 years reflected the changes in Ireland."

Lughnasa and almost all his other plays take place in Ballybeg, a mythical town in Donegal invented by Friel. In Gaelic, it is *baile beag,* and literally means small town. For Friel, it is a Ballybeg of the mind. While he denies it has the specificity of Faulkner's Yoknapatawpha, it is a microcosm of rural Ireland, and, by inference, it represents small towns around the world.

Though he has occasionally written a play with an urban setting, his artistic home is Ballybeg. For this and other reasons, he is often compared with Chekhov. Besides the fact that both are short-story writers as well as playwrights, they share an empathy for those who are trapped in seemingly ordinary lives and for the importance of a provincial place as an adjunct of character. There are societal changes in the background, but the people remain landlocked within their emotional environment.

In *Lughnasa, Philadelphia* and other plays, the author stands within and outside the narrative, commenting sardonically on what in other hands might be regarded as nostalgia. Stylistically he moves away from naturalism, employing striking theatrical devices to shed a more intense light on his subject. In *Lughnasa,* the artist as a boy is played by an adult actor, who becomes a kind of overseer of the family history.

The plays take place at homecomings and leavings, reunions and preludes to exile. Old worlds dissolve and traditional values are questioned. Language is of the utmost concern—not simply the lyrical language that elevates his plays, but in his commentary on communication. He illustrates the power of things spoken and unspoken, language as both divider and bridge.

Friel's plays are not nearly as simple as they might seem (including his few less successful satires and farces). At his best, he creates an intricately interwoven tapestry of character, atmosphere and ideas. It is the kind of work that theatergoers enjoy and academics love to sink their theses into. As with other artists, Friel prefers to let his work speak for itself. He is reluctant to analyze it or himself. As one friend says, trying to capture Friel is like "shifting smoke with a pitchfork."

He has followed his own private course to what has turned out to be a rather public career. To be an artist in his country is to be political, and, living all his life near the border of Northern Ireland, he keeps a foot in each of Ireland's two worlds. For a time, at the invitation of the president of Ireland, he served in the Irish Senate, the first writer since Yeats to be so honored. As a public official, he hardly said a word. But he has discoursed in his work, addressing significant issues, including, in *Translations,* the historic crushing of Irish language and culture by the English.

Because of his closeness to Northern Ireland, some people assume that he is actively anti-British. Politics in Ireland is "a muddy issue," he says. "I do think the problem will always be exacerbated as long as England is in the country. But if England were to go tomorrow morning, that wouldn't solve it. We still have got to find a *modus vivendi* for ourselves within the country."

To questions of a more personal or artistic nature, he can offer the tersest response but, after dodging, he will encourage the questioner by saying, "Persist! Persist!" as if cheering a pole vaulter to leap higher into the air. This is a word that was spoken frequently during our conversations this summer in Ireland and in England. I persisted. He resisted. That resistance was with a certain wryness. He seems professorial, with his thickly tufted hair and eyebrows and his quietly assured manner of speaking. In portraits and photographs, his chin is often resting on his hand as he regards the world with a slyness: the thinker about to spring into a witticism.

During our meetings, the time he was most relaxed was at a long and convivial dinner in Dublin with his producer, Noel Pearson; his wife, Anne Friel; and their youngest daughter, Judy, who is a theater director. With no tape recorder or note pad in sight—and with everyone drinking a fine Bordeaux—he became expansive, even disagreeing with his wife over one of his favorite subjects, the efficacy of presenting English adaptations of foreign classics in Ireland. He insisted the language should be adapted into Irish-English. Anne Friel, quite correctly I think, suggested it might be possible to write a neutral translation that would work for all English speaking countries. "A neutered translation!" Friel countered, and broke into an impassioned defense of his nationalistic position.

One of Friel's favorite recent novels is *Amongst Women* by John McGahern. His own life story could also bear that title, for he has spent his years amongst women, beginning with his Glenties aunts. Actually, there were seven sisters, but he reduced them to five in the play ("Economy is more important than truth," he says with a smile). He has two sisters, one living in Ireland, one in England, and he and his wife have four daughters and one son.

During his boyhood near Omagh in County Tyrone and later in Derry, his mother was a dominant, vivacious presence. Friel's father was a teacher and principal, remembered by his son as a quiet, reserved man. On each side of the family, one grandparent was illiterate, a fact that reminds Friel of his peasant roots. One sign of the closeness of the two families is that Friel's father was best man at the wedding of Anne Friel's parents. Brian and Anne Friel, married for 37 years, have known each other since they were 16.

Friel was born, grew up and still lives within an area of 60 miles. For someone who has resolutely stayed at home, it is interesting that he so often writes about questions of exile and emigration, as in *Philadelphia, Here I Come!* the play that brought him an international reputation at the age of 35.

When asked why he himself has remained homebound, Friel

replied: "I think exile can be acquired sitting in the same place for the rest of your life. Physical exile is not necessary." In his mind, Friel has gone to Philadelphia and farther, questioning his sense of dislocation and reflecting in himself his country's own unsure identity. But by remaining in his own corner of Ireland, he has found his constantly replenished source of inspiration.

He did not set out to be a writer. He went to St. Patrick's College in Maynooth with the idea of studying for the priesthood, but at the age of 17, he changed his mind. When asked if he could imagine himself as a priest, he answered, "It would somehow have been in conflict with my belief in paganism." Instead he followed his father and his sisters into the teaching profession. Gradually he began to divert more of his attention to writing short stories, which soon began appearing regularly in *The New Yorker.* Stories led to radio plays and then to stage plays; his first was presented in Belfast in 1959.

He might have continued quietly on his modest career were it not for Tyrone Guthrie. The legendary stage director, who lived in County Monaghan, sent Friel a fan letter about one of the *New Yorker* stories. They met, and this led to a firm friendship. Guthrie was about to go to America to inaugurate the Tyrone Guthrie Theater in Minneapolis. Friel went with him as an unpaid observer. The months he spent watching Guthrie would prove to be among the most important in his life. Sitting by his side as Guthrie staged *Hamlet, The Miser, The Three Sisters* and other plays, with Hume Cronyn, Jessica Tandy and George Grizzard, Friel was fully immersed in the theater art, its practice as well as its theories.

Searching for a way to describe Guthrie's importance to him, he said, "The experience was enabling to the extent that it gave me courage and daring to attempt things." When Friel's money ran thin, he returned to Ireland, where he wrote *Philadelphia, Here I Come!* a stunning departure in style and artistic authority.

Over the next dozen years, he wrote almost a play a year. Although many of them came to New York, he remained more of a figure in his home country than in England or the U.S. Then came a breakthrough. In a period of about 18 months, beginning in 1979, he wrote three of his best plays, *Aristocrats, Faith Healer* and *Translations.*

Faith Healer, an eloquent metaphorical study of the artist's life-and-death struggle, had a very brief life on Broadway through a combination of unfortuitous circumstances. A play of four seemingly contradictory monologues, it did not sit comfortably on a large Broadway stage. But even in New York it had its ardent admirers. After the final performance, James Mason, who played the title role, addressed the audience. As he began speaking about "the Broadway failure" of the play, theatergoers shouted in protest, "No. Never. Never." Subsequent productions have reclaimed *Faith Healer,* at the center of Friel's canon, as his most personal statement about art and faith. At a climactic moment in the play, the faith healer, Frank Hardy, accepts his fate and faces his assassins: "As I moved across that yard towards them and offered myself to them, then for the first time I had a simple and genuine sense of homecoming. Then for the first time there was no atrophying terror; and the maddening questions were silent. At long last I was renouncing chance."

It was to be 10 years before *Aristocrats,* his most Chekhovian play, came to the U.S., opening at the Manhattan Theater Club, which also produced *Translations.* These two plays reaffirmed the artistry evidenced years before in *Philadelphia.* But the ready acceptance of *Translations* in England prompted the author to an act of self-subversion. He wrote a farce spoofing issues raised in the earlier work. The play, *The Communication Cord,* was not well received.

What followed was a period of silence and frustration. Despite his apparent productivity, there had been fallow times, in the past, but none like the middle 1980's. Ostensibly he was working on an historical play about the Irish hero Hugh O'Neill. Every morning he would go up to his study in his house in Greencastle in County Donegal. That house, a converted temperance hotel, is only a few steps from the sea, the Lough Foyle. He would sit at his desk, with a cigarette in his hand and with his back to the vista. As usual, he wrote in pencil. The play proceeded at a crawl. Looking back on the long, bleak period, he said: "I sat it out. I waited for the rescue." One could imagine him saying to himself, "Persist! Persist!"

Encouraged by his wife to find a divergence, he wrote an adaptation of Turgenev's *Fathers and Sons.* At the end of that labor he journeyed to London and listened to Tom Kilroy's suggestion for writing a play about his aunts. Shortly thereafter, he was buoyed by the delayed opening and success of *Aristocrats* in New York. As he began to write *Dancing at Lughnasa,* he focused the play on the sisters and the homecoming of their brother, a burned-out priest who has served for many years as a missionary in Africa. Although he had written a number of plays with women as central characters, this was the first time he was able to deal so directly with his mother and her family.

Over the years, Friel has become increasingly mobile, flying from Derry to Dublin to London, but the longer he is away from Donegal, the more unsettled he feels. For all his talk of exile-at-home, he is rock-rooted and as indigenous as his art. His home is his refuge. There he is surrounded by familiarity—his books, his collections of Irish paintings and antique clocks, his beehives and the natural beauty of the landscape. Only 75 miles away he has a summer house facing the Atlantic.

Now that the Friel children are grown, with each involved in a profession (the oldest daughter has the euphonious job of being a curator in a castle in Kilkenny; their son recently completed his studies in marine biology), the house is quiet, except at holiday time. Friends from other parts of Ireland, and occasionally America, stop by, and Friel is quick to play the host. One of his most welcome guests is Katharine Hepburn.

His circle of intimates is literary as well as theatrical, beginning with Seamus Heaney, Ireland's premiere poet, with whom he shares both background and artistic sensibility. Heaney and other friends are involved in Field Day, the company that Friel and the actor Stephen Rea founded to tour plays and generate a nationwide, politically conscious theater.

Anne Friel is the first to read her husband's plays, although, she says, he has the annoying habit of giving her a play when it is only half-finished, leaving her to surmise where it might end. For her, her husband has something of a split personality, combining the utmost seriousness with great humor. He is, she says, like the doubled character, the private and public man, in *Philadelphia, Here I Come!*

During one of our talks, referring to the fact that he no longer wrote short stories, I began, "Having moved from fiction to theater. . . ." He interrupted, "Theater is fiction, too." He explained that the characters in *Lughnasa* diverged from precise reality. Speaking of the women of Glenties, he said, "The play provides me with an acceptable fiction for them now."

In his introduction to his adaptation of *The London Vertigo*, an 18th-century comedy by Charles Macklin, Friel says, "The desire to metamorphose oneself, to change everything utterly—names, beliefs, voice, loyalties, language, ambitions, even one's appearance—excites most people at some stage of their lives." The statement seemed curious, coming from one who has remained so firmly in place. But as a playwright, he said, he metamorphoses himself through his work. "You invent an alternative life, a fiction of your life each time you write a play."

To the suggestion that there still might be a real alternative life he would like to lead, he said, with enthusiasm: "I would love to be a very good clarinetist, or trumpeter or organist. But those are pipe-dream alternatives." He continued: "Had I been born 50 years earlier, exile would have certainly been valuable, maybe even necessary. There was no encouragement for artists in those years.

"The question," he said, "is not whether Ireland is harder or easier on its artists. The artist has to acquire his own armor and armory. I don't have a lot of sympathy with people who feel they are silenced by opposition." In his career, he has deliberately moved from theater to theater, from director to director, taking the widest advantage of Ireland's relatively small pool of theatrical talent. If he worked with the same people each time, he said, he "would acquire a dependence, a comfort, a house style." He adds: "You could absorb the style of a director. It's necessary to maintain your freedom, your individuality."

Despite his feelings about Guthrie and several directors with whom he has worked, he has grave doubts about the directorial profession. "I want a director to call rehearsals, to make sure the actors are there on time and to get them to speak their lines clearly and distinctly," he says. "I've no interest whatever in his concept or interpretation. I think it's almost a bogus career. When did these people appear on the scene? One hundred years ago?" And he added, "I think we can dispose of them very easily again." By his measure a director should be "obedient" to the play. If not, all you need is an "efficient stage manager."

He makes his revisions before a play goes into rehearsal. "As far as I'm concerned, there is a final and complete orchestra score. All I want is musicians to play it. I'm not going to rewrite the second movement for the sake of the oboe player." Then he admitted: "I sound very dogmatic and grossly self-assured about this, but I don't feel that way at all. I just think it is a more valuable stance than working on the hoof. For the actor, the score is there and there are musical notations all around. We call them stage directions." For example, the Dionysiac dance in *Lughnasa* is carefully choreographed in the text itself.

To safeguard his work, he attends all rehearsals of a new play. But once the play has opened, he leaves it, and it is with the greatest reluctance that he will look at a second production. Part of that clearly derives from his proximity to his art. To illustrate, he told a story about Ibsen. He said that when Ibsen returned to Norway toward the end of his life, he was given permission to sit in the royal garden. "Every day Ibsen would strut along, this pompous little figure in his frock coat and tall hat." He would sit on a bench, take off his hat and put it on his knee. "Someone realized he was staring into his hat and crept up behind him and saw that inside the crown of the hat was a mirror. And this is how Ibsen spent his day."

"Whether or not that story is true, that is the kind of narcissism writers have. If one takes art as seriously as the faith healer does, as a matter of life and death, that itself is hubristic. You're courting catastrophe." Knowing that, he still persists. "As Auden said, art is not going to save the Jews from the Holocaust. It's not going to make a person any more worthy or noble, but I do think it can make some tiny, thumbscrew adjustment on our psyche."

Friel writes only what he wants to write—plays, not screenplays— and refuses to repeat himself. "If *Dancing at Lughnasa* is about the necessity for paganism," he said, then his next play will deal with "the necessity for mystery. It's a mystery, not religion, but mystery finds its expression in this society mostly in religious practice." The working title is "The Imagined Place."

In one of his early stories, he wrote about a father who reluctantly goes with his wife and children to revisit his birthplace in Donegal and discovers "the ruins of the old place." At first, the father reflects that the past is an "illusion into which one steps in order to escape the present." But by the end of the story, he has come to terms with his memories. "The past did have meaning," he realizes. "It was neither reality nor dreams. . . . It was simply continuance, life repeating itself and surviving."

Dancing at Lughnasa arrives on Broadway in the Abbey Theater production, directed by Patrick Mason and starring the Irish actresses who created the roles or played them at London's National Theater, including Rosaleen Linehan as the oldest sister and Catherine Byrne as the youngest, representing Friel's mother. Joining the company as the missionary is Donal Donnelly. For the actor, the play is itself a homecoming. He has had a long history in the works of Friel, appearing on Broadway in *Philadelphia, Here I Come!* and *Faith Healer.*

Before coming to New York, *Dancing at Lughnasa* gave one special performance in Glenties, the market town in the hills of Donegal that was the setting of the original events in the play. The occasion was a Brian Friel festival, a weeklong series of talks, panel discussions and performances sponsored by the Patrick MacGill Summer School. For weeks before the festival, Friel tormented himself with the question of whether or not he should attend. Although he felt close to many of the people who would participate, the idea made him feel acutely self-conscious. Finally he decided to go, but to avoid all colloquies analyzing Frielian themes, like immigration and return, incipient decay and the illusion of pastoralism, and certainly to avoid the guided bus tour of "Friel country." Still, he felt "like a ghost at the feast."

The festival opened on a Sunday night in August with the performance of *Dancing at Lughnasa* at the Glenties Comprehensive School, with actors gathered from the Abbey company and the current London cast. The lighting and sound equipment came from Dublin, the costumes had been delayed in transit from London and the scenery was makeshift. To give a semblance of reality, several haystacks were brought indoors to stand in for the wheat field in the original production. Every seat in the school hall was taken.

Overcoming his embarrassment at all the attention, Friel addressed the audience before the performance. He said it was "an important occasion" for him because the play had to do with his family, which had lived a half mile from the school hall. In the audience were many neighbors who knew the people behind the characters. After thanking the actors, the playwright stood to one side of the house to watch the brave Glenties women take the stage. The performance began late and was not finished until after midnight, when the audience rose in a wave and cheered. For Friel, it was "a heightened and very moving" experience. Art and life had come together in the real Ballybeg.

In *Dancing at Lughnasa,* Due on Broadway this Month, Brian Friel Celebrates Life's Pagan Joys

John Lahr / 1991

In October 1990 the distinguished theater critic John Lahr reviewed *Dancing at Lughnasa* for the British edition of *Vogue* before the play opened in London. Praising Friel's "subtle memory play" as "the work of a master," Lahr said the play depicts "the collision of the pagan and the Christian spirit as it struggles to celebrate the miracle of life amid enormous impoverishment." Prior to the play's Broadway opening a year later, Lahr's interview with Friel for the American edition of *Vogue* afforded an opportunity for the playwright to reflect on the thematic significances Lahr had seen in Friel's masterpiece. Although Friel again recounts the genesis of the play, he also offers one of the most substantive explorations of his career of the thematic implications of one of his plays. Friel discusses the way he sees a pagan perception of life coexisting with a Christian sense of mystery, his desire to dramatize the spiritual, the significance of contact with other cultures, and the need for each new play to subvert something of the thematic significances of its predecessors.

A field of golden wheat dotted with poppies tilts down from the horizon to the kitchen in the rural Donegal backwater where Brian Friel has set his masterpiece, *Dancing at Lughnasa*. The wheat evokes a sense of bounty and festival in this superb memory play, which stops time in 1936

From *Vogue* (American edition), October 1991, pp. 174, 176, 178–79.

to conjure out of the dutiful bravery of the five unmarried Mundy sisters a moment of fierce pagan joy. The radio in the corner of their family kitchen is the instrument of their liberation, corrupting their threadbare lives with pleasure through music and forcing an extraordinary collision between Christianity and paganism. At various times the sisters dance around the kitchen and in the field, and one character, a retired missionary, reflects on dance as the merging of the secular and the sacred—which is what Friel accomplishes in this play.

"I think there's a need for the pagan in life," says Brian Friel, taking another drag on his cigar amid the din of a Dublin chophouse. "I don't think of it as disrupting Christianity. I think of it as disrupting civility. If too much obeisance is offered to manners, then in some way we lose or suppress the grumbling and dangerous beast that's underneath the ground. This denial is what causes the conflict."

Dancing at Lughnasa has already been performed in Dublin's Abbey Theatre and London's National Theatre and makes its Broadway debut this month with most of its original Irish cast intact. "It began very modestly about three years ago," says Friel, who took eight months to get his first draft. "I was at a play at the National Theatre with the playwright Thomas Kilroy. We walked across the Waterloo Bridge and up the Strand. It was about eleven-thirty at night, and there were homeless sleeping in the doorways. Tom said, 'If you talked to those people, I'm sure many of them are Irish.' And I said, 'I had two aunts, who, I think, ended up something like that.' He said, 'Why don't you write about that?' So that's how it began: backward."

In *Dancing at Lughnasa,* the Mundy sisters live with a sense of loss to which they refuse to capitulate. Possibilities, like food, are thin on the ground, but they persevere with their special brand of bittersweet gaiety. Michael, the seven-year-old love child of sister Christina who observes his aunts and tells the audience about them twenty-five years later, builds kites in the yard that seem as resolutely unable to take flight as the dreams of his aunts. Uncle Jack, returned from a lifetime's work with lepers in Uganda, moves through this Christian household like a sleepwalker, unable after so many years of submersion in a different culture to find words to describe the object world or the spiritual one. For a generation, the sisters' prestige in the community has centered around their missionary brother, but his return to their pious community has brought both the whiff of scandal and scandalous religious ideas. Into this landscape of disappointment, exotic music insinuates itself. The radio has a nickname. The jokey sister, Maggie, suggests calling the radio Lugh, in honor of the Celtic god of the harvest (for whose festival the play is named), but the prim schoolteacher and head of the household, Kate, won't hear of it. So they just call it Marconi "because that was the name of the set." Says Friel, speaking of the "Marconi voodoo" that sends the sisters careening around the kitchen and includes Cole Porter: "I think what's interesting is that it's music from a different culture that liberates them. They haven't absorbed it into their life and into their culture and tamed it. It's still slightly exotic."

Friel's enormous accomplishment in *Dancing at Lughnasa* is to flush out from the humdrum struggles of daily life a sense of wonder and to make the sacramental felt. "I think there is a value in religion," says Friel, who was born a Catholic in the Protestant North in 1929 and who studied for the priesthood for two years, between the ages of sixteen and eighteen. "I think whether we want to call it religion or the acknowledgment of mystery or a salute to the otherness, it can be enriching. I think self-fulfillment is the realization of that otherness. But in Ireland we have perverted that enriching process and made it into some kind of disabling process."

To incarnate the spiritual in his play, Friel has had to forge a language and a method without moral overtones. "The spiritual is difficult to dramatize," says Friel. "I suspect we have lost some of the vocabulary. Conventional religious vocabulary has been so demeaned that it's not appropriate. The audience—a word that has its root in the word for hearing—loses its 'ear'; it either becomes deaf or tone-deaf." *Dancing at Lughnasa* eschews the high moral ground but finds a new way for articulating man's yearning for heaven. Dancing at once evokes and transcends this linguistic stalemate, "as if language had surrendered to movement."

In making a show of the ceremonial aspects of life, Friel points out how men honor the religious instinct in different ways. Uncle Jack gropes for a word to describe the merging of the secular and the sacred in African tribal life and comes up with "ceremony." The ceremonial generates community—not division. And as the sectarian violence in Northern Ireland has long borne witness, sin is separation. Dancing expresses the will to integrate with life, not separate from it.

Ritual, Friel shows, is how human beings impose a sense of order on the awesome disorder of life. "The whole thing is so fragile, it can't be held together much longer," says sister Maggie of the family constellation that will soon be changed forever when two of the sisters lose their piecework-knitting jobs and set off for London. Dancing becomes a bridge to some acknowledgment of the mystical; it traps a sense of otherness, "a wordless ceremony," as the narrator says, "to whisper private things, to be in touch with some otherness."

The Mundy sisters, each with her own private grief, are "beside themselves" in the pleasure of the dance. Uncle Jack describes his lepers, drunk on palm wine, dancing to express thanksgiving for the fact of life. Gerry, the feckless father of Christina's son, dances silently with Christina in the fields, which the narrator-son remembers beautifully: "No singing, no melody, no word. Only the swish and whisper of their feet across grass." Dancing kills time and incarnates grace.

The first line of *Dancing at Lughnasa* is "When are we going to get a decent mirror to see ourselves in?" The play provides such a mirror. Friel's plays have long given Irish life a hearing far beyond the boundaries of the island. His first hit, *Philadelphia, Here I Come!* (1963), was written quickly after a gamble in which Friel at the age of thirty-three packed his wife and two young children off to Minneapolis so he could sit in without pay at the rehearsals for Tyrone Guthrie's first season at his Minneapolis repertory theater.

"Guthrie was a friend of mine," says Friel. "Up to that time, I'd written a few bad plays and had spent ten years teaching secondary and primary school. Guthrie said, 'If you're going to do something in the theater, you've got to live in it, work in it.' So I moved to Minneapolis. I had no function, no role, and no income. I just sat there. My parents thought I was crazy. My wife's people thought I was crazy. But the time I spent in Minneapolis was some kind of explosion in the head. Had to be. I don't know what it was. Guthrie and America released me from the insularity of Ireland."

Friel followed *Philadelphia, Here I Come!* with a score of plays, including *The Loves of Cass McGuire, The Freedom of the City, Faith Healer, Aristocrats,* and *Translations,* the first play to be mounted by Friel and the Irish actor Stephen Rea under the auspices of their touring company, Field Day, which they founded in 1980 and which has since grown into one of Ireland's most influential arts organizations.

"Any life in the arts is delicate," Friel says. "You've got to forge rules for yourself, not for the sake of moral improvement but for the sake of survival. Rule number one would be to not be associated with institutions or directors. I don't want a tandem to develop. Institutions are inclined to enforce characteristics, impose an attitude or a voice or a response. I think you're better to keep away from all of them. It's for that reason that I didn't give *Dancing at Lughnasa* to Field Day to produce.

"Another rule would be to explore different themes in each play you write. I find once you've lived with a play for two years, you become adjusted by the text, that the play adjusts you. It fashions you, it shapes you in a certain way. Once you accomplish a play, it always provides you with a stance. Therefore, that stance has instantly got to be subverted. Otherwise, you could find yourself developing a kind of moral orthodoxy, a theology.

"Trust your voice," Friel tells me as a piece of parting literary advice. "Just sing." And that is what Friel does in the gorgeous fuss of his characters. He masterfully manipulates language, objects, and stage pictures to evoke in dancing a pure place beyond words: "as if," so one of the play's last lines goes, "language no longer existed because words were no longer necessary . . ."

Friel at Last

Julie Kavanagh / 1991

Prior to the Broadway opening of *Dancing at Lughnasa*, Julie Kavanagh spoke with Brian Friel in a series of wide-ranging discussions at Friel's home in Ireland. Friel would eventually grant permission for a film of *Dancing at Lughnasa* to go forward, in a version starring Meryl Streep as Kate. But the proposed film version of *Translations* would join a number of other ultimately abandoned attempts to transfer Friel's plays from stage to celluloid. Friel talks about the limits of language, the element of autobiography in *Lughnasa,* and his perception of the literary fraternity in Ireland.

In Ireland, Brian Friel is the patriarch of the macho literary pack. Even Seamus Heaney, the Irish poet who has been short-listed for the Nobel Prize, calls him "Daddo." He is recognized as the country's greatest living dramatist, creator of such national classics as *Aristocrats* and *Translations.* In America, people still tend to associate Friel mainly with his single Broadway triumph, *Philadelphia, Here I Come!,* which had a run of 326 performances in the mid-sixties.

The reason Friel is not as well known abroad as "Seamus the Famous" is that he chooses not to be. He is notoriously elusive with the media: he routinely declines interviews, and he is uncompromising about having his plays filmed. He has refused several offers to make a "fill-m," as he pronounces it, of *Dancing at Lughnasa,* his current West End hit, which opens on Broadway this month, even though one bidder is Noel Pearson, the producer of *My Left Foot.*

Friel cites the familiar complaint: "You have no control. The writer

---

From *Vanity Fair,* October 1991, pp. 128, 130, 134, 138.

is nobody in the cinema." But all the same, he is allowing Neil Jordan to make a movie of *Translations,* considered to be his masterpiece, because he admires the young director's work. Friel never allows anyone to cut a line or tamper in any other way with his work. He has what his friend David Hammond, the Belfast broadcaster and musician, describes as "an important arrogance in him," which makes him incompatible with Hollywood. He wrote a screenplay of Brian Moore's novel *The Lonely Passion of Judith Hearne,* but when he refused to change his (even more) downbeat ending, his version was scrapped. There was, however, an unexpected bonus for Friel. As a result of the initial discussions, Katharine Hepburn, who was to have starred in the Maggie Smith role, became a close friend and a fan. "He's entertaining, sensitive, and he's goddamn good," she told me. Friel and his wife stay with Hepburn whenever they go to New York.

"Occasionally the film world is tempting to me," admits Friel, "but I don't need the money. It's easy to live here and it's cheap. As writers, we're tax-free." "Here" is a rambling white converted Victorian boarding-house, balanced like a lighthouse above a craggy inlet on the Inishowen Peninsula in the North of Ireland. It is a symbolic location, allowing Friel to live in the republic while retaining a grip on Ulster. Combat-torn Derry (or Londonderry, as the English call it) is about twenty miles from his house in Greencastle, and the border dividing British-owned Northern Ireland from Eire's County Donegal is just minutes away. It is an unsettling contrast. Half an hour before meeting Friel, I saw soldiers on the outskirts of Derry, running and crouching with their machine guns pointed at the road. Yet once you turn down the long drive to the house, you enter a pastoral zone "away from it all," to borrow the title of a Heaney poem. Donegal, famous for the unspoiled beauty of its scenery, has always been an image of possibility for Friel. For the Northern Irish, too, it is magic territory, where people go on holiday. Living where he does stretches Friel's imagination "between politics and transcendence," in Heaney's phrase. This dichotomy is the subject of "Away from It All," in which the poet, in conversation with a friend, chews over lobster claws and aesthetic imperatives confronting every Irish writer: whether to contemplate the "motionless point" or "participate actively in history." The unnamed friend in the poem is Friel.

Stories circulate about how Brian Friel will agree to see a journalist and then change his mind at the last minute, or insist, as Nabokov did, that questions be submitted in writing. But the genial Irishman who comes out to greet me immediately counters his formidable reputation. He is followed by Anne Friel, his wife of thirty-six years, a gentle, engaging woman with a soft Donegal lilt and smiling eyes. Plodding behind is Masha, their geriatric Labrador, named after the middle sister in Chekhov's *Three Sisters,* a play which Friel, often called "the Irish Chekhov," translated ten years ago "as an act of love."

In the living room, with its wide-angle view of the loch and the shadowy hills of Ulster, there is a piano against one wall. Music is extremely important to Friel—stage directions in several of the plays specify popular songs and classical sonatas—but Anne Friel is the pianist in the family. She is also an accomplished gardener, and has created a romantic terraced garden around which her husband takes me with pride. Even a stranger can see they have an enviable rapport. Anne Friel is always the one to whom Friel first shows his work. "He wouldn't change anything, though," she says, laughing. "He'd change it for nobody."

Friel settles in front of a peat fire, lighting up a tycoon-style cigar. He has an awesome boiled ham of a face, like a Francis Bacon self-portrait. A poet acquaintance likens it to "a four-bar electric fire," and I think how apt that is as Friel's complexion glows through the floating carpet of fug which thickens to a pea-souper as the hours pass. The only evidence in the simply furnished room of his huge London success is what he calls "my Lughnasa clock," a George III antique which he says is "more pleasurable than the play itself." But later he shows off a new CD player—bought with the proceeds of his play's long London run—which he hasn't yet used, as he has only a couple of Abba discs, left behind by one of his five grown-up children.

Dancing at Lughnasa is an unlikely hit, with its dreamy, Chekhovian pace and a title few can remember or pronounce. (It sounds like *lunacy.*) Yet when it moved from the Abbey Theatre in Dublin to London's National Theatre in October 1990, it instantly became the most coveted ticket in town. It won this year's Olivier Award for best play, and is still running to full houses. The New York production will feature several members of the original cast, including such superb ensemble actresses from the Abbey as Brid Ní Neachtain, Brid Brennan, and Catherine Byrne. On Broadway, Alec McCowan will be replaced by Donal Donnelly, who starred in the 1966 run of *Philadelphia, Here I Come!*

Noel Pearson, who is producer and chairman of Dublin's Abbey Theatre, fell in love with *Dancing at Lughnasa* as soon as he read it. "I had the same feeling about this as I had with *My Left Foot.* I rang Friel the next morning and said, 'Not only do I want to open the new Abbey with this play, but I'm telling you it's going to go everywhere.'" Friel's response was characteristically laconic: "Noel, I think your *Left Foot* has gone to your head."

Like that film, *Dancing at Lughnasa* focuses on a large Catholic household, in this case five unmarried sisters scraping a living together in County Donegal in the thirties. The story of their last year together as a family is elegiacally narrated by Michael, the illegitimate son of one of the sisters. The play is set during the weeks of Lughnasa, the Irish harvest festival, named after the pagan god Lugh (pronounced Loo). For Michael, the incandescent memories of that summer are the appearance of his ne'er-do-well father, the hopeless charmer Gerry Evans; the effect on his aunts of "Marconi," a radio endowed with contagious, Dionysian powers; and the return from Africa of his missionary uncle, Father Jack, the character Donal Donnelly will play on Broadway.

In the first act, Friel takes a considerable risk with the audience's attention span, concentrating on the mundane routine of the sisters' life—making mash for hens, collecting turf, knitting, shopping, cooking. Their conversation is humdrum, fragmentary. For about half an hour the play doesn't seem to be going anywhere; there is an edginess in the air both on- and offstage. Rosaleen Linehan, who appears as the schoolmistress, Kate, agrees: "The first part is very difficult to perform. It's not till after the dance that the whole play settles. After that we're more relaxed, and the audience settles."

The most extraordinary scene on the London stage is triggered when Michael's mother, Chrissie, switches on the radio. Maggie, standing with her hands in a bowl of flour, is first to respond to the heavy beat of the ceili band. Absorbing the rhythm, she drags her fingers down her cheeks and breasts, streaking her face like a savage. With a wild cry she starts to dance, arms, legs, and bootlaces flying. One by one the sisters follow suit, each one a maenad deranged by the atavistic spirit of the music, all moving in ways that caricature them—like the crude jig danced by Rose, a simpleton, whose Wellington boots "pound out her own erratic rhythm." The circumspect Kate is the last to join in, and her tight-lipped, autistic reel is the most strangely driven of all. When the music ends midphrase, the sisters stop as if snapped out of hypnosis, half embarrassed and half defiant. A few members of the audience titter awkwardly, unsure of how to respond. But from that moment on, Friel has both actors and spectators in his thrall.

In subjecting us to what he has described as the "momentous daily trivia" of life in rural Donegal, Friel forces us to share the boredom and frustration of these five sisters quarantined in a rustic kitchen by circumstances and convention. As his friend Seamus Deane, the poet and academic, has written, "The same blend of disappointment and unyielding pressure is found time and again to characterize the experience of his protagonists." The women in *Dancing at Lughnasa* have surrendered their youth and their dreams to a life from which only the dance can release them. Like music, dance confesses what can't or shouldn't be spoken. "Don't talk any more; no more words," Michael's mother tells his father as, later in the play, they perform a wistful Fred-and-Ginger routine, asserting the triumph of Apollo over Dionysus, which is a central conflict in the play. "When you come to the large elements and mysteries of life," says Friel, "they are ineffable. Words fail us at moments of great emotion. Language has become depleted for me in some way; words have lost their accuracy and precision. So I use dance in the play as a surrogate for language."

Friel has become bolder about allowing himself the freedom to indulge what Seamus Heaney, one of his closest friends, calls "the anti-rational or irrational impulse." Dance, expressing its intuitive, nondiscursive truths, is just one device with which he achieves this. "Stagecraft and plot skills are all in the service of a kind of reverie in *Lughnasa*," says Heaney. "I thought of Monet, late, watery Monet, and not because of the poppies on the set, but because of the fluency and opulence of the mood painting." It was this hazy quality that led the English critics to label *Dancing at Lughnasa* a poignant nostalgia play—"a bogside *Five Sisters*," as *The Independent* called it. Friel sees it as far more barbaric: "It is about the necessity for paganism," he says, and in his narrative he shows how the old pagan customs still impinge on rural life and Catholic propriety.

The old stationmaster's house is up a hill outside the small, pretty town of Glenties in County Donegal. This was the home of the Mundy sisters, "those five brave women of Glenties" to whom Friel has dedicated his text. One of them was his mother. *Dancing at Lughnasa* is Friel's most directly autobiographical play. Like Michael, he was seven in 1936, although his parents were married and his father was a respectable schoolmaster. "I had four aunts with those names and an uncle who came back from being a missionary in Africa. My Aunt Rose was a simple girl." Glenties is also where his wife's family comes from; Friel's father was her parents' best man. When the solid two-story house overlooking the now dilapidated station hut came up for sale, he considered buying it, "but I felt it might have haunted me a bit." Knowing what it meant to him, David Hammond chose a different house when he was asked to host a documentary on the playwright. "I had to do a piece to camera, so I stood in front of a house about five miles away. Nobody knew."

The idea for the play came to Friel one night when he was walking along London's Strand with Tom Kilroy, the theater director. Looking at the cardboard-quilted vagrants sleeping in shop doorways, Friel said, "I'm sure some of those are Irish people," and recounted the story of two of his aunts, who lived rough in London and died young as penniless alcoholics. "Write a play about it," said Kilroy.

Those close to Friel say he feels a certain guilt about *Dancing at Lughnasa,* for he fears he has exploited his family circumstances. But the element of autobiography is just a tracing, which allows him to rework perennial themes from earlier plays: the role of language, the attraction of exile, the hardship of an agrarian life—conventional issues in the Irish theatrical tradition. As Seamus Deane has written, "Irish drama has been heavily populated by people for whom vagrancy and exile have become inescapable conditions about which they can do nothing but talk, endlessly and eloquently and usually to themselves. The tramps of Yeats and Synge and Beckett, the stationless slum dwellers of O'Casey or Behan, bear a striking family resemblance to Friel's exiles."

Friel's disclosure of the existence of the Glenties household is the closest he has come to identifying the whereabouts of Ballybeg, the fictitious setting of *Dancing at Lughnasa* and most of his plays (Heaney compares it to William Faulkner's Yoknapatawpha County). Ballybeg, as Friel's poet friend Tom Paulin puts it, could be "Ballyanywhere." It is a microcosm of Ireland—the *whole* island: there is no place in Friel's writing for "the border." But its location is unmistakably western Donegal. It is a bleak, architectural landscape where Irish is the first language and where many Celtic customs and traditions are preserved. Friel chose to base his characters on the people there, whom he once found "completely untouched by present-day hysteria and hypocrisy," though he now admits that that is too romantic a notion. He is a miniaturist and confines his canvas to the local and the domestic. But parochialism, in Friel's hands, is rarely constricting. Because he deals so accurately and so truthfully with the fundamentals of life, he is able to make the Irish condition a universal one.

In County Donegal, Brian Friel is a local hero. Mention his name in Bunbeg, a two-boat fishing port fifteen miles from his summer retreat, and the young Cockney owner of the only pub will probably recount how he played in an amateur production of *Translations.* At Sharkey's Bar and at the Cope shop, further down the road, beaming proprietors offer Irishly prolix directions to his hideaway in Kincasslagh, which is unmarked on any map. I eventually located it at a spot where a dirt track stops at the edge of a cliff. Far below, Atlantic rollers thrash the long crescent of white strand where Katharine Hepburn went cycling at seven every morning when she stayed with the Friels. She loves the lack of ostentation and the privacy of their life ("something I try to have and fail," she said), and, of course, Friel, the hard-drinking, brilliant Irishman, is exactly her type.

Now that he lives by the sea in Greencastle, Friel rarely visits Ireland's West Coast. The house there is kept as a holiday cottage for his grandchildren. Friel is a terrific grandfather, according to David Hammond, and has always been a tolerant and perceptive father. "He gives his children vast freedom—the freedom to make mistakes." Only his daughter Judy is following him into the theater, as a would-be director. Paddy Friel lives in Kilkenny, where she is curator of the castle; Mary is a housewife in Dublin; Sally lives in Canada and works in the hotel business; and the youngest, David, is completing his studies in marine biology at a university in Wales. Although they are frequently drawn back home, none of the children shares their father's affiliation with Donegal. "They don't have that acute sense of place," he says. "They probably feel smothered by it."

For Friel, though, it is "the ultimate fashioning of experience . . . maybe a substitute for some kind of intellectual rootlessness." There was a time thirty years ago when, like John Millington Synge discovering the uncomplex people of the Aran Islands, Friel consciously integrated himself into the local community, going out with the fishermen and getting seasick "like a stupid townie," feeling his way into the spirit of the place. He drew on that period in wonderful stories like "The Gold in the Sea," first published in *The New Yorker* in the sixties. Friel wrote fourteen stories in all for the magazine, supplementing the small income he earned as a schoolmaster in Derry.

He dismisses his two collections of short stories as "stammerings from the past," but they are just as fresh, intimate, and evocative today as when they were written. It was the *New Yorker* stories that prompted Tyrone Guthrie to write Friel a fan letter—the beginning of a close friendship and an inspired creative partnership.

At Guthrie's invitation, Friel spent the spring of 1963 at the Guthrie Theater in Minneapolis, "learning about the physical elements of plays." Through the director, he became aware of the audience and how to move it, as he does so brilliantly in *Lughnasa*. Friel has described the Minneapolis experience as "a parole" from stifling Derry. Those months in America acted as a catalyst on his imagination, and he came home to write *Philadelphia, Here I Come!,* the play that secured his international reputation.

Success, however, had a reverse effect on Friel. Friends say that after his Broadway triumph he went into a retreat. He began work on what David Hammond describes as his "hinterland" plays, such as *The Gentle Island* (1971), which is almost vengeful in tone and renounces the Celtic Twilight values which he had dramatized in the world of Ballybeg as illusory and sham. Friel has always had what Heaney calls a "subversive intelligence," which he explains as "Friel's need to unsettle pieties (in *The Communication Cord*) and question the stability of myth/memory/history (in *Faith Healer, Making History,* and *Aristocrats*)."

It got him into trouble, particularly in America and England, where he was accused of defending the I.R.A. in his angry, polemical plays *The Freedom of the City* and *Volunteers,* which retaliate against the British army's butcherings in Ulster. Though their subject is still topical, they are not among Friel's best works. He is a master of nuance and suggestion, and therefore any element of pamphleteering is more forceful when he speaks out in a refracted way. *Translations*—about the mapping and renaming of Ireland by the English—is a highly political but very subtle play, written with compassion, not bitterness.

"I don't think Friel is vitally and centrally interested in politics in Northern Ireland," says David Hammond. "He was made a senate in Dublin—the equivalent of England's House of Lords—which is unusual for someone who is apolitical. But he only went once and he didn't speak."

"I bet that's a bloody political table over there," remarks Friel. We are having dinner on the harbor at Kealy's Bar, renowned in the area for the fish it serves straight off the boats. Friel has spotted John Hume, the Social Democratic and Labor Party leader, a convivial fellow who has a weekend cottage nearby. Despite his well-known aversion to the profession (he once declared on television that all politicians were rats), Friel likes Hume and speaks of him as "very skillful—in Irish terms a new politician, a committed European with vision." Hume sits at one of the bar's two Formica tables, and is joined by his "henchman," as Friel calls his companion, their respective wives, and a couple of friends. They are there, Hume says, to "talk about the talks"; the next morning the first round-table talks in sixteen years will take place in Derry.

Kealy's could be the set of a Friel play or the prelude to his story about salmon fishing, "The Gold in the Sea." Sitting around the bar are three or four local fishermen, tanking up before taking the salmon boats out for several nights. A colleague sticks his head in the door and calls, "Half nine, Paddy." But Paddy looks very anchored. Friel has warned about the slow service: "You have to pace your waiting." Jimmy Kealy cooks on two gas rings, but eventually the lobsters and perfectly pink salmon appear. Friel, jovial and relaxed, talks enthusiastically about his friends, particularly Seamus Deane, whose first novel is about to be published and who has just been elected to the Aosdana, the Irish academy of arts. "I think he's the most brilliant man in Ireland. A conversation with him is a kind of epiphany."

Deane and Friel's other good friends—Seamus Heaney, Tom Kilroy, Tom Paulin, the actor Stephen Rea, and David Hammond—are all co-directors of Field Day, the theater company Friel started in 1980 with Rea. The original aim was to take Irish drama to culturally starved areas of the country. Since its inception, Field Day has expanded, and now publishes literary and political pamphlets. Its most ambitious project to date, masterminded by Deane, will be the publication in November (printed and distributed by Faber and Faber in the U.K. and Ireland and W. W. Norton in the U.S.) of *The Field Day Anthology of Irish Writing*, three volumes of poetry, drama, and fiction as well as political, historical, and philosophical articles in Irish and English written between the year 600 and the present day. Deane is overall editor, but the seven Field Day directors and friends have all contributed to the project in some way.

The small literary fraternity in Ireland is both enriching and inhibiting for Friel. The word he uses to describe it is "metabiotic"—which refers to organisms that need other organisms to thrive. So close-knit is the group that the writers—particularly Friel and Heaney—occasionally find themselves sharing the same images, most memorably digging and divining. When Friel sent Heaney the script of *Volunteers*, the poet was so excited by the coincidence of their both being imaginatively at work on the same Viking dig that he spent a weekend typing and ordering his poems and sent off the manuscript immediately to Faber and Faber. "His tunneling and tapping met my tunneling and tapping and set me on my way with the book." The book was *North*, published in 1975.

It is nearly eleven when we leave Kealy's Bar, and "the bloody political table" is still waiting to be served. Friel wishes Hume good luck, both with the arrival of the food and with the next morning. "So much hope is pinned on those talks," he says, leading the way out into the twilight-bright northern night.

Since then, the talks have collapsed. Friel is unsurprised. As Deane says, Friel has always been conscious of the recurrent failures of the political imagination in Ireland—"a whole history of failure." But his anger of twenty years ago has mellowed, and he now acknowledges that human nature provides its own consolations. "The Troubles are a pigmentation in our lives here, a constant irritation that detracts from real life. But life has to do with something else as well, and it's the other things which are the more permanent and real."

How *Dancing with Lughnasa* Writer Put Glenties Squarely on the Map

James Delingpole / 1992

James Delingpole's feature article on Glenties, the town that provides the setting for *Dancing at Lughnasa*, repeats a recollection of Friel saying a standing ovation from the townspeople was the proudest moment of his life. The Abbey Theatre cast of *Lughnasa* came from London to stage one performance in Glenties prior to taking the play to Broadway. The article, however, is primarily of interest for the conversations it records about Friel. Glenties residents comment on the ways Friel's play accurately reflects what they knew of his mother and aunts. But they say Friel offers fabrications in claiming the festival of Lughnasa was known in the area and in representing his missionary uncle as having "gone native."

From Dublin to Donegal and across the border into Londonderry, they have been toasting the health of Brian Friel and his play about five Donegal sisters and their ex-missionary brother.

It seems as if almost every Irish town from Dublin northwards wants to claim the author of *Dancing at Lughnasa* as its favourite son.

But nowhere has a better right to do so than the town of Glenties in the south of Donegal. It was here, after all, that the real life equivalents of the play's heroines, the Mundy sisters, had their home. Their name was McLoone and they were in fact Friel's mother and her sisters. "Mundy" is a common local nickname for the family name of McLoone.

Friel, born in Londonderry and now living 60 miles to the north of Glenties in Greencastle, consistently denies that Ballybeg, the fictional

From the *Daily Telegraph*, 2 June 1992, p. 4.

town where most of his plays are set, is anything more than a composite creation. But share a drink with anyone in Glenties, and they will disagree.

"Sure this is Ballybeg," said Mrs Eilish Herron, as she mulled over her whiskey in Paddy's Bar, one of the 13 pubs in Glenties's only street. Ballybeg means "small town" in Irish—"but Ballybeg is Glenties all right", she added.

Her pride is understandable. The three Tony awards that the play won on Sunday night—best play, best director (Patrick Mason) and best featured actress (Brid Brennan)—are the crowning glory of *Dancing at Lughnasa*'s three-year journey from Dublin's Abbey Theatre via the National Theatre and the West End to Broadway.

Mrs Herron, like most of the town's 900 or so inhabitants, is keen to establish a personal link with the play. Her mother and Friel's imposing aunt Kate taught at the same school, and she remembers young Brian from his holiday visits to Glenties as a "reserved, reticent and shy boy, who was jet black in the hair".

Friel's status as a local hero is never in any doubt. A portrait of the man hangs proudly across the street from Paddy's in the Highlands Hotel, and when he returned last August for a one-off gala performance of the play by the original cast from Dublin's Abbey Theatre, he was rewarded with a standing ovation. "He said it was the proudest moment of his life," says Mrs Herron. The playwright has enjoyed more than a few such moments since the play opened three years ago. In London, *Dancing at Lughnasa* was named best play in the *Evening Standard,* Writer's Guild, *Plays and Players* and Olivier Awards. Before the Tony awards it won the New York Drama Critics, the Drama Desk and Outer Critics Circle awards.

The play which has attracted this adulation is a surprisingly low-key affair. Set in 1936, it tells the story of the five Mundy sisters, one of whom has a son, Michael, who live in poverty with their brother, Father Jack, a missionary recently returned in disgrace from a Ugandan leper colony.

Its title comes from a scene in which the sisters interrupt their household chores to break out into a wild and completely unexpected dance, as they celebrate a pagan Irish festival called Lughnasa (pronounced Loo-na-sa). How much of all this is autobiographical and how much artistic licence has largely been a matter of speculation because Friel is notoriously reluctant to discuss his work. In Glenties they have their own ideas.

"I never heard of the festival of Lughnasa in me life," says Dr Malachy McCloskey, at 77 one of the town's older residents. "And we wouldn't be dancing round fires or anything like that. Not in my time, or my mother's," adds Miss Marie Clare O'Donnell, a supervisor in the town co-op.

Locals are equally surprised at Friel's apparent representation of his own uncle, Father Barney, as a batty priest who "went native" during his time as a missionary. "I think he was just an ordinary priest. He wasn't in any way kinky," says Dr McCloskey, who treated Father Barney for malaria. "Brian was writing about his own so he could take liberties. We do that here," says Miss O'Donnell.

Most agree, however, that Friel's portrait of his mother and four aunts is more or less accurate. This may be why he did not bother to change the Christian names of the sisters—Kate, Maggie, Rose, Agnes and Chris—in the play.

A few hundred yards from the town's comprehensive school, where *Dancing at Lughnasa* was staged last year as part of a Friel festival, stands The Laurels, where the sisters lived alongside four or five brothers (no one can recall exactly how many) who were excluded from the play.

The Laurels, named after the bushes that surround its secluded drive, is a pretty, slate-roofed cottage with creamy walls and brown cornerstones. It scarcely looks big enough to have once housed a family of 10.

Although The Laurels is viewed fairly nostalgically in the play, Nora Cooper, the author's first cousin once removed and his only surviving relative in Glenties, says Friel never much enjoyed the holidays he spent there with his aunts.

"He hated the summer hanging around The Laurels with no one to play with. And his aunt Kate was very strict," Mrs Cooper says.

"It was a beautiful house, very clean with lovely furniture," she adds. "But I used to be scared because there were rats. Maggie used to tell me there were no rats because the priest had blessed the house. But I could hear them scurrying around."

The sisters themselves were not nearly as straitened as the ones in the play. "There was poverty in the area," says Dr McCloskey, recalling the days when, as a young Donegal practitioner, he would leave patients' homes crawling with body lice. "But the McLoones weren't as poor as all that. After all, two of them were teachers and one was a priest."

They have long since passed away. Mrs Nora Breslin, who works for the Mac Gill Summer School, will happily show you where they are buried in the town's crumbling Old Cemetery. The McLoone family vault sits beneath a stone *Scathlan*—an ancient shelter where priests would once say Mass.

Friel himself, a Derry man by birth, may never choose to rest alongside the women who inspired his greatest play. But the people of Glenties are not going to forget their second famous son in a hurry.

A plaque commemorating their first local hero, Patrick Mac Gill, "the navvy poet", stands on one side of a bridge in the middle of Glenties. The wall on the other side lies empty. There can be little doubting whose name it will eventually bear.

Drama of Love: From One Great Master to Another

Eileen Battersby / 1992

Brian Friel had previously translated Chekhov's *Three Sisters* into a distinctively Irish idiom and had adapted Turgenev's novel *Fathers and Sons* for the stage. On the occasion of his producing a distinctively Irish version of Turgenev's *A Month in the Country,* Friel spoke to Eileen Battersby about issues raised by the process of translation, about what attracts him to the world of nineteenth-century Russia, and about the enigmas implicit in Turgenev's text.

Though acknowledged as a master of Russian prose within his own lifetime, Ivan Turgenev (1818–1883) had no confidence in himself as a playwright. He referred to his plays as little more than "scenes and comedies", and after about six years during which he wrote 10 plays, he more or less decided to abandon writing for the stage.

Yet though he made no claims for these scenes and comedies, most of which were experimental in form, he did believe that they contained something worthwhile; he was to write in 1869: "I consider it my duty to explain my motives to my readers. Realizing that I have no dramatic talent, I would not have acceded to the request of my publishers who wished to print the fullest possible edition of my works had I not thought that my plays, although unsatisfactory as pieces for the stage, could be of certain interest as pieces designed for reading."

No doubt his tentativeness towards his stage work was tempered by the success of his six novels. But Turgenev the perennial bachelor—charming sophisticated, handsome, very European—was to remain a

From *The Irish Times,* 1 August 1992, "Weekend" section, p. 2.

bullied son all his life and openly accepted the role of unsuccessful lover. He tended towards self-caricature all his life and wrote about the minor Russian gentry, the last relics of a collapsing semi-feudal regime, from his own experience of belonging to that class himself.

So persuasive were Turgenev's denouncements of his plays that even his friends and supporters shared his views. Yet if Turgenev was critical of his dramatic techniques, the acute psychological insights contained in the works assure their acceptance as intimate psychological theatre.

As a playwright he was born several decades too early. It took the emergence of Chekhov to confirm the theatrical achievement of Turgenev, which rests largely on one play: his seventh, the five-act work *A Month in the Country* (1848–50). It is ironic that this play, which appears so Chekhovian, was completed 10 years before Chekhov was even born. Both *The Seagull* and *Uncle Vanya* are direct descendants of it.

Brian Friel's version of the play opens at the Gate Theatre on Tuesday. Five years after transferring Turgenev's finest novel, *Fathers and Sons*, to the stage, Friel has worked his own version of *A Month in the Country*.

Why re-work an existing play? "I find the process—the exercise—of translating, both interesting and satisfying. Because you are presented with a complete fiction—given characters, given situations, given resolutions. Your 'creative' responsibilities are circumscribed. You may present the characters with situations not in the original text, but if you do, these characters must still be subject to Turgenev's psychological imperatives."

Described by Turgenev as "not really a comedy, but a short story in dramatic form" which, he insisted, "is clearly not suitable for the stage", *A Month in the Country* observes a frustrated and emotionally starved woman, Natalya Petrovna, loved and admired by a boring husband and worshipped by a long-suffering friend and unrequited lover, Rakitin. She falls hopelessly in love with Belyayev, her small son's tutor.

At the time of the play, the young man has been with the family a month and has settled in; he is enjoying life on a country estate—tutoring, making kites for his young charge and harmlessly flirting with Natalya's ward, the 17-year-old Vera. Belyayev does not realise that both women have fallen in love with him.

In the familiar atmosphere of crippling inertia which dominates Chekhov's plays, the characters are finally forced to confront their own complex feelings. Although it is about love, which tears through it like an avenging comet, the play is not a conventional romantic comedy. With the unintentional cruelty of youth, Belyayev dismisses the emotional upheavals of the play's three-day action as having "flared up".

If considered a comedy at all, it is because Turgenev—who, as stated above, consistently denied its comic content—set out to explore the absurdity of human passion. But it also looks at class differences. Shpigelsky, the local doctor, who spends most of his time making silly jokes and ridiculing his ability to heal anyone, explains his relationship with the gentry, describing himself as their "'breath of fresh air'—'comedian'— hah! They're civil to me because I relieve their boredom. But in their hearts they hate the peasant in me. And I clown for them because that masks how deeply I detest them."

And the doctor stresses to the woman he is pestering to marry him: "if you agree to marry me, you must know you're not marrying the laughing, fawning, ingratiating Shpigelsky. You're teaming up with the bitter, angry, cunning peasant." Young Belyayev, an early prototype for Turgenev's later hero Bazarov, also crosses the class divides, but without appearing conscious of it.

Falling in love holds disastrous consequences for Natalya; she is exposed and humiliated and, above all, rejected. According to Friel the play is about a complex and passionate woman's exploration of love: "Natalya's is a 20th-century sensibility that is bruised by and bruises itself against 19th-century morals. That exploration is the enigma of the play."

A distressed Natalya exclaims to Vera near the end of the play, in Friel's version, "For God's sake can't you see it's the normal that's deranging me, child?" For Stanislavsky, of the Moscow Art Theatre, Natalya is "a hot house rose" seeking to become a "field flower . . . from this there came the general catastrophe."

Of the other two love situations which are, he says, "much less complex, much more conventional and hinted at in Turgenev's text", Friel explains: "I have filled them out in order to enrich the overall pattern of the play and as an obligation to the play's main theme."

Turgenev wrote *A Month in the Country* while living in Paris. The period 1848 to 1850 were years of revolution, and at that time the influence of Turgenev's radical friends, such as Belinsky and Herzen, had its strongest hold on him. The radical quality of the play expresses itself through the revealing monologues of both Natalya and of Rakitin.

While acknowledging the existence of "several satisfying translations" of *A Month in the Country,* such as Constance Garnett's or Isaiah Berlin's, Friel points out the dangers of using in Ireland "a score written for English voices and sung by English actors." His version, based on a literal translation by Christopher Heaney, has a noticeable, if refined, Irish idiom.

"My first duty is to transpose the text into a key that is comfortably within the range of Irish actors," Friel explains; he questions the credibility of having an Irish actor, "using his native accent, convincingly deliver a line like, 'I say, old chap, that was a caddish thing to do'."

Friel concedes that "there are, of course, much larger issues at stake here. The practice of translation has to do with matters greater than pitch and range. But the Irish translator's dominant concern is a practical one: a play scored for Irish voices to sing."

Brian Friel, who maintains that Turgenev and Chekhov "change the face of European drama", admits to having "made a play" of Turgenev's *Fathers and Sons*. Why did he return to Turgenev? "I'm not sure. Maybe because he is 19th century Russian and I don't feel at all distant from that world. Because he is great but flawed; and the flaws allow in—maybe invite—the cheeky translation."

He describes the Russian master as "such a decent man who courageously risked more in his life than in his art; and since the play is partly autobiographical, it is good to be able to acknowledge that decency." But while Friel admires Turgenev and understands the psychological intensity of the work, his Ulster practicality adds: "when I began this, I had nothing else in hand. If I had had a new play of my own, I would have pursued that."

Turgenev spent 40 years of his life worshipping a woman, the Spanish singer, Pauline Garcia-Viardot, who was married to another man. It is in keeping with his tragic bad luck that it took 20 years for *A Month in the Country* to reach a Moscow stage, while the first satisfying production of it was not staged until 1909, when Stanislavsky's Moscow Art Theatre performed the work with Stanislavsky playing Rakitin. Although Stanislavsky proved a thorn in Chekhov's side, he identified the greatness of Turgenev's play, which he described as "so psychologically fine that it doesn't allow of any decor."

Playwright Brian Friel Quits Field Day

Gerry Moriarty / 1994

When Friel resigned from Field Day he told reporters that he had "nothing more to say," a phrase that would gather weight as his silence extended into years.

The playwright Brian Friel has resigned from the Derry-based Field Day theatre company which he founded 14 years ago with the actor Stephen Rea. In a typically laconic statement, he simply announced yesterday that his resignation was effective from last Monday.

When contacted at his home in Inishowen, Co Donegal, Mr Friel refused to give any reason for his decision. "I sent Field Day my resignation notice a few days ago and I have nothing more to say," he said.

Mr Friel was involved in an artistic quarrel with Mr Rea over his decision not to allow Field Day to stage his most recent plays, *Dancing at Lughnasa* and *Wonderful Tennessee.* Instead they received their premieres at the Abbey and went on international tour as Abbey productions promoted by Mr Noel Pearson—*Dancing at Lughnasa,* in particular, enjoying huge artistic and financial success.

Mr Rea was deeply annoyed and disappointed that Field Day had not been given the opportunity to show these plays first, as it had with previous Friel works such as *Translations* and *Making History.* Field Day was firmly put on the artistic map with its inaugural production of *Translations* in Derry.

Asked about the resignation yesterday, Mr Rea would merely say, "I think it is a pity." Asked if he and Mr Friel had mended fences since their row, he said: "Things are fine, but I don't want to talk any more about it."

From *The Irish Times,* 3 February 1994, p. 7.

Mr Friel's resignation comes at a time when Field Day, with the motivation of Mr Rea, is planning its first stage production since 1991. It is in the process of selecting a director and designer to present Chekhov's *Uncle Vanya*, adapted by Frank McGuinness, for probable production in the autumn.

Another Field Day director, Mr David Hammond, yesterday praised Mr Friel's contribution to the company. He said that while Mr Friel had been involved in a personal artistic dispute with Mr Rea, the row had not extended to the rest of its directors Seamus Heaney, Seamus Deane and Tom Paulin.

Asked why Mr Friel resigned, Mr Hammond said: "I think it is that he is going on a new artistic journey. All of us directors have changed directions since 1980, and I think it's marvellous that at this stage of our lives we can change." He said when Field Day was formed it was understood that there would be no difficulty in the playwrights on the board bringing their work to other companies. He added that Mr Rea, when he was concentrating on his film career, was away from the hub of Field Day activity for about two years.

Mr Friel is the second Field Day director to resign. In October 1992, the playwright Tom Kilroy left the board because he felt he was not "fully expressing" himself with Field Day.

Brian Friel Never Gives Interviews and Writes with a 2B Pencil

Bobbie Hanvey / 1999

If Friel offended any colleagues in Field Day by letting the Abbey Theatre stage *Dancing at Lughnasa* and *Wonderful Tennessee,* two months after quitting Field Day he was being asked why he sent his next play to the Gate Theatre instead of to the Abbey. With *Molly Sweeney,* the sixty–five-year-old Friel decided that for the first time in his career he would direct a play. But some things stayed the same. Friel refused all requests for interviews regarding *Molly Sweeney* and on opening night offered journalists just two words: "I'm OK." *Molly Sweeney* went to New York (1996) and Friel directed Jason Robards in the Broadway production, but even as a director on the Great White Way he declined all interviews. His silence continued when he directed *Give Me Your Answer, Do!* in Dublin (1997). Friel did give an answer to producer Noel Pearson, who had persuaded him to film *Dancing at Lughnasa.* After a private screening in Dublin of the film starring Meryl Streep, Friel grabbed Pearson and said "Well done, I'm very happy." But Friel's happiness did not change his stance toward the press. When the film version of *Dancing at Lughnasa* was launched in 1998, a major promotional campaign on both sides of the Atlantic included multiple interviews with Streep and several other members of the cast as well as interviews with the director but not one word from the author. But while Friel may refuse to be interviewed, he does allow himself to be photographed. And if a photographer asks him about the weather or writing implements, he just might

From *Belfast News Letter,* 12 June 1999, p. 15.

238

answer. Bobbie Hanvey's contribution to a picture of Friel—apart, that is, from a splendid photograph—has less to do with the playwright's penchant for pencils than his demeanor. Despite Friel's refusal to talk to interviewers, Noel Pearson insists that "he's not like Beckett or anything. He loves a sing song, puffs away on his cigar. He's great company." Although he did not seek to engage Friel in song, Hanvey probably has grounds to agree with Pearson.

I've never met a man like Brian Friel before. Totally dedicated to his work, he guards his privacy with a passion and treats publicity like the plague.

I asked myself why Ireland's greatest playwright doesn't court the limelight but I soon realised the answer. He doesn't have to.

In February past, I was commissioned to take his photograph by the *Irish Echo* in New York, which was making him Man of the Year 1999.

Having arranged to meet Brian in Donegal I knew it would take me two and a half hours to get there so I phoned him at 8 a.m. to check the weather.

"Well, what's the weather like this morning, Brian?"

"Your guess is as good as mine. What do I know about the weather?" he quipped.

I had heard he had a fantastic, wicked sense of humour but not having experienced it at first hand I couldn't be quite sure if he was being funny or straight to the point. I didn't test the waters.

"Is the sky clear or cloudy and overcast?" I continued.

"Wait until I look out."

Now there was a pause and a short silence.

"It looks fine to me, Bobbie."

Now totally convinced he had no interest in the fine art of weather forecasting, I assumed he was happy enough that the day was good enough for a photo session, so off I went making sure the studio lights were in the boot just in case we had to do an inside job.

My appointment was at 11 a.m., and at one minute to eleven, I pulled up in front of his bright yellow door.

Brian Friel celebrated his 70th birthday recently but there was no way he looked or acted his age.

Skipping over rugged rocks which almost invaded his front lawn he doggedly refused to let the camera get the better of him.

Then it was round the back of the house, up a few steps, past the sun dial, through a thicket and there hidden from the world a beautiful plantation of some 200 poplars which he planted 15 years ago and now they were reaching for the sky.

"When you're writing your plays, Brian, do you use a typewriter or pen?"

"I use a pencil," he replied.

"What sort of a pencil do you use. Is it an HB, H or B?" I probed.

He laughed loudly.

"Usually a 2B or a 3B," he replied. "I like a soft pencil."

Having been kindly given an hour to do my work I now had 10 minutes to go as I took the final shots of Brian leaning on the big, black anchor.

I then said I was very happy with the shots I'd got and thanked him very much for his time and cooperation.

"Thank God for that, Bobbie, I'm freezing. Would you like a cup of tea?"

Seated at the kitchen table I looked through the window and over the water and back into Northern Ireland as his wife, Anne, the most friendly of hosts, prepared the tea.

Brian lit up a big Havana and savoured the moment.

Secretly, and presumably unnoticed by him, I quickly inhaled some of the rising cloud. Having been reared in Co Fermanagh I was taught, from an early age, never to let anything go to waste.

What a moment for both of us! Better than Woodbine! Whenever you go to see one of Brian Friel's superb plays, spare a thought for the man who never gives an interview. He doesn't have to.

And in this manic world of hard drives, floppy discs and desk tops, also spare a thought for the knuckle bending reliability of the tried and tested 2B pencil and a scrumptious packet of Jacob's Mikado.

Bibliography

The following bibliography of Brian Friel's works and words about his works is arranged chronologically within each category. Plays are listed in the order of their initial production; short stories and articles appear in the order of their initial publication. Print interviews and broadcast talks and interviews are listed in the order—insofar as it can be determined—in which they were given. Where information about the date of an interview is not available, it is listed according to the date it was published or broadcast. News items and profiles are listed according to date of publication. Omitted are play reviews, news articles about productions with no personal involvement by Friel, audio and video recordings of plays, and acting editions of Friel plays (except for plays not otherwise published).

Plays by Friel

A Sort of Freedom. BBC Radio, Northern Ireland Home Service, 16 January 1958.

To This Hard House. BBC Radio, Northern Ireland Home Service, 24 April 1958.

A Doubtful Paradise. BBC Radio, Northern Ireland Home Service, 2 February 1962.

The Enemy Within (Abbey Theatre production at the Queen's Theatre, Dublin, 6 August 1962; BBC Radio, Northern Ireland Home Service, 6 June 1963, 9 September 1963). Newark, Del.: Proscenium Press, 1975, 1979; Dublin: Gallery, 1979, 1992.

The Blind Mice. (Eblana Theatre, Dublin, 19 February 1963; BBC Radio, Northern Ireland Home Service, 28 November 1963, 18 May 1966). Derry: Ireland, 1963.

Philadelphia, Here I Come! (Gaiety Theatre, Dublin, 28 September 1964; BBC Radio, Third Progamme, 25 February 1965). London: Faber, 1965, 1994; New York: Farrar, Straus and Giroux, 1966; New York: Noonday, 1966.

The Founder Members. BBC Radio, Light Programme, 9 March 1964.

The Loves of Cass McGuire (BBC Radio, Third Programme, 9 August 1966, 29 August 1966); Helen Hayes Theatre, New York, 6 October 1966). London:

Faber, 1967; New York: Farrar, Straus and Giroux, 1967; New York: Noon-
    day, 1967; Dublin: Gallery, 1984.
Lovers: Winners, Losers (Gate Theatre, Dublin, 18 July 1967; *Winners* on BBC
    Radio, Third Programme, 14 April 1968, 7 May 1968). New York: Farrar,
    Straus and Giroux, 1968; London: Faber, 1968, 1969; Dublin: Gallery,
    1984, 1996.
Crystal and Fox (Gaiety Theatre, Dublin, 12 November 1968; BBC Radio, Third
    Programme, 12 March 1969; Radio Four, 10 October 1971). London:
    Faber, 1970; New York: Farrar, Straus and Giroux, 1970 (with *The Mundy
    Scheme*); Dublin: Gallery, 1984.
The Mundy Scheme (Olympia Theatre, Dublin, 1969). New York: French, 1970;
    New York: Farrar, Straus and Giroux, 1970 (with *Crystal and Fox*).
The Gentle Island (Olympia Theatre, Dublin, 30 November 1971; BBC Radio
    Four, 29 October 1973). London: Davis-Poynter, 1974; Loughcrew, Oldcas-
    tle, Co. Meath: Gallery, 1993.
The Freedom of the City (Abbey Theatre, Dublin, 20 February 1973). London:
    Faber, 1974; Loughcrew, Oldcastle, Co. Meath: Gallery, 1992.
Volunteers (Abbey Theatre, Dublin, 5 March 1975). London and Boston: Faber,
    1979; Loughcrew, Oldcastle, Co. Meath: Gallery, 1989.
Farewell to Ardstraw. BBC Television Northern Ireland, 2 December 1976. (On
    Walter Glenn, a carpenter from Ardstraw, Co. Tyrone, who left Ireland in
    August 1744, like hundreds of thousands of other Presbyterians, to seek a
    better life in the New World.)
Living Quarters (Abbey Theatre, Dublin, 24 March 1977). London and Boston:
    Faber, 1978; Loughcrew, Oldcastle, Co. Meath: Gallery, 1992.
Faith Healer (Colonial Theater, Boston, February 1979; Longacre Theatre, New
    York, 5 April 1979; BBC Radio Three, 13 March 1980, 18 May 1980). Lon-
    don and Boston: Faber, 1980; Loughcrew, Oldcastle, Co. Meath: Gallery,
    1991.
Aristocrats (Abbey Theatre, Dublin, 8 March 1979; BBC Radio Four, 1 May 1989,
    6 January 1990). Dublin: Gallery, 1980; London: Faber, 1980.
"American Welcome" (Actors Theatre of Louisville, 27 February 1980). In *Best
    Short Plays 1981,* ed. Stanley Richards. Radnor, Pa.: Chilton Book Co., 1981,
    pp. 112–114.
Translations (Field Day, Guildhall, Derry, 23 September 1980; BBC Radio Three,
    31 January 1982, 10 February 1983). London and Boston: Faber, 1981.
Three Sisters (a version of the play by Anton Chekhov, Field Day, Guildhall, Derry,
    8 September 1981; BBC Radio Three, 23 December 1990). Dublin:
    Gallery, 1981, 1992.
The Communication Cord (Field Day, Guildhall, Derry, 21 September 1982). Lon-
    don and Boston: Faber, 1983; Loughcrew, Oldcastle, Co. Meath: Gallery,
    1989.
Selected Plays. London: Faber, 1984; Washington, D.C.: Catholic University of
    America Press, 1986; Gerrards Cross, Bucks.: Colin Smythe, 1988. (*Philadel-
    phia, Here I Come! The Freedom of the City, Living Quarters, Aristocrats, Faith
    Healer, Translations.*)
Fathers and Sons (a dramatization of the novel by Turgenev, National Theatre,
    London, 8 July 1987). London: Faber, 1987.

Making History (Field Day, Guildhall, Derry, 20 September 1988; BBC Radio
Three, 28 April 1989). London and Boston: Faber, 1989.

Dancing at Lughnasa (Abbey Theatre, Dublin, 24 April 1990). London and
Boston: Faber, 1990.

The London Vertigo (from a play by Charles Macklin, Gate Theatre production at
Andrew's Lane Theatre, Dublin, 23 January 1992). Loughcrew, Oldcastle,
Co. Meath: Gallery, 1990.

A Month in the Country (from the play by Turgenev, Gate Theatre, Dublin, 4
August 1992). Loughcrew, Oldcastle, Co. Meath: Gallery, 1992.

Wonderful Tennessee (Abbey Theatre, Dublin, 30 June 1993). London and Boston:
Faber, 1993; Loughcrew, Oldcastle, Co. Meath: Gallery, 1993.

Molly Sweeney (Gate Theatre, Dublin, 9 August 1994). Loughcrew, Oldcastle, Co.
Meath: Gallery, 1994; London and New York: Penguin, 1994; New York:
Plume, 1995.

Plays One. London: Faber, 1996. (*Philadelphia, Here I Come! The Freedom of the City,
Living Quarters, Aristocrats, Faith Healer, Translations.*)

Give Me Your Answer, Do! (Abbey Theatre, Dublin, 12 March 1997). Loughcrew,
Oldcastle, Co. Meath: Gallery, 1997; London: Penguin, 1997.

Uncle Vanya (Abbey Theatre, Dublin, 6 October 1998). Loughcrew, Oldcastle,
Co. Meath: Gallery, 1998.

Brian Friel's Dancing at Lughnasa: Screenplay. Adapted by Frank McGuinness. London: Faber, 1998.

Plays Two. London: Faber, 1999. (*Dancing at Lughnasa, Fathers and Sons, Making
History, Wonderful Tennessee, Molly Sweeney.*)

Fiction by Friel

"The Child." *The Bell,* 18, no. 4 (July 1952), pp. 232–33.

"The Good Old Days." *Ariel.* BBC Radio, Northern Ireland Home Service, 2 May
1956.

"Red, Red Rose." BBC Radio, Northern Ireland Home Service, 5 April 1957,
read by Friel.

"My True Kinsman." BBC Radio, Northern Ireland Home Service, 5 December
1957.

"The Fishing Lesson." BBC Radio, Northern Ireland Home Service, 18 July
1958.

"The Skelper." *New Yorker,* 1 August 1959, pp. 20–23. (*Morning Story,* BBC Radio
Four, 27 November 1967).

"The Fawn Pup." *New Yorker,* 2 April 1960, pp. 42–46. (*Morning Story,* BBC Radio,
Light Programme, 5 December 1963; Northern Ireland Home Service, 11
March 1964.)

"The Saucer of Larks." *New Yorker,* 24 September 1960, pp. 109–10. (*Morning
Story,* BBC Radio, Light Programme, 5 March 1964.)

"Segova, the Savage Turk." BBC Radio, Northern Ireland Home Service, 27
October 1960; *Morning Story,* Radio Two, 27 August 1971.

"The Potato Gatherers." *New Yorker,* 19 November 1960, pp. 172+. (*Morning Story,*
BBC Radio, Light Programme, 11 March 1965).

"Foundry House." *New Yorker,* 18 November 1961, pp. 50–57.

"My True Kinsman." *New Yorker,* 2 December 1961, pp. 196–200. (BBC Radio, Northern Ireland Home Service, 5 December 1957.)

"The Visitation." *The Kilkenny Magazine,* 5 (Autumn–Winter 1961–62), pp. 8–14.

The Saucer of Larks. New York: Doubleday; London: Victor Gollancz, 1962.

"The Diviner." *New Yorker,* 31 March 1962, pp. 36–42.

"Among the Ruins." *New Yorker,* 19 May 1962, pp. 118–28. (*Morning Story,* BBC Radio Two, 8 March 1968.)

"The Illusionists." *Saturday Evening Post,* 6 April 1963, pp. 56–62.

"A Fine Day at Glenties." *Holiday,* April 1963, pp. 22, 24–26, 28, 30–31.

"Ginger Hero." *Saturday Evening Post,* 18 May 1963, pp. 58–63.

"Everything Neat and Tidy." *New Yorker,* 11 April 1964, pp. 39–42.

"The Widowhood System." *New Yorker,* 5 September 1964, pp. 29–36.

"Death of a Scientific Humanist." *New Yorker,* 14 November 1964, pp. 58–62.

"The Girls from the Pyjama Factory." *The Arts in Ulster.* BBC Radio, Northern Ireland Home Service, 4 February 1965.

"The Gold in the Sea." *New Yorker,* 31 July 1965, pp. 32–37.

"My Own Kinsman." *Morning Story.* BBC Radio, Light Programme, 7 August 1965.

"The Queen of Troy Close." *Morning Story.* BBC Radio, Light Programme, 9 December 1965; *Interval Talk,* Northern Ireland Home Service, 1 April 1966.

The Gold in the Sea. New York: Doubleday; London: Victor Gollancz, 1966.

"Johnny and Nick." *Morning Story.* BBC Radio Two, 12 July 1968.

The Saucer of Larks: Stories of Ireland. London: Arrow Books, 1969.

"Green Peas and Barley O." *The Magic Sovereign.* BBC Television Northern Ireland, 18 May 1979. (Specially written story, fully dramatized, about the meeting between two con men and two simple country folk.)

Selected Stories. Dublin: Gallery Press, 1979, 1994.

The Diviner: The Best Stories of Brian Friel. Dublin: Gallery Books, 1979; Dublin: O'Brien Press, 1982; London: Allison and Busby, 1983; Old Greenwich, Conn.: Devin-Adair, 1983.

"The Giant." *Morning Story.* BBC Radio Four, 20 July 1990, 18 September 1991.

Articles by Friel

1952

"A Visit to Spain." *Irish Monthly,* 80 (November 1952), pp. 342–44. (An account of a trip to Spain with a sympathetic account of life under Franco's regime.)

1957

"For Export Only." *Commonweal,* 15 February 1957, pp. 509–10. (On Irish writers ignoring some facets of Irish life to avoid upsetting "the traditional concept of Irish life which Americans have.")

1961

"NATO at Night." *New Yorker,* 1 April 1961, pp. 105–9. (A humorous article about amorous sailors outside Friel's Derry home.)

1962

"The Lighter Side of Life: Meet Brian Friel: Who Has Undertaken to Entertain You Here Every Saturday." *Irish Press,* 28 April 1962, p. 10.

"The Lighter Side: Hotel Decorum." *Irish Press,* 5 May 1962, p. 10.

"The Lighter Side: Old Memories." *Irish Press,* 12 May 1962, p. 10.

"The Lighter Side: The Life of an Ageing Cyclist." *Irish Press,* 19 May 1962, p. 10.

"The Lighter Side: Cunningly Candid." *Irish Press,* 26 May 1962, p. 10.

"The Lighter Side: When the Bomb Fell on Derry." *Irish Press,* 2 June 1962, p. 10.

"Bringing in the Voters: Brian Friel Tells How He Helped the Party on Election Day." *Irish Press,* 9 June 1962, p. 11.

"The Lighter Side: Music Hath Charms: or, Why My Mother Breeds Greyhounds." *Irish Press,* 16 June 1962, p. 13.

"The Lighter Side: Disposing of the Body." *Irish Press,* 23 June 1962, p. 10.

"The Lighter Side: Waiting in the Rain." *Irish Press,* 30 June 1962, p. 10.

"Man of Action." *Irish Press,* 7 July 1962, p. 6. A review of *Sir Hubert Wilkins, His World of Adventure* by Lowell Thomas.

"The Lighter Side: The Afternoon of a Fawn Pup." *Irish Press,* 7 July 1962, p. 10.

"The Wild Life: Brian Friel Goes to the Country." *Irish Press,* 14 July 1962, p. 10.

"Donegal Diary: Brian Friel's Seaside Adventures: A Memorable Week." *Irish Press,* 21 July 1962, p. 10.

"Seagull in Distress: Brian Friel to the Rescue." *Irish Press,* 28 July 1962, p. 10.

"To the Wee Lake Beyond: A Journey with Brian Friel." *Irish Press,* 4 August 1962, p. 8.

"Brian Friel's Troubles with a Rat in the House." *Irish Press,* 11 August 1962, p. 8.

"A Bird in the Bog: Brian Friel Disappoints the Fans in O'Driscoll's Field." *Irish Press,* 18 August 1962, p. 8.

"It's a Long Way to Dublin." *Irish Press,* 25 August 1962, p. 10.

"Terror on the Rooftop." *Irish Press,* 1 September 1962, p. 8.

"Taught by the Maestro." Irish Press, 8 September 1962, p. 10.

"Lost: A Good Biographer." *Irish Press,* 15 September 1962, p. 8.

"After the Catastrophe." *Irish Press,* 22 September 1962, p. 8.

"Prison—Sanctuary on an Island." *Irish Press,* 29 September 1962, p. 6. A review of *Tide-Race* by Brenda Chamberlain.

"The Gathering Storm: Brian Friel's Preparations for an Evening Out." *Irish Press,* 29 September 1962, p. 8.

"The Play That Never Was." *Irish Press,* 6 October 1962, p. 8.

"Brian Friel's Derry Diary." *Irish Press,* 13 October 1962, p. 13.

"Brian Friel in the Role of—The Demon Fisherman." *Irish Press,* 20 October 1962, p. 10.

"A Thief in the Coal House." *Irish Press,* 27 October 1962, p. 8.

"Stalked by the Police: The Daylight Torture of Brian Friel." *Irish Press,* 3 November 1962, p. 8.

"The Ladies and the Tramp." *Irish Press,* 10 November 1962, p. 8.
"*And Then What Did She Say?:* A Tragic Dialogue." *Irish Press,* 17 November 1962, p. 8.
"A Retreat from the Brink." *Irish Press,* 24 November 1962, p. 8.
"At the Annual P.P.U. Meeting: Brian Friel's Secret Thoughts." *Irish Press,* 1 December 1962, p. 8.
"Social Climbing via the Post." *Irish Press,* 8 December 1962, p. 8.
"The Letter Writers: Solemn and Silent." *Irish Press,* 15 December 1962, p. 8.
"My Friend and Loyal Love: Who Is Out to Ruin My Digestion and My Career." *Irish Press,* 22 December 1962, p. 8.
"Brian Friel's Latest Temptation: To Flee to a Haven for the Harassed." *Irish Press,* 29 December 1962, p. 6.

1963

"A New Year's Diary." *Irish Press,* 5 January 1963, p. 6.
"Now About These Rats . . . Dear Lord Brookeborough." *Irish Press,* 12 January 1963, p. 6.
"Boyhood in Belfast Before Waterloo." *Irish Press,* 19 January 1963, p. 6. (A review of *Little Tom Drennan: Portrait of a Georgian Childhood* by Mary McNeill.)
"Marching with the Nation: By Howard B. Hedges, Junior (alias Brian Friel)." *Irish Press,* 19 January 1963, p. 8.
"A Warm Afternoon in the Cooler." *Irish Press,* 26 January 1963, p. 8.
"The Shameful Road to Glenties." *Irish Press,* 2 February 1963, p. 8.
"In the Waiting Room with Brian Friel." *Irish Press,* 9 February 1963, p. 8.
"Daughter Talk: Doing Down Daddy." *Irish Press,* 16 February 1963, p. 8.
"The Young Friel: The Days of My Glory? NO!" *Irish Press,* 23 February 1963, p. 8.
"An Affair of the Heart: Confessions of a Middle-aged Flirt." *Irish Press,* 2 March 1963, p. 8.
"Brian Friel's Lenten Diary." *Irish Press,* 9 March 1963, p. 8.
"Queen of the Smugglers: Brian Friel's Fond Tribute to His Mother." *Irish Press,* 16 March 1963, p. 8.
"The Importance of Being Frank: Brian Friel Writes from America." *Irish Press,* 23 March 1963, p. 10.
"Labors of Love." *Atlantic Monthly,* April 1963, pp. 130–2. (An autobiographical account of Friel's early notions of romance; also broadcast as "Labours of Love: A Talk by Brian Friel." BBC Radio, Northern Ireland Home Service, 13 August 1963 (recorded 17 March 1963).)
"Brian Friel's American Diary: 1. Arrival in New York." *Irish Press,* 20 April 1963, p. 8.
"Brian Friel's American Diary: 2. Sight-seeing." *Irish Press,* 27 April 1963, p. 10.
"Brian Friel's American Diary: 3. A Moving Lecture." *Irish Press,* 4 May 1963, p. 8.
"Brian Friel's American Diary: 4. The News From Home." *Irish Press,* 11 May 1963, p. 8.
"Brian Friel's American Diary: 5. At the United Nations." *Irish Press,* 18 May 1963, p. 8.

"Brian Friel's American Diary: 6. The Philosopher and I." *Irish Press,* 25 May 1963, p. 6.

"Brian Friel's American Diary: 7. The Checking Account." *Irish Press,* 1 June 1963, p. 10.

"Brian Friel's American Diary: 8. Living a Dog's Life." *Irish Press,* 8 June 1963, p. 8.

"Brian Friel's American Diary: 9. Wings on His Heart." *Irish Press,* 15 June 1963, p. 8.

"Brian Friel's American Diary: 10. 'The Phone Call': A Tragi-comedy in One Act." *Irish Press,* 29 June 1963, p. 10.

"The Returned Yank." *Irish Press,* 10 August 1963, p. 8.

"Downstairs No Upstairs." *New Yorker,* 24 August 1963, pp. 82, 84–85. (Broadcast, in a revised version, as a talk by Friel on BBC Radio, 5 July 1967.)

"Walk to that Exit." *Holiday,* November 1963, pp. 48, 50–52.

1964

"The Giant of Monaghan." *Holiday,* May 1964, pp. 89, 92, 94–96.

"Brian Friel, O'Connor and Edwards." *Sunday Independent,* 11 October 1964, p. 21. Friel's response (alongside that of Hilton Edwards) to Frank O'Connor's review of *Philadelphia, Here I Come!*—"Edwards the magician turns gentle play into rip-roaring review," *Sunday Independent,* 4 October 1964, p. 18.

1967

"The Theatre of Hope and Despair." *The Critic* (The Thomas More Association, Chicago), 26 (August–September 1967), pp. 13–17. Delivered as a lecture at the Thomas More Association Symposium, Chicago. Reprinted in *Everyman* (Servite Priory, Benburb, Co. Tyrone), no. 1 (1968), pp. 17–22.

1970

"A Challenge to *Acorn.*" *Acorn* (English Society, Magee University College, Derry, a campus of the New University of Ulster, now the University of Ulster), no. 14 (Autumn 1970), p. 4.

1972

"Sex in Ireland (The Republic of)." *The Critic* (The Thomas More Association, Chicago), 30, no. 4 (March–April 1972), pp. 20–21.

"Plays Peasant and Unpeasant." *Times Literary Supplement,* 17 March 1972, pp. 305–6.

"Self-Portrait." *Aquarius* (Servite Priory, Benburb, Co. Tyrone), no. 5 (1972), pp. 17–22. A somewhat revised transcript of a talk given on BBC Radio, Northern Ireland Home Service, 19 December 1971.

"Two Playwrights with a Single Theme." In *A Paler Shade of Green,* ed. Des Hickey and Gus Smith, pp. 220–25. London: Leslie Frewin, 1972. U.S. edition, *Flight from the Celtic Twilight.* Indianapolis: Bobbs-Merrill, 1973.

1978

A tribute to Hilton Edwards and Micheál Mac Liammóir. In *Enter Certain Players: Edwards– MacLiammóir and The Gate 1928–1978*, ed. Peter Luke, pp. 21–22. Dublin: Dolmen Press, 1978.

1979

"Salutation." *Pennyburn Boy's Anniversary Magazine 1954–1975* (St. Patrick's Boys' School, Derry), 1979. (Cited by Ulf Dantanus, *Brian Friel: The Growth of an Irish Dramatist.* Gothenburg Studies in English 59. Goteborg, Sweden: Acta Universitatis Gothoburgensis, 1985, p. 66 and p. 217, n. 40.)

1980

"Extracts from a Sporadic Diary." In *The Writers: A Sense of Ireland,* ed. Andrew Carpenter and Peter Fallon, pp. 39–43. Dublin: O'Brien Press; New York: George Braziller, 1980. (On the writing of *Aristocrats.*)

1983

"Extracts from a Sporadic Diary." In *Ireland and the Arts,* A Special Issue of the *Literary Review,* ed. Tim Pat Coogan, pp. 56–61. London: Namara Press, 1983. (On the writing of *Translations.*)
"Address by Brian Friel at the Opening of Annaghmakerrig House." *Threshold* (The Lyric Players Theatre, Belfast), no. 33 (Winter 1983), pp. 58–59. (Transcript of October 1982 speech at the formal opening of the Tyrone Guthrie Centre at Annagh-ma-Kerrig.)

1986

"Important Places." Introduction to *The Last of the Name* by Charles McGlinchey. Belfast: The Blackstaff Press, 1986; Nashville: J. S. Sanders, 1999, pp. 1–4.

1990

"MacLochlainn's Vertigo." Introduction to *The London Vertigo.* Adapted from *The True Born Irishman* by Charles Macklin (a true born Irishman christened Cathal MacLochlainn). Oldcastle: Gallery Press, 1990. Reprinted as "MacLochlainn's Vertigo," *Irish Times,* 12 December 1990, p. 14. Reprinted in an abbreviated version as "MacLochlainn's Vertigo" in the Gate Theatre *London Vertigo* production program, 23 January 1992. Dublin, n.p.

1992

"A New Initiative for Ireland." Letter to the editor cosigned by Simon Lee, Robin Wilson, Jennifer Johnston, Seamus Heaney, et al. *The Guardian,* 11 February

1992, p. 18. (On the deteriorating situation in Northern Ireland and opportunity for dialogue offered by Initiative '92.)

Introduction and Foreword to *A Month in the Country* by Ivan Turgenev in a new version by Brian Friel. Oldcastle: Gallery Press, 1992. Reprinted in the Gate Theatre production program, 4 August 1992. Dublin, n.p.

1997

"I Was Beginning to Wonder What Further Ecstasy Confession Itself Would Bring." *Irish Independent,* 3 May 1997. (A reprint of a 1965 story about an eight-year-old boy approaching his first confession; excerpted from *Great Irish Stories of Childhood.*)

1999

"Words." In *Friel Festival: April–August 1999,* the festival program edited by Noel Pearson. Dublin: Ferndale Theatre Productions, 1999, p. 8.

"Great Actors." In *Friel Festival,* pp. 10–11.

"Amateurs." In *Friel Festival,* p. 13.

"Music." In *Friel Festival,* pp. 14–15.

"Directors." In *Friel Festival,* pp. 16–17.

"Translations." In *Friel Festival,* pp. 18–19.

"Kitezh." In *Friel Festival,* p. 20.

"Brian Friel." *Irish Times,* 11 May 1999, "Education and Living" section, p. 55. (Two paragraphs recalling his student experiences at St. Columb's.)

Print Interviews

1962

"Broadcast of Ulster Author's Play: 'Angry Young Man' is Angrier." *Northern Whig* (Belfast), 22 January 1962. (On *A Doubtful Paradise,* which Friel describes as "a timorous statement of what I now firmly believe: that the majority is *always* wrong.")

"Derry Author Mr. Brian Friel." *Irish Press,* 26 January 1962, p. 3.

Moore, Tom. "People I Meet: He'll Be Glad to Get Back Home." *Irish Press,* 7 August 1962, p. 9. (On the Abbey Theatre opening of *The Enemy Within.*)

1963

"Brian Friel's First Book." *Belfast Telegraph,* 25 February 1963, p. 3. (On *The Saucer of Larks.* Friel, who has spent six months working on a play called "The Ballad of Ballybeg," says his ambition is to write the "great Irish play": "Such a play is one where the author can talk so truthfully and accurately about people in his own neighbourhood and make it so that these folk could be living in Omagh, Omaha or Omansk.")

1964

Smith, Gus. "'I've Yet to Make Money from My Plays' Says Festival Dramatist
  Brian Friel." *Sunday Independent* (Dublin), ca. 4 October 1964. (Undated
  clipping from the *Sunday Independent* clippings library does not appear in
  the edition of the *Sunday Independent* on microfilm. *Philadelphia, Here I Come!*
  opened on 28 September 1964 as part of the Dublin Festival that closed on
  4 October 1964. Internal evidence suggests the interview occurred during
  the Festival.)
Lennon, Peter. "Playwright of the Western World." *The Guardian*, 8 October
  1964, p. 9. (British Humanities Index cites title, perhaps from another edition, as "Derry, Here I Am.")

1965

Hamilton, John. "The 'Big Five' of Ulster Drama." *Ulster Week*, 6 January 1965, p.
  12. (Quotes Friel as having one ambition: "to write the great Irish play.")
McMullen, Desmond. "TV Comment: Fifty Dramatic Minutes in March." *Belfast
  Telegraph*, 5 February 1965, p. 12. (Regarding *The Enemy Within* dealing with
  St. Columba, Friel says he has attempted to analyze the reasons why the man
  became a saint: "But I assure you it is not pious. There are no thous or thees
  in it.")
Morison, Graham. "An Ulster Writer: Brian Friel." *Acorn* (English Department,
  Magee University College, Derry, now a campus of the University of Ulster),
  no. 8 (Spring 1965), pp. 4–15.

1966

Fairleigh, John. "After *Philadelphia*." *Belfast Telegraph*, 9 August 1966, p. 6.

1967

Darina. "The Life and Work of a Playwright." *Irish Press*, 7 April 1967, p. 12. (On
  The Loves of Cass McGuire, his work habits, and a play he was then calling
  "Lovers Keepers.")
"Londoner's Diary: Secluded in Muff." *Evening Standard*, 15 September 1967, p.
  6. (After his move to the village of Muff in the Republic of Ireland, Friel is
  quoted as saying: "All Irishmen are born with the awful burden of being
  physically and spiritually bound up with Ireland. It's inevitable.")
"Friel Adapts Wells Story for Film." *Belfast Telegraph*, 9 October 1967, p. 4. (Friel
  is writing the screenplay for H. G. Wells's short story "The Man Who Could
  Work Miracles.")
"Critics Have No Effect on What I Do, Says Friel." *Belfast Telegraph*, 10 November
  1967, p. 7.

1968

Funke, Lewis. "Interview with Brian Friel." In *Playwrights Talk about Writing: 12
  Interviews with Lewis Funke*. Chicago: Dramatic Publishing Co., 1975, pp.

111–33. (Interview conducted in New York in mid-September 1968 when *Lovers* was already running.)

Tallmer, Jerry. "A Song of Ireland." *New York Post,* 20 September 1968, p. 47. (Asked about Catholicism, Friel says "Well, I don't know how the hell to put it, but don't say: 'Once you're Catholic you're always Catholic.'" Regarding politics, Friel says: "I used to be a violent nationalist. I'm still a nationalist, but it has come to mean a different thing for me.")

Bunce, Alan N. "Frank Talk from Friel." *Christian Science Monitor,* 27 November 1968, p. 13. (On the contrast between American and Irish theatre as well as Friel's view of directors.)

1969

"Press Diary: Unsinkable Brian Friel." *Irish Press,* 11 April 1969, p. 17. (Friel describes *The Mundy Scheme* as "a savage satire on Irish politics.")

"New Friel Play is Not Accepted by Abbey Theatre." *Irish Times,* 23 May 1969, p. 1. (Friel says he is "very angry" about the Abbey's rejection of *The Mundy Scheme.*)

"Abbey 'No' to Friel Play." *Belfast Telegraph,* 23 May 1969, p. 1.

"12 Teachers to Coach Itinerant Pupils." *Belfast Telegraph,* 26 May 1969, p. 5 (Serving as the welfare officer for the Derry Itinerants' Settlement Committee, Friel says "a process of education" is needed for "itinerants to live in the kind of society the rest of us live in.")

Smith, Gus. "Why Friel Doesn't Write about Civil Rights." *Sunday Independent,* 1 June 1969, p. 20.

"What's On: A Look at the Arts: Brian Friel's New Play." *Irish Times,* 9 June 1969, p. 12. (Comparing *The Mundy Scheme* to his earlier plays, Friel says that "in the past I've tried to investigate individuals, but this is an indictment of the general establishment." Of *Crystal and Fox,* faulted by Irish critics, Friel remarks "They say if you've a backward child you love it best of all, so maybe that's why I think it's the best thing I've ever done.")

1970

Rushe, Desmond. "Kathleen Mavourneen, Here Comes Brian Friel." *The Word: An International Catholic Pictorial Magazine* (Divine Word Missionaries, formerly of St. Richard's College, Hadzor, Droitwich, Worcestershire, England; now published at Donamon, Co. Roscommon, Ireland), February 1970, pp. 12–15.

Linehan, Fergus, Hugh Leonard, John B. Keane and Brian Friel. "The Future of Irish Drama." *Irish Times,* 12 February 1970, p. 14.

Boland, Eavan. "The Northern Writers' Crisis of Conscience." A Series of Three Articles. *Irish Times,* 12, 13, and 14 August 1970, p. 12.

1971

Madden, Aodhan. "Brian Friel's Other Island: Aodhan Madden Talks to Ireland's Top Dramatist about His New Play." *Sunday Press,* 28 November 1971, p. 31. (On the opening of *The Gentle Island.*)

1972

Bell, Sam Hanna. *The Theatre in Ulster.* Dublin: Gill and Macmillan; Totowa, N.J.: Rowman and Littlefield, pp. 102–7.

1973

Boland, Eavan. "Brian Friel: Derry's Playwright." *Hibernia* (Dublin), 16 February 1973, p. 18. (On *The Freedom of the City.*)
Rosie, George. "'Whatever I Write About Will Offend Someone." *Radio Times* (Belfast edition), 15 February 1973, p. 10. (On *The Freedom of the City.*)
"I'm Bound to Upset Someone—Friel." *Belfast Telegraph,* 20 February 1973, p. 5. (On *The Freedom of the City.*)
Gilchrist, Roderick. "Play about Ulster Angers the Army." *Daily Mail,* 20 February 1973, p. 3. (Friel responds to Army officers' objections to *The Freedom of the City.*)

1975

O'Kelly, Fachtna. "Can the Critics Kill a Play?" *Irish Press,* 28 March 1975, p. 9. (Friel's comments on theatre critics after having received negative reviews for *Volunteers* at the Abbey Theatre.)

1976

"Twelve Years On." *Belfast Telegraph,* 15 November 1976, p. 8. (On an unproduced play called "Bannermen" that was to have been staged in Belfast as a Queen's Festival production but has been delayed.)

1978

Gillespie, Elgy. "Is the Play Still the Thing?" *Irish Times,* 28 July 1978, p. 8.

1980

"World Premiere Crucial for Derry Theatre Hopes," *Belfast Telegraph,* 3 June 1980, p. 13.
O Connor, Fionnuala. "Derry's Guildhall Opens its Doors." *Irish Times,* 4 June 1980, p. 4.
Farren, Ronan. "Broadway? Who Cares?" *Evening Herald* (Dublin), 28 August 1980, p. 8. (On *Faith Healer* and *Translations.*)
Riddel, Lynne. "Why Friel and Rea are Having a 'Field' Day." *Belfast Telegraph,* 15 September 1980, p. 8. (Friel discusses the genesis of *Translations* and the process of mounting a Field Day production in Derry.)
Robinson, Liam. "New Play to Set Fire to the Foyle?" *Evening Press* (Dublin), 19 September 1980, p. 6. (News account of the opening of *Translations* concludes with a statement from Friel about how he came to write the play.)
McCartney, Noel. "Derry Rallies behind Friel Play Premiere." *Irish Press,* 20 Sep-

tember 1980, p. 5. (Friel comments on support of the Derry City Council and on involvement of Derry people in the production of *Translations*.)

McAuley, Liam. "Something Stirs in the Londonderry Air." *Sunday Times*, 21 September 1980, p. 14.

Dixon, Stephen. "Mapping Cultural Imperialism." *The Guardian*, 27 September 1980, p. 11.

Carty, Ciaran. "Finding Voice in a Language Not Our Own." *Sunday Independent*, 5 October 1980, p. 16.

Agnew, Paddy. "'Talking to Ourselves': Brian Friel Talks to Paddy Agnew." *Magill* (Dublin), 4, no. 3 (December 1980), pp. 59–61.

1981

Walsh, Caroline. "£5,000 Award for Brian Friel." *Irish Times*, 15 January 1981, p. 4. (Friel comments on receiving a writing award and expresses his surprise at the immense success of *Translations:* "Nowadays, to write a three-act naturalistic play set in the 19th century in the Gaeltacht is a recipe for some kind of instant death, so its success astonished me.")

Feeney, John. "Ad Lib: Brian Friel's Present Work Is Top Secret." *Evening Herald* (Dublin), 15 January 1981, p. 13. (Friel alludes to a project that has the full support of the Derry Council but says "I can't tell you what we're doing.")

Radin, Victoria. "Voice from Ireland: Victoria Radin Talks to Brian Friel." *The Observer*, 1 March 1981, p. 34.

Kennedy, Maev. "Friel Grateful for His Bad Telephone Line." *Irish Times*, 3 March 1981, p. 6.

Lowry, Betty. "The Man from Muff." *Belfast Telegraph*, 7 March 1981, p. 6.

O'Hare, Gerry. "After *Translations*." *Irish Press*, 7 March 1981, p. 6. (On Field Day tours and the transfer to Broadway of *Translations*.)

Nowlan, David. "Friel on Off-Broadway." *Irish Times*, 4 April 1981, p. 9 ("Weekend" section, p. 1). (On New York rehearsals of *Translations* prior to 14 April opening.)

Spencer, Charles. "Friels on Wheels . . ." *The Standard* (London), 15 May 1981, pp. 24–25.

Vernon, Michael. "Brian Friel and the Road to Ballybeg." *Fortnight*, no. 181 (May/June 1981), pp. 16–17.

Sennett, Graham. "Theatre: Friel's *Three Sisters*." *Evening Press* (Dublin), 22 August 1981, p. 6. (Friel says Field Day will be performing a translation of *Three Sisters*, not an adaptation of Chekhov's play.)

O'Donnell, Donal. "Friel and a Tale of Three Sisters." *Sunday Press*, 30 August 1981, p. 19. (Friel refers to Irish affinities with Chekhov in discussing his adaptation of *Three Sisters* and says a goal of Field Day is "to be transient in the aesthetic sense as well as in the practical sense.")

Riddel, Lynne. "Three Russian Sisters Go Irish—and Take a Bow in Derry." *Belfast Telegraph*, 2 September 1981, p. 8.

Gillespie, Elgy. "The Saturday Interview: Brian Friel." *Irish Times*, 5 September 1981, p. 14 ("Weekend" section, p. 6).

O'Connor, Ulick. "Friel Takes Derry by Storm." *Sunday Tribune*, 6 September 1981, p. 2. (On *Three Sisters* and *Translations*.)

Moloney, Eugene. "Derry Awaits New Brian Friel Chekov Play." *Irish News,* 7 September 1981, p. 5.

Dowling, Noeleen. "Helicopter Drowns Friel's World Premiere: Lot to Admire, Not Something to Rave About." *Evening Press* (Dublin), 9 September 1981, p. 5. (A news account and review of Friel's *Three Sisters* concluding with comments from Friel about his reaction to car bombs and bomb hoaxes that have disrupted rehearsals.)

Póirtéir, Cathal. "Drámaíocht don bpobal." *Irish Press,* 9 September 1981, p. 8. (Interview published in Irish regarding Friel's version of *The Three Sisters.*)

Kiely, Niall. "An Irishman's Diary." *Irish Times,* 17 September 1981, p. 9. (Friel explains why he refused to allow a bilingual performance of *Translations* in English and Irish.)

Parker, Selwyn. "The Place Is the Thing for the Irish Writer." *The Globe and Mail* (Toronto), 30 September 1981, p. 20. (During Derry rehearsals for *Three Sisters,* Friel says he would never leave the area of Derry and Co. Donegal. He talks about Field Day—"our aim is to be heard on this island"—and of the need for Chekhov to be translated into an Irish idiom.)

"Centre Brings to Life a Vision of Tyrone Guthrie," *Belfast Telegraph,* 10 October 1981, p. 3. (Comments by Friel who officially opened the Tyrone Guthrie Centre for creative artists.)

Gillespie, Elgy. "Writers' Retreat Is Opened." *Irish Times,* 12 October 1981, p. 9.

1982

Edwards, Owen Dudley. "A Question of Communication." *Radio Times,* 30 January 1982, pp. 18, 21.

"Another Guildhall World Premiere," *Derry Journal,* 31 August 1982, p. 7. (Brief comments from Friel about writing his first farce, *The Communication Cord.*)

The Roamer. "Friel's Farce." *News Letter* (Belfast), 9 September 1982, "Around & About" column, p. 4. (Friel says *The Communication Cord* "laughs its way towards seriousness.")

Comiskey, Ray. "Rehearsing Friel's New Farce." *Irish Times,* 14 September 1982, p. 8.

Moloney, Eugene. "*Communication Cord* Set to be a Signal Success." *Irish News,* 17 September 1982, p. 4. (Friel discusses the genesis of *The Communication Cord.*)

Stanfield, Maggie. "Response Cry—Variations of a Catastrophe." *Irish Press,* 17 September 1982, p. 7. (On *The Communication Cord.*)

Article about Brian Friel. *Chicago Tribune,* 24 September 1982. (Cited by *Contemporary Authors,* new revision series, vol. 33 [1991], p. 154.)

O'Toole, Fintan. "The Man from God Knows Where: An Interview with Brian Friel." *In Dublin,* no. 165 (28 October 1982), pp. 20–23.

1983

Friel, Brian, John Andrews and Kevin Barry. "*Translations* and *A Paper Landscape:* Between Fiction and History." *The Crane Bag,* 7, no. 2 (1983), pp. 118–24. (An edited transcription of an exchange between Friel and John Andrews,

author of *A Paper Landscape: The Ordnance Survey in Nineteenth-Century Ireland,* that took place at the Interdisciplinary Seminar at St. Patrick's College, Maynooth, on 20 January 1983.)

"Field Day's New Production: *Boesman and Lena* for the Guildhall," *Derry Journal,*
2 September 1983, p. 7. (Friel explains the selection of an Athol Fugard
play for the current Field Day tour and points out the contemporary social
relevance both of that play and of *Translations.*)

1984

Quilligan, Patrick. "Field Day's New Double Bill." *Irish Times,* 18 September
1984, p. 10.

1986

Cowley, Martin. "Field Day Has Made a Permanent Mark." *Irish Times,* 5 May
1986, p. 12. (Friel interviewed about Field Day's two-volume anthology of
Irish literature.)

Morash, Christopher A. "Flamethrowers: Contemporary Northern Irish Playwrights." M. Phil. diss., Trinity College, Dublin, 1987, pp. 41–42. (Friel talks
about the consequences of language becoming politicized and about the
importance of language as reality for a writer—in an interview conducted
22 August 1986 in the Blarney Room of the Leprechaun Restaurant in
Derry.)

Sheridan, Michael. "Friel's Sense of Conflict." *Irish Press,* 1 October 1986, p. 9.
(Profile concludes with a substantial statement from Friel about the difficulties of forging a language adequate to use in writing about the Northern situation.)

O'Toole, Fintan. "Courage, Integrity and Style." *Magill* (Dublin), 10, no. 4
(December 1986), pp. 46–50. (A tribute to the actress Siobhan McKenna
includes one quotation from Brian Friel's comments at her funeral the previous week.)

1987

"US Field Day for Begging Bowl Big Four." *Irish News,* 30 March 1987, p. 3.
(Upon returning from a fund-raising tour in the United States, Friel discusses Field Day anthology of Irish literature.)

Cowley, Martin. "Senator Brian Friel Won't Swap the Pen for Politics." *Irish Times,*
7 May 1987, p. 12. (Friel, one of the Taoiseach's eleven new nominees to
the Seanad, talks about his appointment as an independent senator and
about the latest projects of Field Day.)

1988

Spillane, Margaret. "Friel's Ireland Avoids Getting Lost in *Translations.*" *In These
Times* (Institute for Public Affairs, Chicago), 14–20 September 1988, p. 21.
(Cited by Marilynn J. Richtarik, *Acting Between the Lines: The Field Day Theatre*

Company and Irish Cultural Politics 1980–1984. Oxford: Clarendon Press, 1994, p. 286, n. 7.)

1989

O'Toole, Fintan. "Friel's Day." *Irish Times,* 7 January 1989, "Weekend" section, pp. 1, 12. (Profile quotes from BBC interviews with Friel.)

Wolf, Matt. "Brian Friel's Ireland: Both Private and Political." *New York Times,* 30 April 1989, sec. 2, pp. 7–8.

Agnew, Paddy. "Irish Theatre on Show in Rome." *Irish Times,* 14 May 1989, p. 12. (Cited by George O'Brien, *Brian Friel: A Reference Guide 1962–1992* [New York: G. K. Hall, 1995], item 1989.1, as a "report on Friel's presence at a production, in Italian, of *Faith Healer,* including some comments by the playwright on the state of Ireland." But the *Irish Times* did not publish on Sunday, 14 May 1989; article not located on microfilm or in the *Irish Times* clippings library.)

1990

Woodworth, Paddy. "Field Day's Men and the Re-making of Ireland." *Irish Times,* 5 November 1990, p. 10.

1991

McCarthy, Justine. "Friel Day: Justine McCarthy Tries to Pin Down the Elusive Genius of Secretive Playwright Brian Friel." *Irish Independent,* 19 January 1991, "Weekender" section, p. 13. (Friel talks about why he does not give interviews.)

Purcell, Bernard. "Friel Wins Play of the Year Award." *Irish Independent,* 8 April 1991. (Friel praises Abbey Theatre company for their production of *Lughnasa,* honored at the Olivier awards in London.)

Gussow, Mel. "From Ballybeg to Broadway." *New York Times Magazine,* 29 September 1991, pp. 30, 55–61. (Partially reprinted as "Broadway, Here Comes Friel . . ." *Irish Independent,* 8 October 1991; and partially reprinted as "Brian Goes Dancing on Broadway," *Sunday Press,* 20 October 1991, sec. 3 "Living.")

Kavanagh, Julie. "Friel at Last." *Vanity Fair,* October 1991, pp. 128, 130, 134, 138.

Lahr, John. "In *Dancing at Lughnasa,* Due on Broadway this Month, Brian Friel Celebrates Life's Pagan Joys." *Vogue* (American), October 1991, pp. 174, 176, 178–79.

"Friel Wins Top Award for Play of the Year." *Irish News,* 13 November 1991. (Brief quotation from Friel in New York regarding *Dancing at Lughnasa* receiving Best Play award in London.)

1992

O'Toole, Fintan. "Keeper of the Faith." *The Guardian,* 16 January 1992, p. 26.

Delingpole, James. "How *Dancing with Lughnasa* Writer Put Glenties Squarely on the Map." *Daily Telegraph*, 2 June 1992, p. 4. (Friel quoted as saying a standing ovation in Glenties for *Dancing at Lughnasa* was the proudest moment of his life. Extensive background information on the town—perhaps the original of Ballybeg—where Friel's aunts lived.)

Battersby, Eileen. "Drama of Love: From One Great Master to Another." *Irish Times*, 1 August 1992, "Weekend" section, p. 2. (Interview regarding Friel's version of Turgenev's *A Month in the Country*.)

Sherlock, John. "Captured by the Spirit of True Lunacy." *Irish Independent*, 21 August 1992. (Friel quoted as saying *Dancing at Lughnasa* is "about the necessity for paganism.")

"New Friel Play for Pearson," *Irish Times*, 10 December 1992, p. 10. (Friel describes *Wonderful Tennessee* as "an Irish *Canterbury Tales*.")

1993

Witchel, Alex. "Life May Be a Madness, but It's Also a Poem." *New York Times*, 17 October 1993, sec. 2, pp. 5, 22–23. (Friel praises Noel Pearson, the producer of *Lughnasa*, for having "the head of a businessman, the heart of a gambler and the untutored intuitions of an artist.")

Holland, Mary. "'There's No Point in Prolonging the Agony, Bleeding It to Death.'" *Irish Times*, 30 October 1993, p. 4. (The Broadway closing of *Wonderful Tennessee* after nine performances evokes one comment from Friel: "Sure, I've had more flops on Broadway than I've had hot dinners. I'm immune. Well, I'm not quite immune, but you just have to get on with it.")

O'Mahony, John. "Early Curtain for New Friel Play." *Irish Independent*, 1 November 1993. (Friel refers to the Broadway closing of *Wonderful Tennessee* after nine performances as "a mishap, just a mishap.")

1994

Moriarty, Gerry. "Playwright Brian Friel Quits Field Day." *Irish Times*, 3 February 1994, p. 7. (Includes comment from Friel that "I sent Field Day my resignation notice a few days ago and I have nothing more to say.")

Wolf, Matt. "Epiphany's Threshold." *American Theatre*, 11, no. 4 (April 1994), pp. 12–17. (Profile includes brief quotations from earlier interviews.)

White, Victoria. "New Friel Play for Gate." *Irish Times*, 28 April 1994, p. 10. (On Friel offering *Molly Sweeney* to the Gate Theatre rather than to the Abbey. Includes comment by Friel that "I have often worked in both places alternately, and perhaps more in the Gate than the Abbey. In this case, I think the play is more suitable to the Gate auditorium.")

Hanvey, Bobbie. "Play Right: Every Picture Tells a Story: The World of Bobbie Hanvey: In a Manic World of Hype and Computers, Brian Friel Never Gives Interviews and Writes with a 2B Pencil." *Belfast News Letter*, 12 June 1999, p. 15. (A photographer reports his exchanges with Friel before and during a photo session.)

Radio and Television Interviews

"Writing Plays and Short Stories." *The Arts in Ulster: A Monthly Magazine.* BBC Radio, Northern Ireland Home Service, 27 April 1962. Program introduced by Alfred Arnold includes John Boyd interview with Brian Friel about writing plays and short stories. (Interview recorded in Derry on 25 April 1962.) Transcript not available. Recording of transmission: BBC tape no. TBE 13474 and TBE 13620; recording of interview: BBC tape no. TBE 13840 on TR 90 (from KBE 13796).

"Some People and Places: A Talk by Brian Friel." BBC Radio, Northern Ireland Home Service, 7 November 1962 (recorded 22 October 1962). Friel describes "some people, places and things that will not appear in my autobiography." Transcript: BBC Written Archives Centre. Recording: BBC tape no. TBE 14790.

"Thoughts on Christmas Eve." *Christmas Garland.* BBC Radio, Northern Ireland Home Service, 24 December 1962.

"The Saucer of Larks." *The Arts in Ulster.* BBC Radio, Northern Ireland Home Service, 26 April 1963.

"Labours of Love: A Talk by Brian Friel." BBC Radio, Northern Ireland Home Service, 13 August 1963 (recorded 17 March 1963). In an autobiographical talk, Friel discusses his early notions of romance. (Also published as "Labors of Love," *Atlantic Monthly,* April 1963, pp. 130–32.) Transcript: BBC Written Archives Centre. Recording: BBC tape no. TBE 15719.

The Arts in Ulster: A Monthly Magazine. BBC Radio, Northern Ireland Home Service, 13 December 1963 (recorded 12 December 1963). Program introduced by Roy McFadden includes Brian Friel reviewing *A Journey to the Seven Streams,* a first volume of short stories by the novelist by Benedict Kiely. Transcript: BBC Written Archives Centre. Recording: BBC tape no. TBE 17596 for program, TBE 17595 for Friel review.

The Arts in Ulster: A Londonderry Edition. BBC Radio, Northern Ireland Home Service, 10 January 1964 (recorded 9 January 1964). Serving as program chairman of "this Derry edition of 'The Arts in Ulster,'" Friel introduces and interviews people from Derry who are involved with music, drama, poetry, and art. Transcript: BBC Written Archives Centre. Recording: BBC tape no. TBE 17900.

The Arts in Ulster: A Monthly Magazine. BBC Radio, Northern Ireland Home Service, 5 March 1964. Program introduced by Alfred Arnold includes Brian Friel reviewing *Sean O'Casey: The Man Behind the Plays,* a biography by Saros Cowasjee. (Review recorded 8 February 1964). Transcript: BBC Written Archives Centre. Recording: BBC tape no. TBE 18242 for program, TBE 18237 for Friel review (from KBE 18306).

"The Green Years: A Talk by Brian Friel." BBC Radio, Northern Ireland Home Service, 30 April 1964 (recorded 30 April 1964). On his boyhood experiences in Derry. Transcript: BBC Written Archives Centre. Recording: National Sound Archive LP 28874.

The Arts in Ulster: North-West Arts Festival Edition. BBC Radio, Northern Ireland Home Service, 1 May 1964 (recorded 30 April 1964). As chairman of the program, Friel introduces speakers who "recall some of the most memo-

rable happenings of the past three weeks" on the night before the first
North-West Arts Festival in Derry "comes to a triumphant close." Partial
transcript: BBC Written Archives Centre. Recording: BBC tape no. TBE
18709.

The Arts in Ulster. BBC Radio, Northern Ireland Home Service, 29 October 1964.
Reviews *Ulster: A Journey through the Six Counties* by Robin Bryans.

The Arts in Ulster: A Monthly Review. BBC Radio, Northern Ireland Home Service,
7 January 1965. Program introduced by Alfred Arnold includes Brian Friel
reviewing *Death of a Chieftain,* a volume of short stories by John Montague.
(Review recorded 9 December 1964.) Transcript: BBC Written Archives
Centre. Recording: BBC tape no. TBE 20278 for program, tape no. TBE
20277 for review (from YBE 20249).

The Arts in Ulster: A Monthly Review. BBC Radio, Northern Ireland Home Service,
23 April 1965. Program introduced by Alfred Arnold includes Brian Friel
reviewing *Vive Moi!* an autobiography by Sean O'Faolain. (Review recorded
14 April 1965). Transcript: BBC Written Archives Centre. Recording: BBC
tape no. TBE 20994 for program, BBC tape no. TBE 20993 for review
(from KBE 21194).

"An Observer in Minneapolis: A Talk by Brian Friel." BBC Radio, Northern Ireland Home Service, 16 August 1965 (recorded 21 May 1965). Friel discusses his trip to Minneapolis to "just hang around" for five months watching Tyrone Guthrie at work in the theatre that bears his name. Transcript:
BBC Written Archives Centre. Recording: BBC tape no. TBE 21333.

The Arts in Ulster: A Monthly Review. BBC Radio, Northern Ireland Home Service,
23 November 1965. Program introduced by Alfred Arnold includes interview by John Boyd with Brian Friel discussing the National Theatre production of *Hobson's Choice* as part of Festival '65. (Interview recorded 19 November 1965.) Transcript not available. Recording: BBC tape no. TBE 22332
for program, tape no. TBE 22330 for interview (from KBE 22559).

"First Night in New York." *The Arts in Ulster: A Monthly Review.* BBC Radio, Northern Ireland Home Service, 11 March 1966. Program introduced by Brian
Baird includes interview by John Boyd with Brian Friel about taking *Philadelphia, Here I Come!* to America. (Interview recorded 5 March 1966). Transcript not available. Recording: BBC tape no. TBE 23075 for program, tape
no. YBE 23409 for interview.

The Arts in Ulster. BBC Radio, Northern Ireland Home Service, 3 June 1966. Friel
reviews *In All Directions* by Sir Tyrone Guthrie.

"Philadelphia, Here the Author Comes!: A Talk by Brian Friel." BBC Northern
Ireland Home Service, 21 July 1966 (recorded 15 June 1966). On taking
Philadelphia, Here I Come! to America. Transcript: BBC Written Archives Cen-
tre. Recording: National Sound Archive LP 31710.

"It Matters to Me." BBC Radio, Northern Ireland Home Service, 30 May 1967 (a
sound recording of a Northern Ireland Television broadcast of 19 March
1967). Brian Friel discusses his career with four sixth-formers. Lawrence
Pitkethly, chairman. Transcript not available. Recording: BBC tape no. TBE
9/UT054U.

"Downstairs No Upstairs: A Talk by Brian Friel." BBC Radio for London and
Northern Ireland Home Service, 5 July 1967 (recorded 15 February 1967).

Friel tells the story of an old-fashioned system of electricity in his boyhood home. (Originally published in *The New Yorker,* 24 August 1963, pp. 82, 84–85.) Transcript: BBC Written Archives Centre. Recording: BBC tape no. TBE 22/UT071 (from TBE 7/UH462).

"The Art of the Short Story." *The Arts.* BBC Radio, Northern Ireland Home Service, 16 February 1968. (Interview of Friel by John Boyd.)

Televised interviews in New York in mid-September 1968 regarding *Lovers.* (Cited by Lewis Funke, "Brian Friel." In *Playwrights Talk about Writing: 12 Interviews with Lewis Funke,* p. 112. Chicago: Dramatic Publishing Co., 1975.)

Soundings. BBC Radio Four Northern Ireland, 2 August 1970 (recorded 17 June 1970). Friel talks with John Boyd about short story writing, his "accidental quartet" of plays on the theme of love, the Irish tradition in drama, and his latest play *The Mundy Scheme.* Transcript not available. Recording: National Sound Archive LP033466 b02.

Self-Portrait. BBC Radio, Northern Ireland, 31 October 1971. Friel introduces a self-portrait by Sir Tyrone Guthrie.

"Sunday Gallery: A Profile of Brian Friel." BBC Television, Northern Ireland, 7 December 1971.

Self-Portrait. BBC Radio Four Northern Ireland, 19 December 1971 (recorded 21 October 1971). Friel offers a mock interview with himself before talking about his boyhood recollections of Glenties, and his experience of going to Minneapolis as an observer at the Guthrie Theatre. John Boyd, producer. Rebroadcast BBC Radio Four Northern Ireland, 7 November 1972. Transcript not available from the BBC. Recording: National Sound Archive T34769. A somewhat revised transcription published as "Self-Portrait," *Aquarius* (Servite Priory, Benburb, Co. Tyrone), no. 5 (1972), 17–22.

"A Life in the Theatre." BBC Radio Three, 2 July 1972 (recorded 26 June 1972). Recollections of Sir Tyrone Guthrie by Friel and seven other contributors; presented by Gary Watson. Recording: National Sound Archive T34643.

February Review. BBC Radio Four Northern Ireland, 20 February 1973 (recorded 18 February 1973). Interview with Denys Hawthorne on *The Mundy Scheme* and *The Freedom of the City.* Transcript not available. Recording: National Sound Archive LP35593 f02–f03.

Round-Up Reports. BBC Radio Northern Ireland, 21 February 1973. On *The Freedom of the City.*

Scan. BBC Radio Four, 1 March 1973. Includes an excerpt of 18 February 1973 Denys Hawthorne interview (previously broadcast on *February Review* of 20 February 1973) with Friel about *The Freedom of the City.* Transcript: BBC Written Archives Centre.

March Review. BBC Radio Four Northern Ireland, 31 March 1974 (recorded 31 March 1974). Interviews with a gathering of Irish writers and poets in Toronto, includes Friel discussing the writer and society. Presenter and interviewer: Brian Barfield. Transcript not available. Recording: National Sound Archive LP36172 b01.

Gallery. BBC Television Northern Ireland, 26 March 1976. (Friel appears on the fiftieth edition of a program about the arts in Ireland.)

"Farewell to Ardstraw." BBC Television Northern Ireland, 2 December 1976.

(On Walter Glenn, a carpenter from Ardstraw, Co. Tyrone, who left Ireland in August 1744, like hundreds of thousands of other Presbyterians, to seek a better life in the New World. Dramatization written by Friel.)

"The Next Parish." BBC Television Northern Ireland, 9 December 1976. (Following the Great Famine of 1846–47, over a million emigrants left Ireland. In this 50-minute program written by Friel and produced by David Hammond, Siobhan McKenna traces the route of the emigrants and what became of some of them in "the next parish," as people on the west coast of Ireland refer to North America.)

Woman's Hour. BBC Radio Four, 18 July 1980. Interview with Margaret Percy about how Friel's attachment to the city of Derry had played an influential part in his development. Partial transcript: BBC Written Archives Centre. Recording: BBC program no. HHH306X702.

Today Tonight. RTÉ, 7 October 1980. Interview by Mary McAleese on the opening of *Translations.* Videotape: RTÉ.

Kaleidoscope. BBC Radio Four, 13 May 1981. Friel comments on some of the meanings of the title of *Translations.* Paul Vaughan, presenter. Transcript: BBC Written Archives Centre. Recording: BBC tape no. YLN19/382P050.

"News: Field Day Present *Three Sisters* at Derry Guildhall." RTÉ, 9 September 1981. Interview with Friel on why he undertook the translation. Videotape: RTÉ.

Interview. Channel Four. 1981. (Cited by Paddy Woodworth, "Field Day's Men and the Re-making of Ireland," *Irish Times,* 5 November 1990, p. 10. Quotes Friel as saying: "In a miniscule way, we are defining how this island may ultimately end up. It's possible that this kind of enterprise—I'm so nervous of using inflated language in these situations—may point the way to some kind of total island to which subscription may be given.")

"Brian Friel and Field Day." RTÉ, 14 February 1983. A documentary report, written by Seamus Deane and narrated by T. P. McKenna, on Friel's career as playwright and as a founding member of the Field Day theatre company. Includes interviews with Friel on at least three occasions. Videotape: RTÉ.

"The Arts in the North." *Live Arts Show.* RTÉ, 12 March 1984. A program, presented by Moya Doherty and John Hutchinson, on poetry, drama and the visual arts in Northern Ireland includes excerpts of an interview from "Brian Friel and Field Day," RTÉ, 14 February 1983. Videotape: RTÉ.

"Profile of Brian Friel." BBC–2, 12 August 1984. (Cited in *Irish News,* 8 August 1984, p. 6. "Brian Friel is the subject of "Profile of a Playwright" on the BBC–2 network at 9.25 pm on Sunday, August 12. . . . Seamus Deane talks to Brian Friel in his house in Donegal, which looks across Lough Foyle to Derry.")

"Cursai." RTÉ, 2 March 1990. A program in Irish offers a report on Friel's career.

"News Bulletin." RTÉ, 11 August 1991. On *Translations,* the Glenties landscape and village, and Friel's connection with Glenties. Includes scenes from *Translations* and *Dancing at Lughnasa* and interviews with townspeople from Glenties.

"1,500 Years of Irish Writing." *Morning Edition.* National Public Radio, 12 December 1991. Interview by Bob Edwards with Seamus Heaney, Brian

Friel, and Seamus Deane on the Field Day anthology of Irish writing and on the Irish as storytellers.

"*Wonderful Tennessee*—From Ballybeg to Broadway." RTÉ 1, 29 December 1993. Televised documentary by Donald Taylor Black—tracing the production of *Wonderful Tennessee* from Abbey Theatre rehearsals to opening night on Broadway—shows how Friel immerses himself in rehearsals and will advise actors on how to play a part or deliver a line. (Cited by Brendan Glacken, "Tale of the Travelling Players," *Irish Times*, 28 December 1993, p. 12.)

News

1963

"Awarded £1,000 Fellowship." *Irish Times*, 6 June 1963. (On Friel receiving the first fellowship for playwriting to be awarded by the Macaulay Foundation.)

1964

White, Sean J. "Theatre: In Search of a *Success*." *Irish Press*, 28 September 1964, p. 9. (Calls *Philadelphia, Here I Come!* the most promising play scheduled for the second week of Dublin's Theatre Festival.)

White, Sean J. "Behind the Scenes at the Theatre Festival: A Success for Friel." *Irish Press*, 2 October 1964, p. 9. (Praises *Philadelphia* as being the success of the Theatre Festival.)

Rushe, Desmond. "Irish Theatre in Stagnation?" *Irish Independent*, 5 October 1964, p. 8. (A review of *Theatre in Ireland* by Micheál Mac Liammóir praises Friel as "a major hope of the Irish theatre.")

White, Sean J. "Theatre: A Pleasant Epilogue to the '64 Festival." *Irish Press*, 12 October 1964, p. 11. (Laments the decision to close *Philadelphia* so that *Laurette* can open at the Gaiety Theatre: "a piece of marshmallow is, for the best commercial reasons, pushing out a very fine Irish play, the success of the Festival.")

1966

"The Dark Preview, Or 'At Your Peril.'" *New York Times*, 16 February 1966, pp. 1, 53. (Speculation that the final preview of *Philadelphia, Here I Come!* was cancelled to prevent Stanley Kauffmann from reviewing a preview performance.)

"New Merrick Play Bows on Schedule: 'Difficulties' Held Corrected by Broadway Producer." *New York Times*, 17 February 1966, p. 28. (*Philadelphia* opening not affected by the "technical difficulties" that caused cancellation of the final preview.)

"Show Cancelled After Dispute." *The Times*, 17 February 1966, p. 10. (Partial reprint of story from *New York Times* about cancellation of the final preview of *Philadelphia*.)

"An Irish Hit." *Evening Standard*, 29 March 1966. (Friel says he is "too busy with my next play to worry about" the Broadway success of *Philadelphia, Here I Come!*)

"Friel Honoured." *Irish Times,* 17 June 1966, p. 11. (On Friel's selection as the most promising playwright of the Broadway season for *Philadelphia, Here I Come!*)

"New Friel Play." *Irish Times,* 30 July 1966. (On *The Loves of Cass McGuire* being broadcast by the BBC on the same day the play goes into rehearsal for its stage debut in New York.)

"Four Closings This Week." *New York Times,* 21 November 1966, p. 59. (*Philadelphia* to close.)

1967

"Back Home." *New York Times,* 4 June 1967, sec. 2, p. 16. (Reports from Dublin are that *The Loves of Cass McGuire* has become a hit and is significantly improved from the production that opened and closed in New York after just twenty performances.)

"By Way of Dublin." *The Times,* 6 September 1967, p. 7. (*Philadelphia, Here I Come!* will open in London on 20 September with most of the original cast from Dublin and New York.)

1968

"200 Teen-agers See Lincoln Center Play." *New York Times,* 25 July 1968, p. 28. (On a group of "teen-agers, from Harlem, Coney Island, Brownsville and East Harlem" coming to see *Lovers.*)

"Tatler's Parade: Brian Friel's Latest Play Opens Next Week." *Irish Independent,* 7 November 1968, p. 12. (Friel says *Crystal and Fox,* to open in Dublin, "is rather sad, with a liberal quota of comedy.")

"*Lovers* Is Closing." *New York Times,* 27 November 1968, p. 38. (Announcement— the day after Clive Barnes's "reappraisal" of *Lovers* as not worth a second viewing—that the play will close on Saturday.)

"Closings." *New York Times,* 1 December 1968, sec. 2, p. 36. (*Lovers* "closed last night after 149 performances.")

1969

"Wilfred Brambell in Friel Play." *The Times,* 27 February 1969, p. 7. (A BBC Radio version of *Crystal and Fox* early next month will be the first production of the play outside Ireland.)

"Tatler's Parade: Abbey Theatre Rejects Latest Friel Play." *Irish Independent,* 21 April 1969, p. 10. (The Abbey has rejected Friel's satirical play *The Mundy Scheme* "not because of writing or theatrical deficiencies, but because of its political content.")

"Donal Donnelly to Direct New Friel Play." *Irish Times,* 27 May 1969, p. 10. (Donnelly says he shares Friel's anger at the Abbey Theatre for rejecting *The Mundy Scheme,* which he describes as a "savage, very funny, brilliant . . . essay on expediency.")

"The Press Diary: Next Century Politicians." *Irish Press*, 6 June 1969, p. 11. (Comment on *The Mundy Scheme*, Friel's satirical play about the Irish government, being staged in the middle of a general election.)

"Buying Rights of Friel's New Play." *Irish Times*, 11 June 1969, p. 1. (On the purchase of British rights to produce *The Mundy Scheme*.)

"New Friel Play for New York." *Irish Times*, 31 July 1969, p. 1. (On *The Mundy Scheme*.)

B., B. "Brian Friel, 1930—." *Belfast Telegraph*, 6 November 1969. (Friel quoted as saying his ambition is to write "the great Irish play.")

"Broadway Drops Friel Play." *Irish Times*, 15 December 1969, p. 11. (A summary of New York reviews that led to the closing of *The Mundy Scheme*.)

1970

"Friel Appointed Visiting Writer at Magee College." *Irish Times*, 7 October 1970.

1972

Quidnunc. "An Irishman's Diary: Shy Man Hits Out." *Irish Times*, 24 March 1972, p. 11. (A response to Friel's essay "Plays Peasant and Unpeasant.")

"Drama by Friel To Open March 21." *New York Times*, 28 December 1972, p. 37. (On *Crystal and Fox* coming to New York.)

1973

Smith, Gus. "Can Friel Crack London Scene?" *Sunday Independent*, 18 February 1973, p. 14. (About imminent opening of *Freedom of the City*.)

"Whiff of Gas at the Court." *Evening Standard*, 23 February 1973. (On Royal Court Theatre rehearsals for *The Freedom of the City* directed by Albert Finney.)

"What Albert Finney Asked Sir Graham Shillington." *Belfast Telegraph*, 1 March 1973, p. 3.

1974

"Marginalia: Tour by Milwaukeeans." *New York Times*, 27 February 1974, p. 27. (*The Freedom of the City* closed after nine performances.)

Cronin, Sean. "Letter from New York: Storm over Friel Play on Broadway." *Irish Times*, 4 March 1974, p. 13. (On the Broadway closing of *The Freedom of the City* after a negative review by London-born Clive Barnes took issue with the play's depiction of the British Army.)

1975

Smith, Hugh G. "For Artists, a Tax Haven in Ireland." *New York Times*, 26 January 1975, sec. 3, p. 34. (Tax haven article erroneously says Friel moved eleven miles from Derry in Northern Ireland to Muff in Co. Donegal to take advantage of the Republic's tax exemption for writers.)

1976

Cathcart, Rex. "Preview." *Radio Times* (Northern Ireland edition), 9 December 1976, p. 19. (On "The Next Parish," Friel's televised documentary about emigration to North America at the time of the Great Famine.)

1978

Walker, John. "Top Playwrights: The Traditionalists." *Sunday Times Magazine,* 26 November 1978, p. 70. (A photo feature on contemporary playwrights refers to Friel's *Freedom of the City* as "the best play to come out of the present Irish troubles.")

1979

Nowlan, David. "Brian Friel Play Hangs in Broadway Balance." *Irish Times,* 7 April 1979, p. 5. (On mixed reviews of *Faith Healer* in New York.)
Nowlan, David. "Irish Shows Defy Critics on Broadway." *Irish Times,* 13/14 April 1979, p. 8. (On the response in New York to *Faith Healer.*)
Cronin, Sean. "Friel Play Closing on Broadway." *Irish Times,* 14 April 1979, p. 1.

1980

"World Premiere Crucial for Derry Theatre Hopes." *Belfast Telegraph,* 3 June 1980, p. 13.
Bryson, Sean. "Fantastic Faith Healing at Abbey." *Irish Press,* 29 August 1980, p. 4.
Rushe, Desmond. "*Faith Healer*—A Triumph of Unconvention." *Irish Independent,* 30 August 1980, p. 3.
Nowlan, David. "Theatre Group in Search of Sponsorship." *Irish Times,* 2 September 1980, p. 6.
"Theatre Group Plea for a £10,000 Sponsor." *Belfast Telegraph* (Northwest edition), 3 September 1980, p. 2.
Myers, Kevin. "An Irishman's Diary: Sensational Opening." *Irish Times,* 4 September 1980, p. 9. (On the "sensational opening" of *Faith Healer* at the Abbey and the upcoming opening of *Translations* in Derry.)
Huckerby, Martin. "Londonderry Theatre Company to Present Productions throughout Ireland." *The Times,* 8 September 1980, p. 2. (On the founding of Field Day.)
Sheridan, Michael. "Translated Logic." *Irish Press,* 23 September 1980, p. 9.
Sheridan, Michael. "Triumph for *Translations.*" *Irish Press,* 24 September 1980, p. 4. (A report on reactions, including that of the Bishop of Derry, to the premiere of *Translations.*)
Nowlan, David. "Electric Love Affair as Play Opens in Derry." *Irish Times,* 24 September 1980, p. 8. (On the emotional intensity of the reception of *Translations* in Derry and the "miracle of emotional brevity" of Friel's curtain speech following the production.)
"Standing Ovation for Friel's *Translations.*" *Derry Journal,* 26 September 1980, p.

7. (Account of Friel's speech to the audience following the triumphant premiere of *Translations*.)

"Friel's Winner." *Irish Press*, 26 September 1980, p. 8. (An editorial praising the courageous decision to stage *Translations* in Derry.)

"Derry Delight at Friel Play Triumph." *Sunday Independent*, 28 September 1980, p. 2.

Gillespie, Elgy. "Festival Profile: Stephen Rea." *Irish Times*, 10 October 1980, p. 8.

Nowlan, David. "Theatre Festival: The Summing-up." *Irish Times*, 24 October 1980, p. 10.

Byrne, Danielle. "A New Excitement Stirs the Irish Theater." *New York Times*, 7 December 1980, sec. 2, pp. 5, 28. (Friel garnered the best reviews of the Dublin Theatre Festival for *Translations*.)

1981

Nowlan, David. "The Year of the Playwright." *Irish Times*, 1–2 January 1981, p. 6.

"Friel Leads in Hope." *Irish Press*, 6 January 1981, p. 9.

"Friel to Make Derry Comeback." *Irish Press*, 15 January 1981, p. 4.

Sheridan, Michael. "Friel Puts His Faith in Dowling." *Irish Press*, 10 February 1981, p. 9.

Shepard, Richard F. "A Day in the Life of George F. Kaufman Coming to the Stage." *New York Times*, 13 March 1981, sec. 3, p. 2. (*Translations* will open next month at the Manhattan Theater Club, directed by Joe Dowling, who talks about the founding of the Abbey Theatre in response to growing Anglicization and about the political situation motivating young writers from Northern Ireland to write.)

Walsh, Caroline. "Friel Plays Scoop Awards." *Irish Times*, 18 May 1981, p. 6. (Includes comment from Friel upon accepting Dublin award for *Translations* as best new play by an Irish playwright.)

"Friel Wins Award." *Irish Times*, 4 June 1981, p. 7.

"Hit Play Transfers." *West Herts and Watford Observer* (Watford, Hertfordshire), 24 July 1981. (*Translations*, a big critical and box-office hit at Hampstead Theatre last month, transfers to the Lyttelton Theatre on August 6.)

Bromley, Michael. "National Help Foot the Bill for Friel." *Belfast Telegraph*, 7 August 1981, p. 8.

Sheridan, Michael. "Great Night in Guildhall as Derry Hails Friel's *Sisters*." *Irish Press*, 10 September 1981, p. 7.

"Memorandum: An Arts Notebook: Derry First Night." *Irish Times*, 12 September 1981. (On the Derry opening of Friel's version of *Three Sisters*.)

Sheridan, Michael. "Field Day Carries On Its Consciousness of History." *Irish Press*, 15 September 1981, p. 9.

Hastings, Tim. "Audiences in Dublin Hit for Criticism." *Irish Press*, 30 September 1981, p. 7. (Stephen Rea, who is directing Friel's version of *Three Sisters*, rejects Dublin complaints that the play is too long.)

Sheridan, Michael. "Friel Work That Grows in Stature." *Irish Press*, 30 September 1981, p. 7.

"Friel and Kee Win Ewart–Biggs Prize." *Irish Times*, 20 November 1981, p. 1.

"Points of View." *Daily Telegraph,* 27 November 1981. (Brief mention of *Translations* winning an award.)

1982

Riddel, Lynne. "In Derry the Talk Is All about a Farce in Donegal." *Belfast Telegraph,* 17 September 1982. (News regarding opening of Friel's *Communication Cord,* includes interview with Stephen Rea.)

Nowlan, David. "New Friel Play Applauded." *Irish Times,* 22 September 1982, p. 6. (Regarding Friel's triumphantly silent curtain call after the opening of *The Communication Cord* in Derry.)

Moloney, Eugene. "'Cord' that Tilts the Fun-bath over All." *Irish News,* 23 September 1982. (Regarding triumphant opening of *The Communication Cord* in Derry.)

O'Toole, Fintan. "Barrier." *In Dublin,* 165 (28 October 1982), p. 52. (An article on *The Communication Cord* in the same issue as O'Toole interview with Friel.)

Rocke, William. "Friel Strikes a Comic Cord." *Sunday Press,* 31 October 1982, p. 13.

Cassidy, Ces. "Playwright Who Stays in the Wings." *Irish Independent,* 2 November 1982, p. 6. (Profile on occasion of *The Communication Cord* opening in Dublin includes a comment from Friel on having worked with Micheál Mac Liammóir and Hilton Edwards.)

1983

"University Honours for Top Trainer." *Irish Press,* 25 March 1983, p. 3. (Friel received an honorary D.Litt. degree conferred by the National University of Ireland.)

1984

"Profile of Brian Friel." *Irish News,* 8 August 1984, p. 6. ("Brian Friel is the subject of "Profile of a Playwright" on the BBC–2 network at 9.25 pm on Sunday August 12. . . . Seamus Deane talks to Brian Friel in his house in Donegal, which looks across Lough Foyle to Derry.")

O'Toole, Fintan. "Stephen Rea: The Great Leap from the Abbey." *Sunday Tribune,* 23 September 1984, p. 16. (Interview with Stephen Rea about his early experience in theatre in Ireland and what the founding of Field Day means to him and to Friel.)

1985

Fitzpatrick, Letitia. "Friel's Favourite Work Comes 'Home.'" *Irish News,* 15 March 1985, p. 5. (News regarding Belfast revival of *Living Quarters* says the play is "a favourite child" of Friel's.)

1986

"The Night Brian Sent His Missus to Philadelphia." *Irish Independent,* 17 April
    1986. (Friel's wife—but not Friel—attended the opening night in Dublin of
    a revival of *Philadelphia, Here I Come!*)
MacDermott, Domhnall. "A Write Honour for Friel." *Irish News,* 5 July 1986, p. 5.
    (News regarding Friel's response to honorary degree from the University of
    Ulster.)

1987

Gillespie, Elgy. "Field Day in Search of American Funds." *Irish Times,* 24 March
    1987, p. 10. (On a fund-raising trip to the U.S. by Friel, Seamus Heaney,
    Seamus Deane, and Tom Paulin.)
"Ulster Writer and Surgeon Given Roles in Eire Senate." *Belfast Telegraph,* 24
    April 1987, p. 4.
Harris, Anne. "Friel Spirit in the Senate." *Sunday Independent,* 3 May 1987, p. 10.
    (A profile one week after Friel was seated in the Senate.)
"Acclaim for New Friel Play." *Irish Times,* 11 July 1987, p. 2. (Summary of London
    reviews of *Fathers and Sons* at the Lyttelton.)
Davie, Michael. "A Novel Way to Write a Play." *The Observer,* 12 July 1987, p. 16.
    (Prior to the National Theatre opening of his adaptation of *Fathers and Sons,*
    Friel "refused to be interviewed last week, though in London for the open-
    ing, and left his telephone off the hook.")
Purcell, Bernard. "Playwright Brian Friel Accomplished a Theatrical Hat-trick
    Last Night." *Irish Independent,* 25 August 1987. (Friel has three plays run-
    ning simultaneously in London: *The Freedom of the City, Fathers and Sons* and
    Translations.)
Finlan, Michael. "Finding Art Venues Seen as Problem." *Irish Times,* 19 Septem-
    ber 1987. (On Friel's remarks at a conference in Galway on funding for the
    arts.)

1988

"New Dispute on MacBride Obituary." *Irish Times,* 25 March 1988, p. 7. (Regard-
    ing a letter Brian Friel and others had written objecting to a *Sunday Tele-
    graph* obituary that referred to Sean MacBride as "a murderer.")
Kingston, Jeremy. "Ireland, Through a Glass Darkly." *The Times,* 25 May 1988, p.
    22. (Sinead Cusack and Niall Buggy will appear in *Aristocrats,* previewing
    from tomorrow at Hampstead. *Translations* will be revived this August in the
    Tent, Chichester's studio theatre.)
"Five Honoured by R. D. S." *Irish Times,* 24 June 1988, p. 11. (Cited by George
    O'Brien, *Brian Friel: A Reference Guide 1962–1992* [New York: G. K. Hall,
    1995], item 1988.36, as an account of Friel receiving an honorary life mem-
    bership in the Royal Dublin Society; item not located.)
Myers, Kevin. "An Irishman's Diary." *Irish Times,* 5 July 1988, p. 11. (On Friel's
    adaptation of *Fathers and Sons.*)
MacDermott, Domhnall. "Friel World Premier Set for Derry Stage." *Irish News,* 16

September 1988. (Interview with Stephen Rea and other actors who comment on the close involvement of Brian Friel in rehearsals of *Making History* for its Derry opening.)

Coyle, Jane. "Making History with Field Day." *Irish Times,* 17 September 1988, "Weekend" section, p. 11.

Cowley, Martin. "Making History with Echo of Today's Politics." *Irish Times,* 21 September 1988, p. 13. (*Making History* had its world premiere at the Guildhall in Derry last night.)

O'Toole, Fintan. "A Hesitant Move into Unknown Territory." *Irish Times,* 24 September 1988, "Weekend" section, p. 5. (On *Making History.*)

TK. "Field Day at Belfast's Grand Opera House." *ABSA Bulletin.* (Northern Ireland), Winter 1988/1989, p. 11. (On a Field Day performance on 4 October 1988 in Belfast to attract corporate sponsorship.)

Holland, Mary. "A Field Day for Irish Theatre." *Observer Magazine,* 30 October 1988, pp. 60–61, 63, 65. (Interview with Stephen Rea on the founding of Field Day, Friel's reaction to Belfast criticism of *Translations* and the playwright's intentions in *Making History,* to open at the Cottesloe on 3 December.)

"National's Hat Trick." *The Times,* 19 November 1988, p. 2. (*Aristocrats* won the award for best play at the *Evening Standard* Drama Awards.)

"Friel Takes London Drama Award." *Irish Times,* 19 November 1988, p. 2. (For *Aristocrats.*)

Billington, Michael. "Critic's Choice: Theatre." *The Guardian,* 2 December 1988, p. 34. (*Making History* arrives at the Cottesloe.)

"Field Day in London: Through Irish Eyes." *Economist,* 309 (3 December 1988), pp. 104–5. (A report on Field Day.)

Heaney, Seamus. "A Field Day for the Irish." *The Times,* 5 December 1988, p. 18. (An account of the founding and purposes of Field Day.)

Vidal, John. "Stronger than Fiction." *The Guardian,* 5 December 1988, p. 36. (On the background of *Making History,* opening at the Cottesloe, includes interview with Stephen Rea.)

McGuinness, Frank. "The Gentle Island." *Sunday Tribune,* 11 December 1988, p. 20.

Battersby, Eileen. "Field Day Pamphlets by Foreign Authors Launched." *Irish Times,* 12 December 1988, p. 10.

Cunningham, Francine. "Getting to the Nuts and Bolts of Theatre." *Irish Times,* 12 December 1988, p. 14. (Interview with Wendy Shea, designer.)

Coulter, Carol. "Field Day Pamphlets Launched in Dublin." *Irish Times,* 17 December 1988, p. 2.

O'Toole, Fintan. "McGuinness Rescues Friel's Lost Island." *Irish Times,* 17 December 1988, "Weekend," p. 5. (Commentary on a revival of *The Gentle Island* directed by Frank McGuinness.)

1989

Brennan, Brian. "Intimate Attentions." *Sunday Independent,* 8 January 1989, "Colour Extra" magazine, p. 7.

Reid, Lorna. "A Birthday Surprise for Playwright." *Irish Independent,* 10 January 1989, p. 11.

Cooney, John. "$10,000 Award for Field Day Anthology." *Irish Times,* 12 January 1989, p. 8.

Radio Times, 8 April 1989. (BBC Radios 3 and 4 will launch a season of plays by Brian Friel, including: *Philadelphia, Here I Come! Winners, Faith Healer, Translations, Making History,* and *Aristocrats.* Dates and times are listed.)

Kelly, Brian. "Raves for *Aristocrats.*" *Irish Times,* 2 May 1989, p. 10. (Summarizes New York critics.)

Gussow, Mel. "*Heidi Chronicles* Wins Critics Circle Prize." *New York Times,* 16 May 1989, sec. C, p. 22. (*Aristocrats* named as the best new foreign play.)

Coughlan, Denis. "FF Likely to Retain Senate Majority." *Irish Times,* 15 August 1989, p. 8. (Friel is not expected to be reappointed to the Senate.)

Brennock, Mark. "Senate Problem Eased for FF." *Irish Times,* 29 August 1989, p. 1. (Friel says he does not wish to be reappointed to the Senate.)

Jackson, Kevin. "Running Wilde on the Road." *The Independent,* 15 September 1989, p. 18. (An account of rehearsals in Derry for Field Day production of *Saint Oscar* by Terry Eagleton. Stephen Rea says he and Brian Friel felt the play "was tailor-made" for Field Day.)

1990

Woodworth, Paddy. "Getting to Know the Score." *Irish Times,* 3 February 1990, "Weekend" section, p. 5. (Interview with actor Tom Hickey, in the Gate production of *Aristocrats.*)

Woodworth, Paddy. "Do We Really Need the Theatre Festival?" *Irish Times,* 26 April 1990, p. 6.

Pyle, Fergus. "Translating Friel into German." *Irish Times,* 28 June 1990, p. 8. (Interview with translator.)

Craine, Debra. "Two More Sisters for *The Three Sisters.*" *The Times,* 1 September 1990, "Saturday Review" section, p. 16. (Dublin's Abbey Theatre production of *Dancing at Lughnasa* opens in London at the Lyttelton on 15 October.)

Linehan, Fergus. "London Welcome for Friel Play." *Irish Times,* 16 October 1990, p. 9.

Linehan, Fergus. "Raves for Friel Play." *Irish Times,* 20 October 1990, "Weekend" section, p. 5.

Woodworth, Paddy. "Field Day's Men and the Re-making of Ireland." *Irish Times,* 5 November 1990, p. 10. (Quotes Friel comments to an English interviewer in 1981 and to Channel 4 in 1981.)

Battersby, Eileen. "An Original Talent Hiding behind the Innocent Smile." *Irish Times,* 24 November 1990, p. 10. (Interview with actor Donal McCann.)

Wallace, Arminta. "Great Faith in Friel, Confidence in His Cast." *Irish Times,* 27 November 1990, p. 8. (Interview with director Joe Dowling.)

"Friel Joins Theatre Greats." *Irish Independent,* 1 December 1990, p. 6. (Cited by George O'Brien, *Brian Friel: A Reference Guide 1962–1992* [New York: G. K. Hall, 1995], item 1990.23, as a "report on the hanging of Basil Blackshaw's portrait of Friel among those of other Irish theatrical notables in the Abbey

Theatre." On 1 December 1990 *Lughnasa* was still playing in London; the return of *Lughnasa* to the Abbey in mid-January 1991 was the occasion of festivities including a reception for Friel by the Lord Mayor. *Stage* reported on 21 February 1991 that the portrait in the Abbey was unveiled "recently"; item not located.)

"Broadway Bound?" *The Times*, 10 December 1990. (On possible transfer to New York for *Dancing at Lughnasa*.)

1991

Linehan, Fergus. "Dancing at the Mansion House." *Irish Times*, 12 January 1991, "Weekend" section, p. 4. (Summary of rave notices in London for *Lughnasa* and lengthy queues at the National. Upon the play's return to the Abbey, the Lord Mayor of Dublin will hold a reception in Mansion House for the author and company.)

Stage, 17 January 1991. ("Following a 13-week run at the Lyttelton, *Dancing at Lughnasa* has returned to the Abbey, Dublin before it transfers to Broadway.")

"The Man Who Might Have . . . and the Girl Who Did." *Evening Standard*, 8 February 1991, p. 21. (Noel Pearson has resigned as artistic director of the Abbey to pursue work in film but will continue to supervise the New York transfer of *Lughnasa*, delayed as a result of the Gulf War situation.)

"Briefing: Shuffle Westwards." *The Times*, 16 February 1991. (*Lughnasa* will return to London on 18 March rather than opening on Broadway on 27 March. The New York transfer has been postponed until the autumn.)

Garvey, Anthony. "Irish Eyebrows Are Raised by a Critic." *Stage*, 21 February 1991. (*Lughnasa* preparing for transfer to New York; Brian Friel becomes the second living theatrical VIP to have his portrait hung in the Abbey foyer.)

"Irish Nominations for Olivier Awards." *Irish Times*, 5 March 1991, p. 10. (*Lughnasa* has four nominations for Olivier awards including play of the year, director of the year, actress in a supporting role and choreographer.)

Boardman, Susan. "Friel Play Nominated." *Irish Independent*, 5 March 1991. (*Lughnasa* nominations for Olivier awards.)

Billington, Michael. "Going On in Good Hands." *The Guardian*, 21 March 1991. (*Lughnasa* returns to London to the Phoenix Theatre after a sell-out season at the National.)

"Critics Name *Aristocrats* Best Play Off-Broadway." *Newsday*, 3 April 1991.

"Danced Off Her Feet." *The Times*, 4 April 1991. (Anita Reeves, the one *Lughnasa* cast member to receive an Olivier award nomination, will leave the production at the end of April. Sorcha Cusack will replace her.)

"*Lughnasa* Wins Play of Year." *Irish Times*, 8 April 1991, p. 1. (*Lughnasa* has won the prestigious BBC award for play of the year at the Olivier awards in London.)

"Step Out Again." *The Times*, 28 May 1991. (*Lughnasa* will play the Abbey in September before opening on Broadway on 17 October.)

Doyle, Martin. "Friel's Play Keeps on Dancing." *Irish News*, 7 June 1991. (*Lughnasa* continues to be a huge success after ten weeks at the Phoenix Theatre in London where auditions are being held for a complete cast change to take place next month. A transfer to Broadway is expected in the autumn.)

Holohan, Renagh. "Theatre for the People." *Irish Times,* 12 August 1991, p. 6. (On a performance in Glenties of *Dancing at Lughnasa* and comments by John Hume of the Patrick MacGill Summer School about Friel.)

Arnold, Bruce. "Abbey Pays Unique Tribute to Friel." *Irish Independent,* 12 August 1991. (On the performance of *Lughnasa* in Glenties and Friel's speech to the packed house.)

Wolf, Matt. "A Five-Sister Play, a Family of Actors." *New York Times,* 20 October 1991, sec. 2, pp. 5, 11.

Pacheco, Patrick. "The High Priest of Irish Theater." *Newsday,* "Fanfare" section, p. 12.

Lay, Richard. "Lughnasa Crew Dances with Joy." *Evening Herald,* 25 October 1991.

McCarthy, Justine. "Dancing for Joy!" *Irish Independent,* 26 October 1991, p. 12. (A backstage account of the preparation for the opening of *Lughnasa* on Broadway and jubilation over the play's reception.)

O'Mahoney, John. "American Critics Sing Praises of Lughnasa." *Irish Independent,* 26 October 1991, p. 7.

"Dancing for *Lughnasa.*" *Sunday Independent,* 27 October 1991. (An account of the opening night parties celebrating the triumphant Broadway reception of *Dancing at Lughnasa.*)

Rocke, William. "Extra Staff for *Lughnasa* Rush." *Sunday Press* (Dublin), 27 October 1991. (On Broadway *Lughnasa* has passed the $1 million advance booking mark and has no seats available until mid-December.)

"Friel Frenzy." *Sunday Press,* 27 October 1991, "Living" section, p. 3. (Cited by William Rocke, "Extra Staff for Lughnasa Rush," *Sunday Press,* 27 October 1991.)

O'Faolain, Nuala. "The Voice that Field Day Didn't Record." *Irish Times,* 11 November 1991, p. 14. (On the Field Day anthology of Irish literature.)

"Friel Play Voted Best of Year." *Daily Telegraph,* 13 November 1991, p. 8. (*Lughnasa* received the Evening Standard drama award as best play.)

Nally, David. "Women Offended by Irish Anthology." *Sunday Tribune,* 1 December 1991, p. 13.

"Morgan Wins Award." *Irish Times,* 30 December 1991, p. 2. (Friel won the Eamonn Andrews special award at the RTÉ awards.)

1992

Peterborough. "Seen and Hurt." *Daily Telegraph,* 11 January 1992, p. 13. (*The London Vertigo,* adapted by Friel, will be directed by the playwright's daughter, Judy Friel.)

"Comedy of Terrors." *Irish Times,* 18 January 1992, "Weekend" section. (In adapting *The True Born Irishman* by eighteenth-century Charles Macklin as *The London Vertigo,* Friel was interested in the way Macklin wrote "almost autobiographically about his self-invention: from Donegal peasant to the toast of the noble classes.")

"Honorary Degree for Brian Friel." *Irish Times,* 22 January 1992, p. 4.

"European of the Year Award Goes to Field Day Playwright Friel." *Irish Press*, 11 February 1992, p. 9.

Boland, Colm. "President Presents Friel with European Award." *Irish Times*, 11 February 1992, p. 5. (Includes brief comments by Friel.)

Healy, John. "Playwright Friel Following CJ's Footsteps." *Irish Independent*, 11 February 1992. (Friel's comments upon receiving the European of the Year award.)

Crowe, Maire. "Second Coming of *Lughnasa*." *Sunday Tribune*, 8 March 1992, p. 89. (News regarding changeover from Irish cast to predominantly American cast in Broadway production of *Lughnasa*.)

Moriarty, Gerry. "Field Day Refused Grant for Friel Play." *Irish Times*, 23 April 1992, p. 7. (Derry City Council withdrew a grant for £65,000 because they were expecting a new play from Brian Friel rather than a revival of *The Freedom of the City*, a "19-year-old" drama. Article includes one comment by Friel.)

"*Dancing at Lughnasa* Wins Outer Critics Circle Award." *New York Times*, 28 April 1992, sec. C, p. 15. (For best Broadway play.)

Collins, Glenn. "Jelly's Last Jam, With 11, Leads in Tony Nominations." *New York Times*, 5 May 1992, sec. C, pp. 13, 17. (*Dancing at Lughnasa* received eight Tony nominations, more than any other straight play.)

McEneaney, Annemaria. "*Lughnasa* Hot Favourite for Play 'Oscars.'" *Irish Independent*, 5 May 1992. (The eight Tony nominations for *Lughnasa* are the most a new play has ever received in the history of the Tony awards.)

"Performing Arts Award for Friel." *Irish Times*, 7 May 1992, p. 8.

Rocke, William. "Film May Be Next for *Dancing at Lughnasa*." *Sunday Press*, 10 May 1992. (Noel Pearson says a film of *Lughnasa* may be in the offing, but Friel does not want a film made "at present.")

"Critics Honor *Lughnasa*." *New York Times*, 12 May 1992, sec. C, p. 17. (*Lughnasa* was named the best new play by the New York Drama Critics Circle.)

Cunningham, Francine. "Map-maker Hovering on Border." *Sunday Business Post*, 24 May 1992, p. 14. (Profile regarding Friel's limited participation in the Senate, his reticence and geniality, and his response to fame and fortune from *Dancing at Lughnasa*.)

Phelan, Angela. "Dancing with Delight . . ." *Irish Independent*, 30 May 1992, p. 11. (Anticipation of possible Tony awards for *Lughnasa*.)

Collins, Glenn. "*Dancing at Lughnasa* and *Crazy for You* Win Top Tony Awards." *New York Times*, 1 June 1992, sec. C, pp. 11, 16. (*Lughnasa* won three Tonys including best play.)

O'Mahony, John. "Friel's *Lughnasa* Takes Tony Awards." *Irish Independent*, 1 June 1992.

Moriarty, Gerry. "Derry Festival Affected by Offstage Drama." *Irish Times*, 1 June 1992, p. 4.

Fitz-simon, Christopher. "Ambassador Brian . . . : Irish Team Dancing with Delight at Tony Awards." *Irish Independent*, 2 June 1992.

"Talking to the World." *Irish Times*, 2 June 1992, p. 13. (An editorial.)

Mulkerns, Helena. "Lughnasa Goes Dancing to the Tonys." *Irish Times*, 2 June 1992, p. 10.

"Topics of The Times: Dancing at *What?*" *New York Times*, 2 June 1992, sec. A, p.

20. (An editorial criticizes Tony Awards presenters who mispronounced "Lughnasa.")

O'Mahony, John. "Friel's Broadway Triumph: Happy Noel's over Galaxy for Joy." *Irish Independent*, 2 June 1992.

Kerr, Angela. "Friel Gets Honorary Degree." *Irish News*, 3 July 1992, p. 4.

Murdoch, Alan. "Shy Friel Shows Up." *Independent on Sunday*, 2 August 1992, "Home News," p. 6. (Friel made a public appearance at the dress rehearsals for his version of Turgenev's *A Month in the Country*, opening at Dublin's Gate Theatre.)

Carty, Ciaran. "Abbey Reaps Lughnasa Harvest." *Sunday Tribune*, 23 August 1992, sec. B, p. 3.

Clarke, Jocelyn. "Putting the Dance in Lughnasa." *Sunday Tribune*, 23 August 1992, sec. B, p. 3. (Interview with the choreographer.)

Johnston, Neil. "An Ulster Diary: Scene: A Train. Enter Mr Friel." *Belfast Telegraph*, 27 October 1992, p. 9. (As a result of a chance encounter on a train, Friel gave permission to an Ulster amateur drama group, the Holywood Players, to perform the world premiere of *London Vertigo*.)

1993

Hemming, Sarah. "King of the Cabbage Patch." *The Independent*, 19 May 1993, p. 15. (Director Joe Dowling speaks of his work with Friel saying that "when the history of 20th-century Irish theatre comes to be written, we're going to be talking about O'Casey, Synge and Friel.")

Carr, Mary. "Is There Life after Lughnasa?" *Evening Herald*, 24 June 1993. (Those associated with the production of *Wonderful Tennessee* say they are "taking our cue from Brian Friel": "He rarely talks to anyone and he keeps telling us not to talk to the press or anyone about the play until it opens.")

McGee, Harry. "In Search of the Real Brian Friel." *Sunday Press*, 27 June 1993, sec. 2 "Leisure," p. 1. (Preparations for *Wonderful Tennessee* are being "conducted in a shroud of secrecy.")

Moroney, Mic. "Myth in Modern Dress." *Irish Times*, 30 June 1993, p. 10. (An account of preparation for the opening of *Wonderful Tennessee* at the Abbey mentions Friel's presence at preview performances; says Donald Taylor Black is shooting a film on the making of the show; and offers an extended interview with the designer, Joe Vanek.)

McMahon, Paula. "Stars Flock to Friel Opening." *Irish Independent*, 1 July 1993. (News of the opening night of *Wonderful Tennessee*.)

Siggins, Lorna. "Brilliant Acting in Friel Play, Says 'NY Times.'" *Irish Independent*, 19 July 1993. (A summary of Frank Rich's *New York Times* review of two plays in Dublin—*Wonderful Tennessee* at the Abbey and *A Midsummer Night's Dream* at the Gate.)

Murphy, Haydn. "The Abbey Changes Its Habits." *The Herald*, 26 July 1993, p. 8. (On *Wonderful Tennessee* being directed by Patrick Mason, the new artistic director of the Abbey Theatre.)

O'Byrne, Robert. "*Tennessee* on Broadway." *Irish Times*, 27 October 1993. (Anticipation of the Broadway opening of *Wonderful Tennessee* and an account of the New York reviews.)

"Friel Play to Close in NY." *Irish Times,* 27 October 1993, p. 9. (On *Wonderful Tennessee* closing after just nine performances.)

Phelan, Angela. "Closure of New Friel Play to Cost $1m." *Irish Independent,* 27 October 1993. (Although *Tennessee* received "very worthy" reviews, they "just weren't money reviews.")

O'Byrne, Robert. "Unenthusiastic Tennessee." *Irish Times,* 28 October 1993, p. 12. (Quotes director Patrick Mason on closing of *Wonderful Tennessee.*)

Cronin, Sean. "Broadway Is Not So Wonderful for Friel." *Irish Times,* 30 October 1993, p. 4. (Appeared alongside Mary Holland interview with Friel: "There's no Point in Prolonging.")

Dodd, Stephen and Kyran Fitzgerald. "Friel's Light Goes Down on Broadway." *Sunday Independent,* 31 October 1993, p. 4. (An examination of the factors contributing to the closing of *Wonderful Tennessee.*)

O'Kelly, Emer. "Time Will Confirm a Classic." *Sunday Independent,* 31 October 1993, p. 4. (A defense of *Wonderful Tennessee* as a masterwork of Friel's, comparable to *Waiting for Godot* in audiences finding its trappings bewildering.)

McCann, Donal. "Tennessee Waltz—Wonderful Tennessee. Terrible New York?" *Irish Times,* 27 November 1993, "Supplement," p. 5. (A member of the cast of *Wonderful Tennessee* gives his feelings on "a week of opening highs and closing lows on Broadway.")

Glacken, Brendan. "Tale of the Travelling Players." *Irish Times,* 28 December 1993, p. 12. (On the RTÉ documentary "*Wonderful Tennessee*—From Ballybeg to Broadway.")

1994

Moriarty, Gerry. "Playwright Brian Friel Quits Field Day." *Irish Times,* 3 February 1994, p. 7.

Duffield, Aislinn. "Lyric Stages Northern Premiere of Friel Play." *Irish News,* 7 June 1994, p. 8. (News regarding opening of *Volunteers* in the north, two decades after its Abbey premiere. *Volunteers* was one of four plays that Friel "said he would be pleased to see staged.")

Carty, Ciaran. "The Life of Brian: Actor's Eye View." *Sunday Tribune,* 24 July 1994, section B, p. 7. (Interview with actor Catherine Byrne of *Molly Sweeney.*)

Clancy, Luke. "What Do Directors Do for Playwrights?" *Irish Times,* 9 August 1994, p. 8. (On Friel directing *Molly Sweeney* at the Gate Theatre; interviews with other directors and playwrights.)

O'Byrne, Robert. "Friel Pins His Hopes, Brooches on Cast and Crew." *Irish Times,* 10 August 1994, p. 3. (On Friel having brooches made for members of the cast and crew of *Molly Sweeney* and, on opening night, making a brief appearance in the foyer to say "I'm OK," before slipping backstage to watch "from the privacy of the theatre's wings.")

Clarity, James F. "In His New Play, a Message for Friel's Critics." *New York Times,* 13 August 1994, sec. I, p. 17. (*Molly Sweeney,* which Friel gave to the Gate rather than to the Abbey, will run there for two months before moving to the Almeida in London.)

Cunningham, Francine. "Friel's Vision of Seeing and Nothingness." *Sunday Busi-*

ness Post, 14 August 1994. (News regarding world premiere of *Molly Sweeney,* directed by Friel, at the Gate Theatre.)

O'Byrne, Robert. "On the Town: Culture Shots." *Irish Times,* 1 October 1994, "Supplement," p. 2. (Richard Avedon in Dublin to photograph Brian Friel for *The New Yorker,* went to see *Molly Sweeney* in the Gate Theatre on the eve of shooting the playwright.)

O'Byrne, Robert. "London Audience Expectant about Brian Friel's *Molly Sweeney.*" *Irish Times,* 4 November 1994, p. 10. (On the opening at the Almeida Theatre.)

1995

White, Victoria. "Public and Private, Now and Then." *Irish Times,* 15 February 1995, p. 12. (Interview with actors who play Gar Public and Gar Private in revival of *Philadelphia, Here I Come!* at the Abbey Theatre.)

Ryan, Paul. "A Field Day Once Again." *Irish Times,* 16 February 1995, p. 14. (On Field Day opening Frank McGuinness's version of *Uncle Vanya* in Derry one year after Brian Friel's resignation from the board.)

O'Byrne, Robert. "On the Town: Once Again, with Frieling." *Irish Times,* 18 February 1995, "Supplement," p. 2. (Friel was absent from the Abbey opening night of a revival of *Philadelphia* but will be going to New York for the Broadway opening of *Translations.*)

Holland, Mary. "The Trouble with Peace: Times Have Changed for Derry's 'Cultural Provos.'" *Observer,* 26 February 1995, p. 4. (Friel, in New York for *Translations,* was not present for the Derry opening of the Field Day production of *Uncle Vanya* [adapted by Frank McGuinness and starring Stephen Rea].)

"*Translations* Sets New York Buzzing." *Evening Herald* (Dublin), 21 March 1995. (A summary of New York reviews of *Translations.*)

White, Victoria. "No Broadway Triumph for Pearson with *Translations.*" *Irish Times,* 23 March 1995, p. 10. (A summary of mixed reviews from New York despite a rave review for the same production in Boston.)

Nemy, Enid. "Chronicle." *New York Times,* 25 March 1995, sec. I, p. 24. (A brief item about Rufus Sewell, appearing in *Translations.*)

Hand, Michael. "Pearson Upbeat about NY Play despite Reviews." *Sunday Tribune,* 26 March 1995. (News regarding continuation of *Translations* in New York despite a negative *New York Times* review.)

Fricker, Karen. "Friel Loses Something in Translation to Broadway." *Sunday Tribune Magazine,* 26 March 1995, p. 35. (On producer Pearson's response to mixed reviews of *Translations.*)

"*Translations* Closing." *New York Times,* 5 April 1995, sec. C, p. 24.

O'Hanlon, Ray. "Friel Play Closes on Broadway after Luke-warm Reviews." *Irish Press,* 7 April 1995.

"Friel's Broadway Cast Named." *Irish Times,* 7 July 1995. (For *Molly Sweeney.*)

"Writers Sign Derry Advert Calling on Britain to Initiate All-Party Talks." *Irish Times,* 30 August 1995, p. 4. (Friel is among 100 signers of an advertisement in the *Derry Journal* saying "We the undersigned, concerned at the lack of progress towards a political solution in Northern Ireland, call on the British government to establish all-party talks immediately.")

1996

"Brian Has Another." *Evening Herald* (Dublin), 4 January 1996, p. 10. (*Molly Sweeney* will open on Broadway in a production directed by Friel.)

Mulkerns, Helena. "Friel's Play Opens on Cold Broadway." *Irish Times,* 8 January 1996, p. 4. (Opening of *Molly Sweeney.*)

Mulkerns, Helena. "Chilly Critics Warm to Molly on Broadway." *Irish Times,* 9 January 1996, p. 5. (Summary of New York critics' responses to *Molly Sweeney.*)

"Molly Bán." *Irish Times,* 10 January 1996, p. 12. (On New York opening of *Molly Sweeney.*)

"Last Chance." *New York Times,* 10 May 1996, sec. C, p. 25. (*Molly Sweeney* to close on 12 May.)

"*Seven Guitars* Chosen Best Play by New York Drama Critics Circle." Associated Press, 13 May 1996. (*Molly Sweeney* named best foreign play.)

Holland, Kitty. "What's in a Name? *Translations* at the Abbey." *Irish Times,* 3 August 1996, "Weekend" section, Supplement p. 2. (Friel's wife, but not Friel, attends the opening of an Abbey revival of *Translations* directed by Robin LeFèvre.)

"Lughnasa, the Movie." *Irish Times,* 14 November 1996, p. 12. (Noel Pearson will make a film of *Dancing at Lughnasa* with a screenplay by Frank McGuinness.)

1997

Meany, Helen. "Questions of Creation." *Irish Times,* 12 March 1997, p. 16. (On *Give Me Your Answer, Do!* which opens at the Abbey tonight.)

"Friel Cargo." *Irish Times,* 15 March 1997, "Weekend" section, "Supplement," p. 2. (Account of the opening night audience at the Abbey Theatre for *Give Me Your Answer, Do!* directed by Friel.)

Dwyer, Michael. "Meryl Streep to Star in Film of *Dancing at Lughnasa*." *Irish Times,* 14 May 1997, p. 1. (Meryl Streep will play Kate in *Dancing at Lughnasa* to be filmed in Ireland in August; producer Noel Pearson interviewed.)

Dwyer, Michael. "Ready for Lughnasa." *Irish Times,* 8 August 1997, "Arts" section, p. 13. (Casting is complete for *Lughnasa* and filming will begin on 18 August.)

1998

"Irish Plays, London Stage." *Irish Times,* 26 February 1998, p. 14. (*Give Me Your Answer, Do!* will open in London on 30 March in a production directed by Robin LeFèvre.)

Ross, Michael. "The Other Side of the Streep." *Sunday Times,* 15 March 1998. (An account of casting and filming *Dancing at Lughnasa* and Friel's enthusiastic reaction to a private screening of the film in Dublin.)

"Friel Accepts UCD Honour." *Irish Times,* 17 March 1998, "Education and Living" section, p. 55. (As a senior fellow at the Department of English in University College, Dublin.)

Rees, Jasper. "A Bright Light in Search of the Shadows." *The Independent,* 26 March 1998, "Features" section, p. 6. (Friel agreed to the filming of *Lughnasa* after four years of badgering by Noel Pearson, who comments on the playwright's avoidance of interviews.)

Rosenthal, Daniel. "America Buys the Write Stuff." *The Times,* 26 March 1998. (For a report on British writers selling their archives to U.S. libraries—a question posed by *Give Me Your Answer, Do!*—Friel declines to be interviewed but says through his agent that he has not sold his papers.)

Michael, Neil. "Streep to Visit Ireland." *The Mirror,* 20 July 1998, p. 11. (The Irish premiere of *Dancing at Lughnasa* in Dublin in September will be followed by a special screening of the film in Glenties, Co. Donegal, where the play is set.)

White, Victoria. "Golden October." *Irish Times,* 20 August 1998, "Arts" section, p. 16. (Friel's version of Chekhov's *Uncle Vanya* will be staged during the Dublin Theatre Festival.)

Dwyer, Michael. "Donegal's Daughter." *Irish Times,* 12 September 1998, "Weekend" section, p. 60. (Interview with Meryl Streep regarding *Dancing at Lughnasa.*)

Binchy, Maeve. "Five Sisters Alone Against Their World." *New York Times,* 13 September 1998, sec. 2, p. 41; reprinted as "Gone with the Wind of Change," *Irish Times,* 26 September 1998, "Weekend" section, p. 64. (On what Ireland was like for women in the 1930s when *Lughnasa* is set.)

"Black Stuff Loosens Up Act." *Belfast News Letter,* 24 September 1998, p. 9. (Meryl Streep on appearing in *Dancing at Lughnasa.*)

Holland, Kitty. "Elegant Meryl Streep Glides in for Film Premiere." *Irish Times,* 24 September 1998, p. 8.

Rodgers, Suzanne. "Glenties Glitters as Tinseltown Queen Takes Starring Role." *Belfast Telegraph,* 24 September 1998.

"Hollywood Dances into Glenties." Irish Times, 25 September 1998, p. 8. (Friel and Meryl Streep attend the screening in Glenties of *Dancing at Lughnasa.*)

Starrett, Ian. "Farewell to the Hills of Donegal: Superstar Streep Has Time of Her Life at Glenties Film Premiere." *Belfast News Letter,* 26 September 1998, p. 3. (Streep talks about *Lughnasa* after special screening in Glenties.)

Ross, Michael. "Modest Festival, Fringe Benefits." *Sunday Times,* 27 September 1998. (Friel's version of *Uncle Vanya* will be in the Dublin Theatre Festival, but Friel "lost his appetite for directing after the hammering given to *Give Me Your Answer, Do!*")

Walsh, Maeve. "The Life of Brian and His Volunteers." *The Independent,* 18 October 1998, p. 15. (*Volunteers* is receiving its British premiere at the Gate Theatre in London.)

O'Haire, Patricia. "Kin-Do Spirit of *Lughnasa:* Five Virtual Strangers Become Sisters for Film Version of Tony-Winner." *Daily News* (New York), 12 November 1998, "New York Now" section, p. 44. (Interview with actresses Catherine McCormack and Brid Brennan.)

Markey, Patrick. "*Lughnasa* Film Gets Mixed US Reviews." *Irish Times,* 14 November 1998, p. 5. (A summary of New York reviews of the film.)

Owen, Michael. "A Woman of Donegal, at Least by Adoption." *New York Times*, 15 November 1998, sec. 2A, p. 30. (A feature on the 24 September screening of *Dancing at Lughnasa*, attended by Friel and Meryl Streep, in Glenties the night after its world premiere in Dublin. Includes one comment by Friel declining to confirm how *Lughnasa* is autobiographical.)

Hartl, John. "Filming *Lughnasa* Was a Delicate Dance between Director and Playwright." *Seattle Times*, 20 December 1998, sec. N, p. 1. (Interview with director Pat O'Connor on Friel's reluctance to allow *Lughnasa* to be filmed.)

Schaefer, Stephen. "Stepping Up: Brid Brennan Takes Her *Dancing at Lughnasa* Role from Stage to Screen." *Boston Herald*, 22 December 1998, p. 47. (Interview with actress Brid Brennan on the differences between the stage and film versions.)

Rosen, Steven. "Director Stresses Irish Reality: Hard Existence Crux of *Lughnasa* Movie." *Denver Post*, 26 December 1998, sec. F, p. 5. (Interview with director Pat O'Connor on Ireland in the 1930s.)

1999

McGarry, Patsy. "Friel's Work Both Censure and Celebration, Says McGuinness." *Irish Times*, 8 February 1999, p. 7. (Friel on hand to receive a Special Tribute Award presented by Frank McGuinness at the *Irish Times* / ESB Theatre Awards.)

Ross, Michael. "A Friel for Failure." *Sunday Times*, 28 March 1999. (On a possible connection between Friel's refusal to grant interviews and the ferocity of recent attacks on his work by Dublin critics.)

Maguire, Stephen. "Village Plans a Reel Tribute." *The People*, 28 March 1999, p. 29. (Villagers in Glenties plan to turn The Laurels, the house where Friel was born, into a museum.)

"Details of Brian Friel Festival Announced." *Irish Times*, 1 April 1999, p. 7.

"What a Frielin'." *Irish Times*, 3 April 1999, "Weekend" section, p. 61. (Friel present when the Friel Festival is opened by Noel Pearson whose company will produce a documentary on the festival.)

Battersby, Eileen. "Echoes in the Dacha: Unrequited Love, Psychological Crises, Hothouse Emotions: All in an Irish Idiom." *Irish Times*, 1 June 1999, "Arts" section, p. 14. (Michael Attenborough, director of Friel's adaptation of *A Month in the Country*, explains his attraction to Friel's version.)

Clarity, James F. "A Time for Calm in Ireland and a New View of Friel." *New York Times*, 9 June 1999, sec. E, p. 2. (On the reasons for the Abbey Theatre's "26 years of neglect" of *The Freedom of the City* and the often overlooked political dimension of Friel.)

Bushe, Andrew. "Home Support Saves Cottage." *The Mirror*, 19 July 1999, p. 10. (Friel will open J. M. Synge's restored Aran Islands cottage.)

Kiberd, Declan. "The Austere Settings of Synge's Harvest." *New York Times*, 8 August 1999, sec. 2, p. 5. (Friel to open Synge's cottage on Inis Meain.)

Donnellan, Eithne. "Paying Homage to Synge around Turf Fire." *Irish Times*, 9 August 1999, p. 4. (Opening J. M. Synge's restored Aran Islands cottage to the public, Friel saluted Synge as "the man who made Irish theatre . . . a man before whom we all genuflect.")

Profiles

"Brian Friel." *Current Biography Yearbook 1974.* New York: The H.W. Wilson Publishing Company, 1974, pp. 127–30.

Kilroy, Thomas. "Writing in the West: Brian Friel: Playwright." *Connacht Tribune,* 31 October 1980, p. 15.

O'Toole, Fintan. "Brian Friel: The Healing Art." *Magill,* 8 (January 1985), pp. 31–35.

Gray, John. "Field Day Five Years On." *Linen Hall Review,* 2, no. 2 (Summer 1985), pp. 4–10.

Harris, Anne. "Friel Spirit in the Senate." *Sunday Independent,* 3 May 1987, p. 8.

Kennedy, Douglas. "Brian Friel: Delighting in Mischief, Wary of Praise." *Irish Times,* 4 July 1987, "Weekend" section, p. 9.

O'Toole, Fintan. "Friel's Day." *Irish Times,* 7 January 1989, "Weekend" section, pp. 1, 12.

Pine, Richard. "Brian Friel at Sixty." *Sunday Independent,* 8 January 1989, p. 19.

Battersby, Eileen. "Intimate Stranger." *Sunday Tribune,* 22 April 1990, p. 11.

O'Toole, Fintan. "Neither Priest nor Politician, but Observer and Playwright." *Irish Times,* 23 April 1990, p. 8.

Kennedy, Douglas. "Success Went to His Feet." *Sunday Telegraph,* 14 October 1990, "Review" section, p. VIII.

Toibin, Colm. "The Derry Magician." *Sunday Independent,* 14 April 1991, p. 14.

Rocke, William. "Newsmaker: Brian Friel." *Sunday Press,* 14 April 1991, p. 4.

O'Toole, Fintan. "Keeper of the Faith." *The Guardian,* 16 January 1992, p. 26. (Partially reprinted and revised as "The Life of Brian," *Irish Press,* 6 May 1992.)

Cunningham, Francine. "Map-maker Hovering on Border." *Sunday Business Post,* 24 May 1992, p. 14.

McGarry, Patrick. "Fluency and Opulence." *Sunday Independent,* 9 August 1992, p. 10L.

Clarke, Jocelyn. "Field Day." *Sunday Tribune,* 27 June 1993, sec. B, p. 5.

McGee, Harry. "In Search of the Real Brian Friel." *Sunday Press,* 27 June 1993, sec. 2 "Leisure."

Christiansen, Richard. "Friel's Gift to Theater's Soul." *Chicago Tribune,* 16 December 1994, sec. 5 "Tempo," pp. 1, 3.

Kilroy, Thomas. "The Life and Art of Brian." *Irish Times,* 24 April 1999, "Weekend" section, p. 60. (An article written for the special edition of the *Irish University Review* devoted to Brian Friel's career.)

Nightingale, Benedict. "Power to Friel's People." *The Times,* 4 May 1999.

Kiberd, Declan. "The Universal Borders of Brian Friel's Ireland." *New York Times,* 4 July 1999, sec. 2, p. 1.

O'Toole, Fintan. "Ireland's Master Storyteller Memories—True and Otherwise—Are Raw Material for the Great Playwright Brian Friel." *Daily News* (New York), 4 July 1999, "Showtime" section, p. 15.

Index